Y0-DVA-069

Approaches to World Studies
A Handbook for Curriculum Planners

Edited by

Robert B. Woyach
Mershon Center, The Ohio State University

Richard C. Remy
Mershon Center, The Ohio State University

Allyn and Bacon
Boston   London   Sydney   Toronto

Tennessee Tech. Library
Cookeville, Tenn.

388663

Copyright ©1989 by Allyn and Bacon
A Division of Simon & Schuster
160 Gould Street
Needham Heights, Massachusetts 02194

All rights reserved. No part of the material protected by
this copyright notice may be reproduced or
utilized in any form or by any means, electronic
or mechanical, including photocopying, recording,
or by any information storage and retrieval system,
without written permission from the copyright owner.

Library of Congress Cataloging-in-Publication Data

Approaches to world studies : a handbook for curriculum planners /
  edited by Robert B. Woyach, Richard C. Remy.
    p. cm.
  Includes bibliographies and index.
  ISBN 0-205-11722-8
    1. World history—Study and teaching (Secondary)—United States.
  I. Woyach, Robert B. II. Remy, Richard C.
  D16.3.A7 1989
  907'.1273—dc19   88-23323
                                                                CIP
Printed in the United States of America
10 9 8 7 6 5 4 3 2 1 92 91 90 89 88

Contents

7. Measuring the Effectiveness of World Studies Courses 209

Judith Torney-Purta

Preface

In September, 1984, the Mershon Center held a national conference on Strengthening High School World Studies Courses. With support from The Danforth and Johnson Foundations, thirty-nine leading educators, scholars, and representatives of professional organizations met at the Wingspread Conference Center in Racine, Wisconsin. The working conference was convened because of a growing awareness of the problems schools were encountering in fulfilling new mandates for teaching world studies. The goal of the conference was to identify practical ways to help schools around the nation strengthen their world studies courses.

Conference working groups made several recommendations regarding national programs, services, and resources that could be useful to local and state education agencies. A key recommendation called for the preparation of a handbook on alternative approaches to world studies. As conceived of by conference participants, the handbook would be based on the latest scholarship in world history, geography, anthropology, and international relations. It would make that scholarship available to curriculum planners in a way that could help them take on the task of conceptualizing and organizing their world studies courses.

Approaches to World Studies: A Handbook for Curriculum Planners implements this conference recommendation. It has come about through a two-year process of discussion, writing, review, and rewriting, made possible by the generous support of Gene Schwilck and The Danforth Foundation. The handbook reflects the impressive knowledge of the multidisciplinary team of scholars who worked on it. It also reflects the wisdom of a great many individual educators, school administrators, and scholars who served on the National Advisory Board for the project and who reviewed draft chapters.

In particular, we would like to acknowledge the contribution of the following individuals:

NATIONAL ADVISORY BOARD

Gordon Cawelti, Executive Director, Association for Supervision and Curriculum Development

Harry I. Chernotsky, International Studies Association; Professor of Political Science, University of North Carolina at Charlotte

O.L. Davis, Professor, Department of Curriculum and Instruction, University of Texas at Austin

Thomas Elliott, Virginia State Department of Education; Council of State Social Studies Specialists

Roy Erickson, Program Specialist, Social Studies, San Juan Unified School District, California

Charles Fox, former President, Social Studies Supervisors' Association

Francis Haley, Executive Director, National Council for the Social Studies

James E. Harf, Executive Director, Consortium for International Studies Education; Professor of Political Science and Mershon Center Senior Faculty, The Ohio State University

Marilynn Jo Hitchens, Teacher of World History, Wheat Ridge High School, Denver, Colorado; World History Association

Gwen Hutcheson, former President, Council of State Social Studies Specialists; Secondary Coordinator—Social Studies, Georgia Department of Education

Salvatore J. Natoli, former Educational Affairs Director, Association of American Geographers

Judith S. Wooster, Associate, Bureau of Social Studies Education, New York State Department of Education; Council of State Social Studies Specialists

Jamil Zainaldin, former Deputy Executive Director, American Historical Association

CHAPTER REVIEWERS

The following individuals read and critiqued one or more of the handbook chapters:

Lee F. Anderson, Professor of Political Science and Education, Northwestern University

Alan Backler, Director, Teaching Resources Center, Indiana University

Regis Birckbichler, Teacher of Social Studies, Westerville South High School, Westerville, Ohio

Jeffrey J. Blaga, Director of Social Studies, Racine Unified School District, Racine, Wisconsin

Jennifer Farkas, Global Education Coordinator, Dublin City Schools, Dublin, Ohio; Adjunct Assistant Professor, Colleges of Education and Medicine, The Ohio State University

Miriam Glessner, Social Studies Consultant, Columbus City Schools, Columbus, Ohio

Louis Grigar, Director of Programs, Texas Educational Agency

David L. Grossman, former Director, Stanford Program on International and Cross-Cultural Education (SPICE), Stanford University

Carol M. Hallman, Social Studies Coordinator, West Clermont Local School District, Cincinnati, Ohio

Phyllis Harris, Teacher of Social Studies, Upper Arlington High School, Upper Arlington, Ohio

Don R. Hoy, Professor Emeritus of Geography, University of Georgia

Julius Knebel, Executive Director of Secondary Curriculum, Pasadena Independent School District, Pasadena, California

Jean Lantz, Professor of Social Studies Education, University of St. Thomas

Robert S. Lopez, Sterling Professor Emeritus of History, Yale University

William S. Maltby, Professor and Chairman, Department of History, University of Missouri-St. Louis

Mary McFarland, Instructional Coordinator for Social Studies, K–12, and Director of Staff Development, Parkway School District, Chesterfield, Missouri

William H. McNeil, Professor of History, The University of Chicago

June Nash, Professor of Anthropology, The City College of the City University of New York

Nancy S. Norman, Teacher of Social Studies and Department Chairperson, Bonn American High School, Bonn, West Germany

George A. Peterson, Director, Educational Media Division, National Geographic Society

Richard Lee Ritchey, Teacher of World History, Cleveland High School, Cleveland, Texas

Bruce Russett, Dean Acheson Professor of International Relations and Political Science, Yale University

Arnold Schrier, Walter C. Langsam Professor of History, University of Cincinnati

Lynda Norene Shaffer, Associate Professor of History, Tufts University

Jeanne Slaydon, Social Studies Coordinator, Spring Branch Independent School District, Houston, Texas

Angene H. Wilson, Associate Professor, College of Education, University of Kentucky

Barbara J. Winston, Professor of Geography, Northeastern Illinois University

Acknowledgements are also due to Charles F. Hermann, Director of the Mershon Center, who has been a valued source of support for our work, and Steven D. Lavine, formerly of the Rockefeller Foundation, whose early and continued interest in this endeavor contributed greatly to its success.

Robert B. Woyach
Richard C. Remy

About the Authors

PAUL BOHANNAN received a Doctorate of Philosophy (1951) and a Bachelor of Science (1949) from Oxford University. Dr. Bohannan has been President of the American Anthropological Association and the African Studies Association. With Philip Curtin, he has co-authored *Africa and Africans* (3rd edition, 1987) and has written numerous other works as well. Until 1987 Dr. Bohannan served as Dean of Social Sciences and Communications at the University of Southern California. He is currently a Professor Emeritus.

MICHAEL GORDON is a Professor of History at Denison University. He received his B.A. (1964), M.A. (1965), and Ph.D. (1972) degrees in history from The University of Chicago. Dr. Gordon is a member of several professional organizations, including the American Historical Association and the Selcon Society. His published works cover such areas as Early Modern Spanish history, the legal history of Tudor and Stuart England, and the comparative legal history of Late Medieval Europe.

PATRICK McGOWAN has received degrees in political science and education from the University of the South (B.A., 1961), Makerere College of the University of East Africa (Diploma in Education, 1962), The Johns Hopkins University School of Advanced International Studies (M.A., 1966), and Northwestern University (Ph.D., 1970). Professor McGowan has taught international relations at Arizona State University since 1979. Before that he taught at Syracuse University (1969–1974) and the University of Southern California (1974–1979). A former Peace Corps volunteer in Uganda and Kenya (1961–1964) and a frequent consultant to U.S. government agencies, Dr. McGowan is also the author of over fifty articles and monographs on international and comparative politics. He is currently an editor of the *International Studies Quarterly*, the journal of the International Studies Association.

KEVIN REILLY received his B.A. in 1963 and M.A. in 1969 from Rutgers University. He will complete a Ph.D. from Rutgers University in 1988. Reilly is a founder and past President of the World History Association. He has published several works, including a college text entitled *The West and the World: Topical History of Civilization,* and a two-volume anthology of world history, *Readings in World Civilizations,* to be published in 1988. He is currently Professor of History at Raritan Valley Community College (formerly Somerset County College).

RICHARD C. REMY is an Associate Director of the Mershon Center at The Ohio

State University, where he also holds appointments in the Department of Political Science and the College of Education. He received a Bachelor of Arts degree in history and education from Loyola University (1964), and an M.A. (1968) and Ph.D. (1971) in political science from Northwestern University. He is the author of numerous research publications on political socialization and citizenship education and is co-author of an elementary grade social studies textbook series, a leading high school civics textbook, and a widely used senior high school American government textbook. He serves on numerous boards and commissions, including the National Advisory Board of the ERIC Clearinghouse for Social Studies/Social Science Education.

W. RANDY SMITH received his M.A. (1975) and Ph.D. (1978) in Geography from York University in Toronto, Canada. He joined the faculty of the Department of Geography at The Ohio State University in 1978 and currently holds a position as Associate Professor. He is a member of the Association of American Geographers, Canadian Association of Geographers, and the National Council for Geographic Education. His research and publications focus on urban geography, especially the development and structure of national and regional urban systems. He currently serves as a member of the Board of Directors and Vice Chairperson of the Urban Geography Specialty Group of the Association of American Geographers.

JUDITH TORNEY-PURTA received her B.A. in Psychology from Stanford University in 1959. She has also received an M.A. (1962) and Ph.D. (1965) in Human Development from The University of Chicago. Dr. Torney-Purta is Chair of the International Relations Committee of the American Educational Research Association and is a member of the Research Committee of the National Council for Social Studies. One focus of her research is the socialization and development of young people's attitudes concerning international issues. She has co-authored *Civic Education in Ten Countries: An Empirical Study* (1975) and has written a number of chapters and articles dealing with evaluation and research on global and international education.

ROBERT B. WOYACH has received degrees in political science and international relations from Marquette University (B.A., 1971), Yale University (M.A., 1973), and The Ohio State University (Ph.D., 1981). He is currently a Faculty Associate of the Mershon Center and an Adjunct Assistant Professor of Political Science at The Ohio State University. Among other works, Dr. Woyach has written and edited eight volumes of instructional materials for secondary education, including *World History and National Security, Bringing a Global Perspective to World History,* and *Making Decisions: Our Global Connection.* He has served as a consultant on international studies for numerous school systems and chaired committees on education for the International Studies Association and the Columbus Council on World Affairs.

Chapter **1**
The Need for Alternative Conceptual Approaches to World Studies

Robert B. Woyach
Richard C. Remy

1. Introduction

This is an exciting time for educators interested in world studies, and also a challenging one. In the past few years increasing numbers of state and local school districts have returned to a curriculum pattern that mandates a year of world history or world civilizations for graduation from high school. In most cases this world history course represents the only opportunity students have after the seventh grade to learn about the world in an integrated and concentrated way. In short, for most students this will be their last world studies course.

At the same time there has been a growing recognition that existing models of the world history course suffer from critical problems. To some, the world history course remains too centered on the Western experience to be relevant to today's complex world. To others, recent attempts to broaden the coverage of other civilizations have exaggerated the difficulties of teaching an already complex and demanding course. One result of this dissatisfaction has been a unique openness to new ideas about this critical part of the social studies curriculum.

This handbook was written to help curriculum planners make more systematic and informed decisions about the goals, organization, and content of a course that can fill the current world history slot within the curriculum. In essence the book provides a conceptual road map to five distinct approaches to the course. Three of these approaches are historical in nature and represent alternative ways of teaching about the history of the world. Two other approaches are essentially non-historical and thus constitute radically different ways of thinking about the goals of the course. For each of the five approaches, the handbook outlines a set of basic goals and a rationale that candidly recognizes the limits as well as the potential of the approach. A final chapter looks at how program evaluation can facilitate the curriculum planning process and ensure that courses meet their intended goals.

This handbook is not meant to provide a ready-made course of study for any of the five approaches, nor does it advocate any one approach over the others. However, by providing relatively concrete images of alternative approaches, the book can help curriculum planners select a basic direction for their course. The descriptions of the individual approaches can also help promote consensus about the specific goals and priorities of a course, once the basic direction has been selected.

Thus the handbook represents a resource, not a substitute, for local and state curriculum planning. Implicit in this handbook, however, are several assumptions about the role of world history/world studies in the high school curriculum and about the importance of sound conceptual models in the curriculum planning process itself.

2. World studies in the high school curriculum

The goal of the traditional world history course has always been to prepare young people for citizenship. But what are the demands of citizenship to which this course about the world must respond? What is the role of this course as opposed to other strategies for introducing international studies into the secondary curriculum?

CITIZENSHIP AND THE NEED TO LEARN ABOUT THE WORLD

Immediately after World War II, Americans found themselves in a new and in some respects uncomfortable position of leadership within the world. Yet the very dominance of the United States politically, militarily, and economically allowed Americans to exercise world leadership successfully even though most knew relatively little about the world.

Over the past three decades, however, the world has changed in some significant ways, and we can no longer be complacent about our ignorance. Since 1945 over a hundred new nations have emerged in Asia, Africa, and the Caribbean and Pacific Basins. Social and economic philosophies that are opposed to the contemporary world order have appealed to many people in these states and elsewhere. At the same time the very success of the postwar economic order has eroded American dominance in manufacturing, finance, science, and engineering. Technological developments such as supersonic jets, space satellites, and computers have intimately joined the far corners of the globe. So have cultural changes as the greater availability of international news and the increasing recognition of universal human rights.

Today the impact of economic and political events in distant places shows up in American communities more quickly and more profoundly than ever before. American policymakers must coordinate the most intimate details of economic policy with other industrialized states in order to accomplish their most basic social and economic goals. Global political forums like the United Nations and the World Court are not always congenial places for American interests.

These changes in the world community have significantly complicated the task of world leadership for Americans. With the erosion of American dominance has come the need for better understanding of the global environment and our place within it. As the American leadership role within the world matures and changes in coming decades, an even higher premium will be placed on our vision, our understanding, and our skill. Nor can the vision and understanding emanate solely from a narrow foreign policy elite. If our democratic institutions and free enterprise economy are to flourish in the future, the challenges of world leadership must be borne by all Americans.

World studies education generally plays a critical role in preparing youth for these challenges. If Americans sometimes appear globally "dumb, deaf, and blind," they do so because of a failure of American society—especially of leaders within the media, education, government, and business—to come to grips with the need for a citizenry able to make educated judgments about world affairs.

THE ROLE OF THE WORLD HISTORY COURSE

Various movements have arisen over the last decades to meet the educational challenge posed by the changing nature of America's leadership role in the world. Most educational leaders and organizations, including the National Council for the Social Studies, the Association for Supervision and Curriculum Development, the Council of Chief State School Officers, the National School Boards Association, and the National PTA, have accepted the rationale for infusing world studies into the elementary and secondary curriculum (Collins and Zakariya, 1982, pp. 22–23). Yet practice lags behind theory. We understand the need for infusing a world view into the curriculum far better than we understand how to go about it.

The most common strategy for increasing students' understanding of the world has been the infusion of international studies or global education materials throughout the curriculum (Woyach, 1983). The infusion strategy can play a vital role in the overall effort to expand international understanding. Perhaps most importantly, the infusion of international perspectives throughout the curriculum can help break down the now artificial boundary between learning about the world and learning about our own society.

However, the infusion strategy also has its limits. Materials infused into non-international studies courses build understanding of the world in piecemeal fashion, so this strategy can go only so far in building a representation or understanding of the world as a whole. American history, for example, should be seen within a global context, but if an American history course seeks primarily to build a representation of world history, it ceases to be American history.

Preparation for citizenship in a global age requires more than the infusion of a global perspective within the curriculum. It requires that students have an opportunity to develop an integrated understanding of the world in which they live. This integrated representation of the world is similar to the architect's drawing of a complex office building. The different rooms on the drawing provide readily recognized places into which students can place new facts or information about current events. The drawing as a whole is vitally important because it, and only it, shows the relationship among the different rooms. In short, the world studies course provides an integrated frame of reference, which students need if they are to see the relationships among discrete events or make informed decisions and judgments about complex international issues.

For all those students who do not go on to college, and for many of those who do, the high school world history course represents the last opportunity to learn about the world in an integrated and focused way. It thus constitutes a cornerstone for citizenship education. In some school districts it can help tie together the threads of what students have learned up to that point through infused materials, giving them the "whole picture" of which those threads were parts. In other school districts the course may serve as the sole foundation for future learning, understanding, and decisionmaking. In either case, the course plays a critical role in helping students understand the world in which they live.

3. The need for better conceptualization

The role of the world history course as a key foundation for citizenship education with respect to world affairs places great demands upon the course. It also creates a dilemma for curriculum planners. Unlike American history or government, world history today has no generally accepted and teachable approach. Those models of world history that appear in major textbooks, and thus pass as conceptualizations of world history, are in reality the parallel regional and national histories of the various civilizations of the world.

There is no conceptual integration to these parallel histories: as a result, they do not add up to a world history in any meaningful sense.

To a large extent, the failure to conceptualize a more integrated and teachable approach to world history underlies many of the problems and criticisms of the world history course today (Alder and Downey, 1985, pp. 13–18). Indeed, this failure has led to a malaise in the teaching of world history that approaches crisis proportions.

THE CHANGING IMAGE OF WORLD HISTORY

The traditional world history course was unabashedly a course in Western civilization. At the end of the last century, when the course was first introduced, it was in fact a two-year course of study that focused solely on Europe. Even when restricted to a single year, that course remained teachable because there existed a reasonably broad agreement about the essential elements in the story of Western civilization (Hertzberg, 1981).

That consensus collapsed over two decades ago, as Americans became more aware of the reality of interdependence and the importance of non-Western peoples in the global milieu. Throughout the 1970s efforts were made to expand the treatment of Asian, African, and Latin American history. In most cases, however, these non-Western histories were simply grafted onto what essentially remained a story of the Western world. The result was an ungainly set of parallel regional histories that lacked coherence for students, demanded almost superhuman teacher competence, and actually compromised the pedagogical values inherent in the study of history—such as the graphic representation of change and continuity in human affairs.

The failure to conceptualize an adequate approach to the world history course means that individual teachers rarely have much help in making difficult choices about content. Indeed, when teachers do receive input on the content of world history, they typically find themselves pressured to include additional discrete topics or units. They almost never find help in conceptualizing the overall course or in establishing criteria for excluding material (Hertzberg, 1985, pp. 27–28). The result is an array of practical dilemmas related to both content and process.

DILEMMAS RELATED TO COURSE CONTENT

World history teachers and curriculum administrators face three distinct but related dilemmas with respect to the content of their world history courses.

CHOOSING BETWEEN THE GENERAL AND THE CONCRETE.   One of the most important and probably most difficult dilemmas that world history teachers face is the strategic choice of emphasizing the general or the concrete in their instruction.

On the one hand, teachers can elect to emphasize the broad chronology of world history, giving students an image of key turning points and major epochs. This choice has considerable merit. The contribution that historical approaches make to education in world studies is a clear image of the flow of the human past. However, at this level the story of human history can remain fairly abstract and even superficial. Many students may find it difficult to understand, visualize, or internalize what is taught. Abstractions can also be equated with irrelevance, leading to lower student interest.

Alternatively, teachers can choose to deemphasize the larger patterns and spend class time primarily on the concrete stories and specific lessons that abound in history. While this strategy can be more exciting for students, it can also fail to achieve larger objectives at the heart of the world studies course. The stories of history can become mere anecdotes. Students may fail to develop the larger, integrated representation of their world that they need in order to understand current and future events. Thus the course may fail in its primary goal: to build a foundation for citizenship.

There is no simple solution to this dilemma. The balance between the general and the concrete should result from an overall understanding of world history or the world history course. However, since teachers tend to face this dilemma with little help from curriculum administrators, scholars, or other relevant groups, they tend to make idiosyncratic and even least-effort choices. Indeed, the mix between the general and the concrete can become essentially haphazard. It can become the *de facto* result of more concrete choices about specific content or specific teaching materials.

SELECTING SPECIFIC CONTENT. A second dilemma, and one self-consciously faced by all world history teachers, is that of selecting what specific content to emphasize or deemphasize in the course.

Making choices about specific content can be an overwhelming experience for teachers, especially those with relatively weak backgrounds in world history. As a result, many simply "teach the text." In other words, they ignore school district guidelines regarding course objectives and content and rely on the textbook as the arbiter of content.

Other teachers, especially those with more experience or stronger backgrounds, may make their own decisions about content, but they are likely to do so in essentially idiosyncratic ways. They may emphasize content related to their personal interests and experiences. Alternatively, they may rely on a variety of supplementary materials that have come their way through the years. They may, in short, fashion their world history course around their personal interests and strengths, not around school district guidelines or any real conceptualization of world history.

INCREASING INSTRUCTIONAL ACCOUNTABILITY. Over time most teachers become relatively comfortable with their compromises between the expected and the possible, however idiosyncratic these compromises may be. It is not clear, however, that school boards, administrators, and local communities should be similarly comfortable. In most states and communities the reality of classroom world history instruction is likely to depart in significant ways from the learning objectives established by the local or state curriculum policymakers. Courses that are meant to teach world history may in reality teach the history of Western civilization. Particular teachers may focus their instruction on regional cultures, not on history at all.

The idiosyncratic nature of world history instruction has rarely been a salient problem in the past. However, the current interest in reinstating a core curriculum into the schools (Robinson and Kirman, 1986, p. 19) has been accompanied by a movement to introduce greater teacher accountability within local and state school districts as well. A number of school districts throughout the nation are experimenting with exit tests or common testing in an effort to ensure that all students leave high school with the same basic foundation. This interest in accountability will necessarily make the idiosyncratic nature of world history instruction a more salient issue.

Parents, school boards, and school administrators do have a right to expect that mandated courses will achieve mandated objectives, but a school district cannot expect teachers to teach an impossible course of study or to teach what they do not know. Thus school districts have a responsibility to define minimum expectations for courses clearly and realistically. They must, in short, provide clear guidance for how teachers should handle the challenge of too much content. If they continue to present teachers with impossible tasks, they should not be surprised if teachers define the task in ways that are personally amenable.

DILEMMAS RELATED TO TEACHING STYLE

The content-related dilemmas that world history teachers face are familiar to anyone who has attempted to teach world history. More subtle, but just as real, are the dilemmas related to teaching style which the failure to adequately conceptualize world history has created.

While research clearly indicates the value of instructional diversity to student learning, most world history teachers devote virtually all their class time to lectures or lecture-discussions (Hertzberg, 1985, pp. 34–36). It is likely that most world history teachers have a natural inclination toward lecturing as an instructional strategy. Similarly, their dominant role models (that is, the history teachers they had in high school and college) almost certainly relied primarily on lecture methods.

However, the lack of conceptualization of world history reinforces this reliance on lecturing as the primary instructional strategy. While instructional strategies involving greater student participation may be more conducive to student learning, especially the learning of skills and the internalization of cognitive knowledge, lectures remain the most efficient way to transmit a given body of information from teacher to student. Some teachers' natural attraction to lecture styles is powerfully reinforced by the need to "cover the material."

The dependence on lectures and the lack of variety in instructional strategies may have a number of impacts on students taking world history. The overreliance on lecture methods may diminish the overall learning that students achieve. While lectures communicate information well, they do not encourage students to internalize content. If students are not required to confront and use information learned in a world history course, they are unlikely to retain it over the long term.

Similarly, unless students are required to use information in more participatory ways, they are unlikely to develop critical thinking skills and other skills intrinsic to social studies education. They may perceive history as a catalogue of facts to be memorized and never learn to hypothesize about alternative explanations for historical trends. They may never learn to look at historical facts and assess their significance or to analyze historical decisions and make judgments about them. They may never learn to work in small groups or to tolerate divergent opinions.

The reliance on lecture methods may also be a key reason for the often-observed lack of student motivation and interest in history. Some students will never share the typical historian's joy in the study of the past. Yet in studying history students should experience the joy of discovery as they learn the patterns of the past and the ways in which different people and forces have shaped our world. Unfortunately, for most students lectures may not be the instructional strategy that best motivates high levels of interest and involvement in the study of history.

Whatever its potentially negative impact, world history teachers can hardly be faulted for their tendency to rely on the lecture method of instruction. As with the dilemmas related to content, this is a dilemma that teachers cannot be expected to resolve satisfactorily on their own. As long as there is no accepted conceptualization of a teachable world history, there will be no legitimate way for teachers to make radical reductions in the content they attempt to cover. As long as that content remains overwhelming, they will be encouraged to depend on lecturing as the most efficient method for transferring information from teacher to student.

THE NEED FOR CONCEPTUALIZATION
IN OTHER APPROACHES TO WORLD STUDIES

The need to conceptualize teachable approaches to content is hardly unique to world history. American history, mathematics, science—indeed virtually every conceivable area of human inquiry—face a similar problem. What could and perhaps should be taught to students is always more than what can be taught in the time available within the curriculum.

What may be unique about world history, and indeed all of world studies, is that we have collectively failed to come to grips with the need for better conceptualization. We have failed to look seriously for new approaches to world history that are at the same time teachable, academically sound, and politically acceptable to curriculum planners, teachers, and interested community groups alike.

Nor is this simply a problem for world history. Alternative models of world studies based on geography and anthropology have exhibited similar problems. Existing models of world geography and world cultures are like the proverbial Cook's tour. They go from country to country or from region to region, attempting to teach students everything important about each particular place. Like the parallel regional history model, these models of world studies fail to provide teachers with a basis for distinguishing more important from less important material. In short, they fail to come to grips with the problem of conceptualization.

4. Clarifying basic conceptual approaches

THE SCHOLARLY DISCIPLINES
AS REPRESENTATIONS OF THE WORLD

Most world history teachers will readily acknowledge that the need to cover large amounts of material results in various problems. At the same time many teachers may not clearly perceive that these problems can only be solved with a better conceptualization of the course. Yet only when teachers are armed with an academically sound, integrated, and teachable conceptual framework for their course can they be expected to strike an appropriate balance between the general and the concrete, to devote class time to more time-consuming instructional strategies, or to become motivated to learn unfamiliar content.

What is the basic and shared knowledge that students should learn about the world? It is here that the discussion of world history flounders. Indeed, this question will probably never be answered in an absolute sense. However, school districts that want to strengthen their world studies courses must wrestle with it, and to succeed they must accept two fundamental and inescapable facts.

First, educators must recognize that the source of our understanding of the world, for better or worse, is rooted in the scholarly disciplines. Our knowledge of the world depends on the methodologies, questions, and organization of knowledge implicit in the social sciences, history, and the other humanities. Any attempt to comprehend the basic and shared knowledge that students should obtain from a world studies course must at some point go back to those disciplines that generated the knowledge. While the structure of knowledge in the various disciplines should not dictate the curriculum of secondary schools, it does provide critical insight into what knowledge is most basic and why (Bellack, 1978, pp. 101–102).

Second, school districts must accept the fact that there is more than one legitimate, discipline-based way to view and study about the world. None of these alternatives is intrinsically correct or intrinsically superior. Each has important strengths; each has equally important weaknesses. Any serious effort to design a high school world studies course must match the goals and priorities of the local community or state with the strengths and weaknesses of the various approaches.

FIVE ALTERNATIVE APPROACHES

This handbook describes five distinct conceptual approaches to world studies. We have labeled these approaches world history, Western civilization, historical cultures, world geography, and international relations. Subsequent chapters analyze each of these approaches in turn, assessing both their pedagogical strengths and their pedagogical weaknesses. Sample topical outlines for courses that faithfully implement the rationale of each approach are presented, along with criteria for selecting specific content.

In most respects each of the five approaches constitutes a starkly different image of the most appropriate goals and priorities for a high school world studies course. While the three "historical" approaches (world history, Western civilization, and historical cultures) all help students understand the sweep and progression of human history, each tells a different story. The world history approach stresses the diversity of human history by giving more even-handed treatment to the various non-Western experiences. The Western civilization approach focuses on the Western experience in constructing its representation of history, although it places the Western experience within a global context. The historical cultures approach uses the epochs of history to differentiate types of culture, showing how humans throughout history have adapted culture to changing situations.

The final two approaches, world geography and international relations, describe alternatives that are essentially non-historical. In other words, both focus primarily on the contemporary world. The world geography approach helps students "think geographically," using geographic perspectives, concepts, and skills to understand the patterns of differences and interactions within the world community. The international relations approach helps students understand how governments, multinational corporations, and other decisionmakers interact and try to achieve their goals within the international system.

For each of these conceptual approaches, the handbook seeks to provide a foundation upon which a local consensus about the goals and organization of a specific course can be built. Each chapter provides a reasoned answer to questions about what subject matter is most basic and how it can best be organized if the world is seen through the lenses of a historian, a geographer, a political scientist, or an anthropologist.

While the handbook does not assume that course principles and specific content are related in lock-step fashion, it does assume that there is an inherent logic to the various approaches, which implicitly establishes criteria for setting priorities about specific course content. Some of the content implications of course goals are relatively clear-cut. For example, it is not surprising that the basic conceptualization of the Western civilization approach suggests that material on Indian civilization has a relatively low priority in the course. However, other content implications of the approaches are more subtle. For example, a key goal of the Western civilization approach is to demonstrate the uniqueness of the Western culture that emerged out of the Middle Ages. It does this in part by demonstrating the fundamental similarity among classical civilizations. With respect to content, this learning goal argues for giving greater priority to teaching about life within the Roman Empire rather than the Roman Republic or Greece. The similarity of Imperial Rome to other classical civilizations is striking. Republican Rome and Greece are less similar to the rest of the classical world.

COMMON THEMES AMONG THE FIVE APPROACHES

While it is important to stress the obvious differences among the five approaches, common elements do appear in the representations of the world they seek to build. Five such elements appear to be the most important. Most of these common elements reflect key dimensions of the contemporary world with which all five approaches must in some way deal.

INTERDEPENDENCE. Each of the five approaches takes as a key knowledge goal helping students to perceive themselves and their nation as part of a larger whole that is global in scope and bound together in various ways. All three of the historical approaches help students understand how our globally interdependent world emerged historically. The world geography approach uses geographical ways of thinking about the world to understand why regions and societies come to depend on each other. The international relations approach, in effect, looks at the implications of interdependence for how nations solve those problems that emerge on the global agenda. Thus, while each approach looks at interdependence from its own perspective, each sees it as a critical element of contemporary life that must be dealt with in the course.

UNEVEN DEVELOPMENT. All five approaches also build an understanding of the relationship between what can be called the less developed world and the more developed countries, including the United States. Like interdependence, uneven development is an aspect of the world community that has a tremendous though often unnoticed impact on our lives. The fact of uneven development reinforces the need to look at Western civilization from a global perspective. Explaining what uneven development means, how it affects international affairs, and how it might be addressed constitute major portions of the world geography and international relations approaches. Even the historical cultures approach looks at the colonial experience and uneven development as an example of how cultural growth and change can be inhibited or distorted.

COMPLEXITY. One of the key goals of citizenship education is to help students appreciate the complexity of social problems and the futility of simplistic solutions. In its own way, each of the five approaches demonstrates the complexity of the world. Each approach helps students comprehend that the world is a complex place with widely divergent cultures, contrasting political and economic systems, and conflicting perspectives on the common good. All the approaches strive to show students that events and problems result from complex causes and require complex solutions.

SOCIAL AND HISTORICAL CHANGE. A fourth theme common to all five approaches is that of change. While there are clear differences in how the reality of change is treated, all the approaches give students an image of the world as a constantly changing environment. The historical and cultural approaches embed the image of change within historical chronology. They describe culture change, the sequence of ages, and the changing relationships among the major civilizations. The international relations approach looks at change primarily within the conflict over broad issues. It focuses on the dynamic tension between the need for order in the world system and those technological and political forces that consistently produce and pursue change. Even the world geography approach, in its treatment of uneven economic development, points to the changing nature of relationships among different regions and societies.

HISTORICAL PERSPECTIVE. Finally, building a historical perspective on the contemporary world is an important element in all but one of the five approaches. The world history, Western civilization, and historical cultures approaches all help students perceive and appreciate the chronological progression of history. They show how key features of the contemporary world, including our cultural diversity, our interdependence, and the major rifts that divide us, have emerged from the distant as well as the near past. The international relations approach uses historical material more selectively, but it too shows the historical origins of key features of the international system, such as the nation-state, world economic interdependence, and underdevelopment.

5. Curriculum planning

This handbook is designed to be a resource for use in the curriculum planning process. The scholars who have contributed to this handbook have knowledge of and perspectives on subject matter that can be very useful in the process of designing integrated and academically sound courses. They are well equipped to recognize the larger patterns of meaning that give coherence to a course.

At the same time curriculum planning is more than an intellectual process. Curriculum planners must be sensitive to and ultimately join together various concerns and perspectives to create the instructional goals, objectives, and strategies that make up a specific course. Good curriculum planning should be based on the conceptual understandings and frameworks available from the social sciences, history, and the other humanities, but pedagogical concerns must be added to conceptual validity if courses are to be successful. Likewise, curriculum planners must come to grips with the ultimately conflicting demands placed on the schools and the social studies curriculum by students, teachers, parents, and interest groups. In short, curriculum planning can be an intensely political process.

The politics of curriculum planning can threaten the conceptual integrity of courses designed by the most well-intentioned, well-informed, and rigorous curriculum planners. Two distinct type of pressure are particularly troublesome: (1) the pressure of local interest groups to include special content within the course, and (2) the temptation to resolve conflicting demands by making courses interdisciplinary.

RESPONDING TO LOCAL INTERESTS AND DEMANDS

Local interest groups often demand that content or materials about their particular ethnic group or issue be included in the world studies curriculum. Courses that are conceptualized in terms of parallel regional histories or the study of the different geographical or cultural areas are quite vulnerable to these demands. There is no good reason to ignore any one cultural, ethnic or racial group when world studies is defined simply as the parallel stories of various national and cultural groups.

The demands of local interest groups may be compelling for most curriculum planners. The public schools are both funded by and meant to serve the local community. Unless local demands actually conflict with the educational goals of the school district, it may be hard not to respond to them in some way. Local demands also have a positive aspect: Interested local groups represent potential resources. The schools almost always benefit from strong local support for a particular curriculum. Students may benefit directly from unique learning experiences that local people and organizations might be able to provide.

However, all too often curriculum planners respond to local pressures in dysfunctional ways. They simply add extra instructional objectives to an already overcrowded course. More to the point, they add content in ways that diminish the overall integrity of the course. The result can be a rich but disjointed learning experience that may not provide students with a well-integrated understanding of the world. This type of learning experience, however successful and exciting it may be in the short run, may not prepare students for active and responsible citizenship in the long run.

Conceptually integrated courses are rarely if ever constructed inductively on the basis of the discrete demands of local interest groups. The challenge facing curriculum planners is thus how to transform local "demands" into local "resources" without sacrificing the conceptual integrity of the course.

A first step is clearly to take local needs, interests, and resources into account in choosing among the different conceptual approaches to world studies. This handbook does not advocate any one approach as better than the others, because it assumes that different local and state school districts face different challenges and have different needs. Simply put, the best approach in one place may not be the best in another.

The demands of local interest groups probably only begin to be addressed through the selection of a particular approach. But having a solid conceptual model for a course may help planners respond appropriately to local demands regarding specific content as well. When courses are poorly conceptualized, there is no guidance as to how new content might be integrated into the course in ways that contribute to the overall learning experience. On the other hand, if curriculum planners have a well-defined image of the course, they can more readily identify how the specific concerns of special interest groups can be fit into the "big picture." For example, the history of a particular ethnic group may be used to show students how feudalism worked, or how states emerged in Europe, or how imperialism affected local societies. The ways in which the ethnic history is used, however, will be determined by the framework of the course, not simply the parochial history of the group.

MAINTAINING THE INTEGRITY OF LEARNING EXPERIENCES

A second threat to the conceptual integrity of world studies courses is the temptation to use the different approaches as the basis for constructing interdisciplinary courses.

The appeal of interdisciplinary courses is obvious. No single approach to world studies can ever encompass all the learning goals that educators or community interest groups would like to see accomplished. With few opportunities to teach world studies in the curriculum, it is tempting to try to pack as much into the course as possible. Likewise, calling for interdisciplinary approaches to the course can serve to reduce conflict. When there are deep-seated disagreements about the basic direction and goals of the course, it is easier to say the course should serve everyone's goals than to make hard choices among approaches.

Despite their appeal, however, successful interdisciplinary courses have proven quite elusive in practice (Cremin, 1964, p. 348; Bellack, 1978, pp. 101–102; Hertzberg, 1981, pp. 80–81). Indeed, the effort to integrate differing conceptual approaches can have unfortunate results. While it is eminently possible to integrate some of the specific goals of one approach into another, it is less likely that integrated learning experiences can be constructed by combining the different approaches themselves. After all, the different approaches represent fundamentally different ways of understanding and learning about reality.

In a sense, the different disciplines, and the conceptual approaches based on them, replicate reality in the same way that the plasticine overlays in a high school biology text replicate the reality of the human body. One sheet diagrams the cardiovascular system; another the skeletal system; another the nervous system. Each sheet describes a good deal about one aspect of the human body, but it describes its particular content well precisely because it ignores most other aspects of the body. Similarly, each approach to world studies represents a distinct set of educational goals and core content.

The challenge of creating interdisciplinary courses is analogous to putting together an integrated or holistic representation of the human body using the various plasticine overlays. There is virtually no guidance in the scholarly disciplines or elsewhere as to how the different layers can be put together into a coherent picture. Even eminent scholars have generally failed in their attempts to create coherent interdisciplinary courses. In most cases such courses simply pile the different ways of studying the world, the different plasticine overlays, atop each other. In the process, information about some things begins to hide or distort information about others. The overall picture becomes increasingly complex and confusing.

In short, courses that attempt to do too much can fail to provide an intelligible learning experience. They can require students with little experience or understanding of the world to sort out a confusing array of facts and images, essentially on their own. In the end, students who have less rich but more focused learning experiences may actually learn more than students who go through richer but more complex interdisciplinary and multidisciplinary courses.

6. Conclusion

This handbook explicitly assumes that one of the key needs for successful curriculum planning in world studies today is better conceptualization of the various alternative ways of teaching world studies. A better conceptualization of world history may address many of the fundamental problems that have plagued teachers of that course; a conceptualization of non-historical approaches may be equally essential in giving educators a fuller image of their options.

If there is one assumption that this handbook does not make, it is that the process of curriculum planning is made easy or straightforward simply as a result of having these alternative conceptualizations. On the contrary, the need to make hard choices and to find satisfactory ways to deal with the conflicting demands placed upon the world history course will forever make curriculum planning a political as well as an intellectual art. In most cases, the quality of a local world studies curriculum will still be measured by the "blood, sweat, and tears" that have gone into creating it.

7. Bibliography

Alder, Douglas D., and Downey, Matthew T. "Problem Areas in the History Curriculum," in Matthew T. Downey, ed., *History in the Schools.* Bulletin No. 74. Washington, D.C.: National Council for the Social Studies, 1985.

Bellack, Arno, "What Knowledge is of Most Worth?" in Donald E. Orlosky and B. Othanel Smith, eds., *Curriculum Development.* Chicago: Rand McNally, 1978.

Collins, H. Thomas and Zakariya, Sally Banks. *Getting Started in Global Education: A Primer for Principals and Teachers.* Arlington, Va.: National Association of Elementary School Principals, 1982.

Cremin, Lawrence. *Transformation of the School.* New York: Random House, 1964.

Downey, Matthew T., ed. *History in the Schools.* Bulletin No. 74. Washington, D.C.: National Council for the Social Studies, 1985.

Educational Commission of the States. *A Summary of Major Reports on Education.* Denver, Colo.: 1983.

Hertzberg, Hazel Whitman. *Social Studies Reform: 1880–1980.* Boulder, Colo.: Social Science Education Consortium, 1981.

Hertzberg, Hazel W., "Students, Methods and Materials of Instruction," in Matthew T. Downey, ed., *History in the Schools.* Bulletin No. 74. Washington, D.C.: National Council for the Social Studies, 1985.

Leinwand, Gerald. *Teaching of World History.* Bulletin No. 54. Washington, D.C.: National Council for the Social Studies, 1978.

Remy, Richard C., et al. *International Learning and International Education in a Global Age.* Bulletin No. 47. Washington, D.C.: National Council for the Social Studies, 1975.

Remy, Richard C., and Woyach, Robert B. *Strengthening High School World Studies Courses: Conference Report.* Mershon Center, Citizenship Development for a Global Age Program, 1984.

Robinson, Paul, and Kirman, Joseph M. "From Monopoly to Dominance," in Stanley P. Wronski and Donald H. Bragaw, eds., *Social Studies and Social Sciences: A Fifty-Year Perspective.* Bulletin No. 78. Washington, D.C.: National Council for the Social Studies, 1986.
Woyach, Robert B. "Curriculum Efforts in Pre-Collegiate Global Perspectives Education: An Analytical Review," Mershon Center, Citizenship Development for a Global Age Program, 1983.

Chapter **2**
A World History Approach

Kevin Reilly

1. Rationale

At the beginning of this century the historian James Harvey Robinson said that the introductory history course ought to prepare students to read the daily newspaper. With only slight modifications that statement still offers the best rationale for a world history course today. To understand the news, to be concerned with local and world events, to develop opinions on current issues—these are marks of good citizenship, and preparing students to be good citizens is central to the mission of social studies education.

Since Robinson's time the number of news-gathering institutions has increased enormously. Today the news is more plentiful but also more controlled; more remote but also more immediate. This has increased our awareness of the complexity of events but decreased our confidence in being able to understand and influence them. Thus the task of turning students into citizens has become considerably more complicated.

WHY WORLD HISTORY?

World history is a study of change on a global scale. Both the study of change and the global vision are essential for students today.

Since 1900 humanity has become a single community, spread to the most remote interiors of continents and the most distant islands of the globe. At the same time human technology has vastly increased our dependence on one another. In different ways, the atomic bomb, the multinational corporation, the satellite, and the evening news have created what Marshall McLuhan so aptly called a "global village." Messages can circle the globe in seconds, missiles in minutes. Men, women, and microbes take only slightly longer. Events in Iran, Nicaragua, South Africa, or the Philippines are as immediate as events in our own country.

Ours is not only the first global age, but also the most rapidly changing in human history. The accelerated pace of change in modern society is our one clear certainty. History, the study of change, is our one certain antidote to the vertigo of the modern roller-coaster ride. Knowledge of how things change—of the past and its relation to the present—keeps us on track.

The study of history also shows us what does not change. It helps us to distinguish between continuity and change, between the parameters and possibilities of the present. Thus it is our most valuable tool for shaping a better future.

THE THIRD STAGE OF CITIZENSHIP

American education has completed two important stages in its approach to citizenship training. The first was the development of American history. Since the second half of the nineteenth century, American history, along with civics, has been the primary vehicle for molding a nation of immigrants into a nation of Americans.

The young nation found national history sufficient for its citizens, but the emergence of America as a world power made a more cosmopolitan identity for Americans equally necessary in the early twentieth century. This second stage of citizenship saw the emergence of a new view of history that was eventually called "Western Civilization."

The course on Western civilization was the invention of an America preoccupied with its relation to Europe between two world wars. "Europe" was always a more meaningful concept to Americans than to Europeans, who study their own national histories, but "Western Civilization" gave America and Europe a common identity and a rationale for weathering the stormy seas of world war and economic collapse together.

Since World War II the United States has emerged from the shadow of Europe. As citizens of a "superpower," Americans have needed a still broader identity. American foreign policy and economic activity have become more concerned with Asia and Latin America. Far more headlines in the daily newspaper originate in Asia, Africa, and Latin America than in Europe, and there are even more immigrants from Asia and Latin America than from Europe.

"Europe was no longer the world," Gilbert Allardyce has written. "Emerging were other peoples, other histories, a globe of historic diversity beyond the imagination of earlier Westerners, a cosmos where pluralism replaced the 'oneness' of history and where human experience could not be ordered into a unilineal pattern of development. As educators came to recognize the world in this way, they recognized, at the same time, the poverty of the Western Civilization course."

The approach to world studies outlined in this chapter aims at preparing students more effectively for the global reach of this third stage of citizenship. It does not help students understand only their country or just Western civilization; it helps them understand the place of Americans in the entire world.

Teaching world history for the third stage of citizenship means reducing the centrality of Western history. The world history course must become less Western as it becomes more global. Thus it requires new perspectives, new approaches, and new questions that accommodate its wider vision. This will be troubling for some.

The story of Western civilization was a classic. It had dramatic tension: the struggles between Athens and Jerusalem, reason and religion, enlightenment and faith. It had a happy ending: the advance of progress and the victory of liberty. The setting was also ideal: The historical advance of Western civilization culminated in America. However, the mythic power of that story was shaped at the cost of historical accuracy. The story is no longer compelling because it ignores too much of the historic reality.

At the same time, for most Americans the story of Western civilization encompasses much of what we know about "the world." Herein lies a dilemma. We must teach elements of the old story while we develop and learn the new one. Teachers would do a greater disservice to their students if they taught world history as if it were a foreign language they had only recently learned than if they taught their course on the basis of an imperfect vision of the world. We must teach what we know. Thus an effective approach to "world" history will use the foundation that teachers already have and provide a framework within which they can progressively fit a broader and more useful understanding of the past.

ADVANTAGES OF THE APPROACH

The advantages of a world history approach to world studies stem from the basic strengths of history and the global perspective that the approach provides.

The key advantages of the historical approach in general are its completeness, its impartiality, and its relative timelessness. History is in a sense more basic than other approaches to world studies. It makes no assumptions about the relative importance or relevance of political, economic, social, or geographical phenomena. The story of history depends on interpretation, but there are no discipline-based blinders preordaining the focus or key dimensions of the story.

Since history tries to present material in ordinary language, and typically in story form, it also has greater permanence. The absence of "scientific" jargon means that history weathers the whims of fashion better than social science. That is one reason why we still read Thucydides but not Thales.

The advantages of world history as opposed to narrower approaches to history, such as the Western civilization approach, have already been discussed. Less global approaches to history do not provide students with an image of the world or a sense of history that is adequate to the challenges and responsibilities inherent in American citizenship today.

DISADVANTAGES OF THE APPROACH

The disadvantages of the world history approach stem from the same sources as its advantages. Indeed, they are like mirror images and represent the tradeoffs involved in selecting any particular approach to world studies.

The key weakness of the historical approach in general is that it encourages a focus on factual material at the expense of a broader understanding. Historical studies are factually dense. They focus on specific contexts rather than general laws. Nonetheless, history without interpretation is not history. While the temptation to focus on facts to the exclusion of concepts is ever present, it can be guarded against by remembering that there is no one story within history. Even selecting the facts needed to tell a coherent history requires interpretation.

Specifically, there are two key disadvantages to a world history approach. First, the subject is too big. There is too much material to cover. Second, it is too new. World history lacks the architectural dimensions and the unimpeachable credentials of a classic. Both of these criticisms must be accepted, but neither is an adequate reason for abandoning the world history approach.

Simply because world history entails a broader vision does not necessarily mean it must contain more information. The simple fact is that no course, even on the most narrow of topics, avoids the problem of selectivity.

An example may make the point. One could easily envision an 8 × 10-inch photograph of (1) a 4 × 5-inch patch of grass, (2) a house, (3) a neighborhood, or (4) an entire city. Each picture requires a different perspective, but none requires a frame equivalent to its size. Nor is there only one perspective possible for each of these pictures. Many different pictures, taken from many different angles, can show the same city, for example. Some pictures can even "suggest" or "represent" the entire city by focusing on a detail or microcosm of it.

The same is true of world history. World history can be taught on some meaningful level in any amount of time or space. Carlo Cipolla, for example, has written a book called *The Economic History of World Population*. In it he tells a history of the world in a hundred pages, most of which are filled with tables and graphs detailing changing population and energy use through time. One page in the book shows a graph of world population over the last 10,000 years: a gradual increase until the eighteenth century, then a right angle turn off the page. That graph in itself is a world history, and an important one. Thus the issue is not whether world history can be taught in a two-semester high school course, but rather what kind of world history can be taught.

The fact that world history is a relatively new field complicates this issue and can be seen as a distinct disadvantage to adopting a world history approach. No view of world history has yet become so widely accepted that it represents a paradigm for the field. Thus curriculum planners and teachers do not have clearly fixed guideposts as to what constitutes an academically sound world history. They do not have a safe and comfortable vision of the "story" of world history.

At the same time educators have a Carthesian freedom to design their image of world history from scratch. They have the opportunity to determine what is most valuable for their students to know, to focus the course on the real problems of our students and our society. Thus we can create world history courses that are truly alive and pertinent.

2. Goals for students

MAJOR KNOWLEDGE GOALS

In a world history approach to the high school world studies course, the major knowledge goals should be to help students:

1. Deepen their historical perspective on the contemporary world and their appreciation of the present as part of a historical process linking past, present, and future
2. Appreciate that peoples of the past, including people in the Western world, behaved and thought differently than we do
3. Understand the enormity of the span of human history and at the same time appreciate its brevity in relation to geological time
4. Recognize continuity and change in human history
5. Learn to distinguish among historical periods and recognize key characteristics that distinguish the context of those periods
6. Appreciate that great cultural traditions have arisen on every continent and understand that many of them still represent classical traditions that people see as models for cultural ideals
7. Realize that various great religions have arisen in the world and understand the importance of these religions to their civilizations
8. Understand the stages in the development and expansion of human interaction throughout the world and appreciate both the positive and negative implications of this interaction
9. Understand the political and economic dimensions of the rise of the West and its critical importance to world history
10. Deepen their understanding of the impact of Western domination on world history, especially from the perspective of non-Western peoples

11. Know the technological and scientific turning points in world history and understand the importance of technological change

MAJOR SKILL GOALS

A world history course should help students:

1. Learn to evaluate and judge, independently and critically, among differing interpretations of events
2. Evaluate and weigh evidence in order to arrive at independent explanations of historical change
3. Synthesize historical facts, interpretations, and explanations to arrive at larger concepts and patterns
4. Critically assess and check sources of historical information
5. Become aware of biases, partisanship, and perspective in themselves and others
6. Make linkages between past and present so that they can draw on past example in order to understand and explain current trends and events

3. Organization of subject matter

World history courses can be organized according to one of three basic criteria: (1) by chronological period, (2) by topic, or (3) by cultural/geographic region. All three approaches have long traditions. Arnold Toynbee's great work might be considered a regional approach, in that it treats each civilization separately. Each "challenge" and "response" is seen as a unique unit of historical investigation. On the other hand, histories written for popular consumption have most often taken a topical approach. Chapters or whole books may focus on "the conquering Balkan Orthodox merchant" or "sex in history." However, most historians and teachers of history prefer a chronological approach. Rather than study each civilization from its origins to the present, chronological histories begin with the "ancient world." Within that time frame they explore key civilizations and themes and then move on to the next chronological period.

In reality, of course, no history can be purely chronological, topical, or regional. Time, place, and subject are intrinsic to any story, but there can be only one principal criterion for organizing subject matter. A recent survey of high school world history teachers indicates that the overwhelming majority prefer a chronological approach. The topical approach was a rather distant second, and the regional approach, which had been popular in the 1960s, was a remote third.

Because of the clear preference of teachers, this chapter will focus on a chronological approach to world history. However, it will also briefly describe an alternative model, which is primarily topical but also follows a general chronology for world history. While it provides an alternative to the chronological model, it also suggests substantive foci than can be used as criteria for selecting course content within a chronological model.

A TOPICAL MODEL

One of the critical dilemmas for teachers using a topical approach to teach world history is the issue of topic selection. What kind of topics are appropriate? Of what order of generality should they be? Should they be "historians'" topics or come from other sources? Should the topics be construed as "issues," "problems," or "subjects"?

The specific selection of topics probably should be guided by the following four criteria. First, they should be topics that interest students. Second, they should provide learning opportunities that help students become better citizens. Third, they should help students grow and understand their world. Finally, since a critical part of citizenship education involves teaching students to think independently, the topics probably should be presented as social, personal, political, or cultural "issues" that the students themselves will confront in one way or another as citizens and human beings.

A topical approach to world history, guided by these criteria and organized to follow a general chronology of world history, might look as follows:

First semester
   Gender and family (Human origins–1000 B.C.)
   City and civilization (3000 B.C.–A.D. 1000)
   Religion and society (1000 B.C.–A.D. 1000)
   War and peace (500 B.C.–A.D. 1500)
Second semester
   Politics and states (1500–1800)
   Economics and ecology (1500–1900)
   Race and nationality (1600–present)
   Individual and mass society (1800–present)

These eight issues are neither so broad as to be meaningless nor so specific as to focus attention on very narrow technical detail. They are generally recognized as issues of broad social significance, and some are of perennial importance. Since all eight issues are of current interest, they provide considerable opportunity to achieve the goals of citizenship education, including encouraging independent thought and helping students learn to use historical knowledge and thinking skills in dealing with contemporary social issues.

Although the issues are organized in terms of a chronology of world history, the structure of each division, or unit, is meant to be topical. Thus it would probably be desirable to begin the treatment of each topic with a discussion of the current issue. Treatment of the issue within the appropriate historical period should be prefaced with a brief review of its historical background. Finally, it would be valuable to bring the topic back to the present at the end of the unit.

Topic 1: Gender and family

One of the most useful things a history course can do is to show students how differently people in the distant past thought and acted. This can increase the students' sense of the variety and plasticity of human behavior. It can also suggest the possibilities of change: Things have not always been as they are now and are unlikely to remain exactly the same.

The study of gender and family in ancient societies offers such an opportunity. While early agricultural or "neolithic" societies were probably not "matriarchal," they probably did honor woman's work more than our own. There is evidence of this both in contemporary neolithic societies studied by anthropologists and in ancient myth.

Above all, however, historical knowledge is knowledge of process, not variety. It is knowledge of how things change through time. Students should see how gender roles changed historically, and by implication how history can be every bit as important as biology in determining what it means to be a "man" or a "woman."

It seems clear that the status of women declined with the rise of urban civilization. "Sky fathers" replaced "earth mothers" in religious hierarchies, and patriarchal families replaced maternal clans. The key new roles brought on by urban living became dominated by men. Students should be asked how the roles of men and women have changed through time. What caused women's roles to be so important in neolithic society, and what caused the rise of patriarchy in the first civilizations? Prepared with a historical understanding of preliterate societies and a long-term view of historical change, students can better debate the relative impact of history and biology and the persistence of gender role stereotypes in the contemporary world.

The role of technology can be introduced at this point. The terms "paleolithic," "neolithic," and "bronze age" refer to technological stages of human development. In defining the cultural context of neolithic and urban gender roles, students should be introduced to the overriding importance of technology in historical change.

Topic 2: City and civilization

The focus of this issue is on the nature of citizenship, the characteristics of civilization, and the problems and accomplishments of city life.

Students should see both sides of ancient urban civilizations: their creative dynamism and their tendency toward inequality. On the one hand, urban living represented a great improvement over neolithic life. Students should see the monumental art, the improvement in security from marauding nomads and others, the greater variety of life, the greater possibility for individuality, and the evolution of law. The dynamism of urban living can be seen in the remains of ancient Indian cities as well as those of Mesopotamia. The development of writing and art can be shown in Shang China as well as Egypt.

On the other hand, urban living created new problems. Kings, armies, police, taxes, forced labor, priests, and class divisions all emerged with cities.

They created not only inequality but also the means for violent and arbitrary rule. Students should examine the role of slavery and colonialism in the maintenance of ancient cities.

Some ancient cities were radically different from others, some more successful than others. Students could be asked to account for the differences between a Rome and an Alexandria. They can explore the evolution of a city like Rome from a city-state to the imperial capital of a classical empire.

The study of ancient cities and civilizations can also suggest much about modern urban problems. Many of the problems facing ancient cities are familiar in nature, if not degree: population density, sanitation, growth, decline, class differences, and internal security. Urban living also created relevant challenges for governance. Students might examine the ancient city as a modern state in miniature and ask how effective the lottery, the public assembly, and the election of generals were in maintaining Athenian democracy. They could compare the territory-based *polis* with the Indian guild (caste) as a basis for social and political organization.

The relationship between cities and citizenship is an important dimension of this topic. Our idea of citizenship began to develop in the European medieval city. What did civic life look like in the typical medieval and Renaissance city of Europe? How is it different today? To what extent are our modern urban problems due to a loss of civic participation? Can we restore this civic spirit? Might the methods of communal responsibility and participation developed in non-territory-based societies like India present meaningful alternatives? Does democracy depend on civic participation? These questions can encourage students to explore the meaning and conditions of citizenship.

Topic 3: Religion and society

One of the most important reasons for studying ancient history is that all the great religious traditions of the world took shape between 600 B.C. and A.D. 700. The list includes Buddhism, Jainism, Hinduism, Confucianism, Taoism, Zoroastrianism, Manicheanism, prophetic Judaism, Christianity, Greek philosophy, Roman stoicism, and Islam.

The development of universal religions of salvation can best be understood within the context of the expanding Eurasian political empires of Alexander, Rome, Han China, and India. This was a time when political empires as well as universalist regions were bringing "salvation" to ever wider and more disparate populations. Here history also saw the first cultural joining of Europe and Asia. This was the first time when all of Eurasia, from the Atlantic to the Pacific, constituted a single intercommunicating zone.

Students should know what it means to be a Buddhist, or a Confucian, or a Muslim. They should be encouraged to ask why all these religions developed at nearly the same time. What did they have in common? What created these commonalities? At the very least, students should understand the distinction between tribal and universal religions, and between ritualistic and salvationist traditions.

Topic 4: War and peace

Probably no issue is more compelling than that of war and peace. Today's students have grown up in the shadow of nuclear weapons. They are approaching the age of military service. They want to understand why war exists and whether it is inevitable.

It is commonplace for students and adults in modern society to throw up their hands in despair and declare that nothing can be done about war. Wars are natural! People are genetically prone to violence! There have always been wars and always will be! Such despair can at least be tempered if students understand that past societies have been less and more warlike than our own. They should understand that wars have historical causes that can be understood, controlled, and even prevented.

Students might be encouraged to examine the status of the soldier in classical China. Why was the military held in such low esteem by the Chinese? What was the impact of this? Was Chinese society less violent or aggressive as a result?

On the other hand, Roman society provides an excellent example of the way in which the "citizen soldier" has been transformed into a "mercenary" by the relentless expansion of imperial frontiers. Students might consider the ways in which "a strong defense" causes trouble spots and enemies to proliferate. They might ask whether a militarized society undermines citizenship.

Feudal societies are, of course, military societies, as students could see by examining Chou China, medieval Europe, or feudal Japan. The European knight and the Japanese samurai in particular are strikingly similar. Does the centralized state reduce this militarization of society? It did in Tokugawa Japan but not in Europe. What differences between the two places might explain this?

Finally, students should look at the apparent change in the relative degree or temper of war between the premodern world and today. When one reads about the Mongol invasions of the ninth century A.D., one is overwhelmed by the callousness towards death and suffering in traditional society. Are we becoming more humane? Are we trying to control our violence through treaties such as the Geneva conventions and the recognition of universal human rights? How do such twentieth-century experiences as Dachau and Dresden fit into this picture of change?

What causes war? Are we becoming more warlike or less? These core questions of this unit cannot be answered definitively, but the process of considering such questions can make students much more aware of how history can help us understand the present.

Topic 5: Politics and states

This unit, the first of the second semester, returns to the issue of citizenship. The unit introduces students to the modern state and the modern democratic political process. Students should be aware that both are relatively recent creations. The development of the modern state begins only in the sixteenth and seventeenth centuries. The development of modern democratic process begins shortly thereafter.

One way to raise this issue is to look at the idea of political morality and corruption. To show the modern meaning of these terms, students need only read Machiavelli or learn about the Ottoman court. The secular rationale for the territorial state served as the basis for the ideas of political morality and "political science" that Machiavelli described in *The Prince*.

Almost coincident with the origins of the modern territorial state is the democratic, middle-class revolution. It is this revolution that has led to our separation of the ideas of state and government, rule and orthodoxy, office and individual. It is also the source of the modern democratic ideology of citizenship.

Students are not born with an understanding of the importance of civic participation, suffrage, jury duty, draft armies, and public service. To see these ideas evolve despite the opposition of Kings Charles I, Louis XVI, and George III is to observe the ideas in historical struggle as well as in current practice. The writings that came out of the Western democratic revolution, from Hobbes and Locke to Jefferson and Paine, can make these issues come alive.

Topic 6: Economy and ecology

Human economic activity has always been linked to human exploitation of the environment. What is unique about modern industrial society is our self-consciousness about economic life and the scope of our impact on the environment.

This unit should focus on three chief concerns. First, it should survey the role of economic behavior in traditional society. In the process it should examine the impact that traditional societies had on their local environments. Second, the unit should explore the enormous economic, scientific, and technological transformation that occurred in Western society with the scientific, commercial, and industrial revolutions. The unit should help students understand the development of modern capitalist, industrial society and the socialist reaction to it. Finally, the unit should examine the ecological impact of industrial society in comparison with that of traditional societies.

Topic 7: Race and nation

This unit examines the concepts and problems of racism, nationalism, ethnocentrism, prejudice, and internationalism in modern society. Students should see the degree to which consciousness of "race" and "racism" have increased since the abolition of slavery. They should understand that nationalism and internationalism are relatively modern phenomena.

A history of racism begins with the slave trade. It should include comparisons of slavery in Africa, the Middle East, North and South America, and South Africa. Finally, it should assess the ways in which racism has declined or increased since the abolition of slavery.

Racism should be distinguished from three other concepts: consciousness of race, ethnocentrism, and nationalism. This can be done by looking at the substitution of European workers for slaves in the nineteenth century, the rise of nationalism, and the development of racial and ethnic stereotypes. Students should see these issues as part of a larger set of developments related to Western imperialism, the development of an international economy, and the international migrations of labor and capital. The coincidental rise of nationalist sentiment, colonization, and international economic integration at the end of the nineteenth century is as striking as the collapse of internationalism due to immigration restrictions and war after 1914.

Students can see how these issues live on today in recent demands for immigration restriction, economic protectionism, and a vigorously interventionist foreign policy. The continuing impact of imperialism can be seen in debates over Third World debt, foreign aid, and the often strained relationship between more-developed and less-developed countries. The struggle between internationalism and nationalism continues in debates over the proper role for the United Nations and international law.

Topic 8: The individual and mass society

To what extent is individuality threatened by mass society? Are people becoming more or less individualistic? These questions are related to students' personal development as well as to citizenship.

Students can gain a perspective on the meaning of "self" in modern mass society by looking at the ways in which human identity has been transformed historically by such new techniques as printing, the assembly line, advertising, and television. They should understand that modern society provides greater opportunities to express individuality and to develop personal values and identity than was the case in traditional societies. At the same time, they should see that modern society encourages conformity and has created a variety of means for surveillance and control. Students should judge whether such developments as fascism, the emergence of an automobile-based society, and welfare have impeded or encouraged the development of individuality.

Ultimately, students should be able to understand their own struggles toward self-definition as historical struggles. They should be able to judge the degree to which their own culture satisfies the need for "self-realization" by comparing modern Western society with modern India or Japan.

A CHRONOLOGICAL MODEL

A chronological model necessarily teaches major concepts less directly than a topical model. This is because a chronological model has as its primary goal the teaching of the chronology. Dates are not necessarily the main lesson of the chronological model, but other conceptual or factual material is presented in the context of the chronology. Thus a chronological model discusses prior events before subsequent events and normally discusses them in the context of a particular geographical or cultural area.

At its worst this basic chronological approach leads to a rather mechanical "meanwhile in China during this period" type of organization. At its best it suggests an impartial overview in which the process of change emerges without a superimposed doctrine or straitjacket.

An alternative to this basic chronological approach is the more thoroughly conceptualized story of the world in which one turns to consider China or the Sudan in order to illustrate a thesis or theme that unifies the story. "Great histories" are always more like this. The problem with great histories is that they are also idiosyncratic. The more brilliant they are, the further they depart from the common understanding of the subject matter, and the more they disagree with each other. The world histories of H.G. Wells, Arnold Toynbee, and William H. McNeill were all highly imaginative conceptualizations of the subject, but each completely redefined the field. This type of thoroughly conceptualized history rarely if ever fits well with what teachers already know, so they find it difficult to use these approaches in the classroom.

For this reason, a more conventional approach to the chronological model is presented here. It is not simply an "if this is Tuesday" approach. It presents a simple overall story of world history, which borrows from some of the more recent conceptual approaches. However, it is hoped that teachers will find this approach easy to use, if not startlingly innovative.

The seven principal divisions of the model are:

   I. The agricultural revolution
   II. The urban revolution
   III. The great traditions
   IV. The rise of the West
   V. The world in Western shadow
   VI. The world in conflict
   VII. Problems of the integrated world

Each heading signals an emphasis on a certain subject-matter goal. Parts I and II are especially concerned with showing the importance of technological "turning points" and acquainting students with long-term historical processes. Part III is mainly concerned with developing the student's understanding and appreciation of other cultures. Parts IV and V are principally directed toward an explanation of the "rise of the West" and its effects on the rest of the world. Parts VI and VII are mainly directed toward understanding current problems in a richer historical framework.

Part I: Human origins and the agricultural revolution (to 4000 B.C.)

A world history course should tell "the whole story" from the beginning. This is especially important in a culture like our own, which often asks questions about causes but rarely answers those questions with any historical perspective. Students should have their sense of time expanded. They should confront the temporal enormity of human history. They should know that the earth is billions of years old, that homonids are millions of years old, and that homo sapiens is hundreds of thousands of years old. They should hear of Neanderthals and Cro-Magnons, and they should know that great glacial and climatic changes have occurred.

This is also the place to tell of the development of the skills and tools that separated humans from the animal world. From an historical perspective, the toolkit of paleolithic hunters and gatherers was only slightly less dramatic than our own. Fire and language are crucial to this story, but cave art may prompt questions about Old Stone Age religion and daily life. The methods of archaeology and anthropology can be introduced to show ways of understanding prehistory and to raise questions about the similarities between our "ancient ancestors" and contemporary Stone Age people.

The agricultural or neolithic revolution is one of the most important turning points in human history. The domestication of wheat and barley in the Middle East, of rice in South East Asia, and of corn in Middle America between 10,000 and 5000 B.C. drastically transformed human society. The rise of population density, village settlement, and production of textiles accompanied the development of agricultural tools and technology. So did earth goddesses, fertility cults, and rudimentary science and government.

The development of metallurgy, especially bronze, and the invention of the wheel, carts, and potter's wheels around 4000 B.C. can be seen as a further elaboration of the neolithic revolution or as the first stage of the urban revolution. In either case, they demonstrate the scope and importance of technological innovation in preliterate societies.

Part II: The urban revolution

THE URBAN REVOLUTION AND EARLY CIVILIZATIONS: THE MIDDLE EAST AND NORTH AFRICA (4000 B.C.–500 B.C.). In the broadest historical perspective, the urban revolution is one of the three most significant changes in human history. Only the agricultural revolution 5000 years before it and the industrial revolution 5000 years after it changed the world as much.

The urban revolution created what we call "civilization." The elements of civilization should be addressed. The division of labor, non-farming specialists (such as artisans, priests, scribes, tax collectors, engineers, court officials, and soldiers), and social class itself were as much a product of Mesopotamian cities as irrigation canals and dams. Government, law, police, citizenship, markets, and war were the political contributions. Astronomy, calendars, writing, recordkeeping, temples, monuments, and the concept of immortality may be some of the cultural results.

The story of Egypt contrasts sharply with the turmoil of Mesopotamia, possibly due to the regular flooding of the Nile as opposed to the fury of the Euphrates. Egyptian civilization was more placid, stable, and conservative. The Nile and the relative separateness of Egypt may also account for the continuity between the Old, Middle, and New Kingdoms and the centralization of the Pharaoh's realm. Egyptian confidence in their civilization and their future was expressed in the science and engineering that built the pyramids. While Egyptian society became calcified by the time of the New Kingdom, its culture had also became less elitist. Instead of tombs for a few, Osiris offered salvation for all, and Ikhnaton, at least briefly, challenged the power of the priests. Knowledge and immortality could not remain the monopoly of the ruling class.

EARLY CIVILIZATIONS OF SOUTH AND EAST ASIA (2500 B.C.–500 B.C.). The importance of geography in the origins and history of civilization should be stressed. The rivers of India (the Indus and Ganges) and China (the Hwang Ho and Yangtse) should be as familiar as the Euphrates and the Nile. In addition to its great rivers, students should perceive the enormity of China. They should understand its diversity, from the mountains and deserts of the west to the great river valleys of the east, from the dry wheat- and barley-producing lands of the north to the wet rice-producing lands of the south. The importance of the monsoons to Asian history should also be described.

The sophistication of Harapa and Mohenjo-daro in India deserves attention. They are planned cities. Private brick houses were two to three stories high and had private bathrooms. The sewer system was the best of its time, better than those of many subsequent civilizations.

The Aryan invasion of about 1500 B.C. imposed a new religion (Brahmanism) and a new language (Indo-European Sanskrit) on the darker Dravidian inhabitants of the Indian subcontinent. The Vedas, especially the Rig Veda, reveal Aryan society and culture during this conquest. Its prayers and poems show the importance of the caste system, based on the dominance of lighter-colored Brahman priests over warriors and subordinate farmers and serfs.

In China, the Hwang Ho (Yellow) River dominates early history. The first two Chinese dynasties, the Shang (1766–1027 B.C.) and the Chou (1027–

256 B.C.) both developed near it. The Shang oracle bones offer valuable glimpses of everyday concerns. The considerable written record of the Chou Dynasty, the longest in Chinese history, includes the writings attributed to Confucius and to Lao Tzu.

The writings of the Chou philosophers suggest the importance of the family and ancestor worship. They articulate the idea that the emperor was father of the entire Chinese family and had the "mandate of heaven" to govern as long as he observed humanity, wisdom, and courage. Students should be impressed with the longevity and continuity of these ideas within Chinese civilization.

Part III: The classical and great traditions

Virtually all of the great cultural traditions of the world developed their defining characteristics between 2000 B.C. and 1500 A.D. A two-semester course cannot look at each and every one of these great traditions in depth, as desirable as that might be. At the same time it is important that students learn about a variety of these traditions, including but not limited to their own.

The following section outlines major concepts and themes that should be the focus for exploring each of the major traditions that might be considered. Any one course would presumably select several of them, as time, materials, and the knowledge of teachers permit. Thus the specific traditions on which the course focuses may differ from one school district to another, but the selection should be guided by clear criteria.

Most historians regard the classical civilizations of Eurasia (the Greco-Roman, Indian, and Chinese), along with the Islamic and European, as the essential core of world history. Indeed, the chronology of world history is normally conceptualized in terms of these classical traditions. The historical records for other civilizations (sub-Saharan African, Meso-American, and Southeast Asian) are less well elaborated and documented. Nonetheless, local standards and interests may suggest that more than passing attention be given to one or more of these civilizations as well. Thus districts with many black students probably should devote time to the history of sub-Saharan Africa. Districts in the southwest may well want to devote more attention to Meso-American history. In any event all students should be exposed in some depth to cultural traditions that arose outside the Western world. Likewise, all students should understand that great cultural traditions emerged on every continent during this broad historical period.

CLASSICAL GREECE (2000 B.C.–31 B.C.).   Beginning the discussion of the Greek world in 2000 B.C. breaks with normative treatments of classical Greek culture. It represents a decision to include Minoan history here as a prelude to the Greek world. This organization allows for the integration of Minoan and Mycenaean civilization within a geographical introduction to Greece. A discussion of Homer and the Dorian invasion should be included as well.

Ancient Greece played two roles in the survey of Western civilization. On the one hand, ancient Greece served to distinguish "us" from "them." The Greeks at Marathon represented Western/European civilization defending itself from Oriental despotism. On the other hand, ancient Greece served to introduce Western notions of politics and citizenship. The latter role is equally important and appropriate to world history.

Athens and Sparta have traditionally been paired in order to contrast their respective open and closed societies. This still has a certain value, but the significance of the Greek city-state lies primarily in its territorially based notion of polity. This is the source of Western ideas of citizenship, the nation-state, and law. The organization of politics around territory is far more important than the differences between Athens and Sparta. A look at the Indian caste or the Chinese family, clan, and empire brings that importance into sharp focus.

The *polis* as a place and a political form should be explored in some detail. Athens is both special and representative. Its democracy should be discussed as an historical development from tyranny, in terms of its Periclean ideal, and in light of its reliance on slavery and empire.

CLASSICAL ROME (1000 B.C.–A.D. 476). Rome is important to Western civilization as a source of law and language, as a transmitter of Greek and Christian culture, and as an innovator in architecture and engineering. All of these contributions are of global importance as well, but when we shift our focus from Western to world history, other developments gain significance.

From a global perspective, the Roman Empire represents the first conquest of tribal Europe and the final extension of the band of civilization from the Atlantic across the Eurasian landmass to Han China. Within this band of civilization, the Eurasian landmass became a single interacting zone for the first time in history.

The struggle between Roman civilization and the barbarian tribes is one of the central themes of Roman history. It marks the limits of Rome's rise and fall. The struggle also helps to explain Rome's transformation from a small city-state into a Mediterranean empire. Students should see the characteristics of this empire: its huge landed estates, the tributary nations, the displaced farmers in the cities, and the dominating presence of generals who had to keep soldiers permanently employed. The militarization of Roman politics and society is a story that is quite relevant to modern students and the modern world.

Also important to Roman history is the emergence of Christianity from a minor Jewish sect to the official religion of the Roman Empire. The spread of Christianity should be treated in conjunction with the contemporaneous spread of Mahayana Buddhism.

CLASSICAL INDIA (500 B.C.–A.D. 500). The two most important aspects of Indian history during this period are the various religious reforms, especially the emergence of Buddhism and the reform of Brahmanism into Hinduism, and the economic and cultural achievements of the classical Gupta empire.

The story of Indian religious reform and development should be told against the background of the limitations of Brahmanism. These include the caste system, the burden of continual reincarnation, Brahman domination of society, and the quest for a deeper emotional and philosophical satisfaction. Religious reform might also be set in the context of the new kingdoms of northern India, such as Magadha, and the tensions between the warrior caste and the Brahmans.

Buddhism is probably the most important of the religious reform movements. Traditional stories of Buddha may help students understand the essential features of Buddhist philosophy. In particular they might compare Buddhist notions of suffering and desire with the Judeo-Christian tradition and with modern American attitudes. While Buddha's life suggests the role of fasting and asceticism in religious traditions generally, the concept of the "middle way" or "eightfold path" should be used to highlight the less demanding religious obligations of Buddhism and its moral universalism.

The Gupta Empire (320–550 A.D.) should also be a focal point for looking at classical India. The Gupta Empire became a hub of trade routes linking Asia, Africa, and Europe. The visiting Chinese Buddhist monk Fa Xian tells of the wealth of its capital, Pataliputra, where free hospital care attracted "the poor of all countries." The university at Nalanda, with its libraries, astronomers, and mathematicians, was more advanced than any other in the world. The scholars of the Gupta Empire gave us our numerical system of notation, negative quantities, quadratics, and square roots.

Textiles, dyeing, and steel and iron manufacture gave an impressive vitality to Gupta economic life. A private sector of merchant and artisan guilds even developed a kind of private commercial law. Some historians have suggested that the economic transformation of Western Europe after A.D. 1000 had its roots in Gupta India.

CLASSICAL CHINA (500 B.C.–A.D. 220). The Han Dynasty, which ruled China during this period, represents the eastern anchor of the band of Eurasian civilization that stretched across the Eurasian landmass during this period. The striking parallels between the Han and the Roman Empires should probably not be surprising.

Like Rome, the Han Empire originated in the need for a unified defense against barbarian invasions. During the Han Dynasty, Buddhism spread through China, just as Christianity spread through the Roman Empire. The monastic movements of both religions played an important role in maintaining the cultural continuity after barbarian conquests had broken up and overrun both empires.

Other parallels exist. The administration of the Roman Empire owed much to the spread of Roman law and magistrates. The governance of the Han Empire was similarly stabilized by the creation of a bureaucracy chosen through the world's first civil service exams. Just as Roman emperors styled themselves "Augustus," so did the Chinese Emperor rule according to the "mandate of heaven." Neither the Roman judicial class nor the Chinese "scholar-bureaucrat" managed to wrest power from older landed aristocracies.

In one critical respect Chinese society under the Han was different from Roman society. Confucian social structure, at least its ideal, was markedly different from the Roman ideal or reality. Confucian thought divided society into four hierarchical classes. At the top was the scholar, followed in turn by the farmer, the craftsman, and the merchant. Soldiers were despised as outsiders, garrisoned at a safe distance on the frontier.

Chinese culture during the Han dynasty reflected the rule of scholars. Paper was invented in 105 A.D. and used in the writing of tens of thousands of volumes by thousands of authors. Scientists charted the moon's movement around the Earth and predicted solar eclipses. They also invented a magnetic compass.

THE WORLD OF BYZANTIUM (500–1453). The Eastern Roman Empire was one of the few centers of civilization able to withstand the barbarian invasions of the fourth and fifth centuries. At first the empire centered at Constantinople retained much of its Latin tradition. However, the seventh-century invasions of the Moslems, Slavs, Avars, and Persians progressively isolated Constantinople. Greek and Eastern influence strengthened, creating the more distinct Byzantine civilization.

The important elements of Byzantine civilization were (1) the military, an armored cavalry with stirrups and spears, (2) the emperor, a divinely anointed autocrat who was the head of church and state, (3) the cities, especially Constantinople, with their wealthy merchant class and sophisticated Greco-Roman culture, and (4) the church, whose missionaries imparted Byzantine law and culture (along with religion) to Bulgars, Slavs, and others.

The Byzantine Empire represented a highly centralized state. While it borrowed the successful Persian military armored cavalry, it supported the army with taxes and plunder rather than feudal grants of land as in Sassanian Persia and later in western Europe. This might reflect an anti-aristocratic bias in Byzantium, and/or the priorities of a sea-based power. It resulted in strengthening the emperor over the army and the church and gave the city clear priority over the countryside.

THE WORLD OF WESTERN EUROPE (500–1500). From a global perspective, relatively little attention should be given to Western Europe before 1000 A.D. The story of the barbarian invasions can be told elsewhere. The story of the church's theological debates, monasticism, and missionary activity can be told better as part of the history of Byzantine civilization. Feudalism and manorialism are hardly unique to western Europe and should be studied as part of a larger story that includes feudalism in China, Japan, and Persia.

It is the weakness, disorganization, and decentralization of western Europe that is most striking during this period. compared to the wealth, power, and sophistication of the Asian civilizations, the kingdoms of western Europe were like today's "developing countries." Western European weakness becomes interesting, however, because it helps to explain the "European miracle" that occurred between 1000 and 1500 A.D.

The rise of Western Europe by 1500 was due in large part to its lack of a powerful, centralized empire. The "weakness" of Europe (that is, the persistence of local aristocratic power) became its strength. A part of the world that had prized its heterogeneity since the Greeks now became a hothouse of mercantile, technological, and intellectual experimentation.

In this light, the church-state controversy that is a traditional part of a Western civilization course is relevant, because of the elbow room it provided. The growth of towns and the development of urban autonomy are also important parts of the story. So is the expanding agricultural productivity of the north, the revival of trade, the spread of markets and capitalist techniques, and the Crusades. These elements of transformation help to explain how this remote peninsula became capable of changing the world.

THE WORLD OF ISLAM (622–1500). Students should be able to distinguish the Arabs from Islam. They should understand something about the origins of Islam in the conflict between nomadic groups and the urban merchants of Arabia. They should know about the geography and culture of the Arabian peninsula and about the much broader geography of Islam's expansion. They should understand that followers of Islam see their religion as the culmination of the Judeo-Christian tradition and see Mohammed as the last in a line of prophets going back to Abraham.

The vigor and vitality of the early expansion should be made clear to students. Maps might show the enormity and rapidity of the Arab conquest. Some attempt might be made to distinguish the Umayyad and Abbasid Caliphates, seeing them respectively as a more Arab stage at Damascus (600–750) and a more bureaucratic, Persian-influenced stage at Baghdad (750–1100). Students should also be given some basis for understanding differences between Sunni and Shi'ite versions of Islam. The Sunni can be seen as an orthodox, traditional, and communal sect, and the Shi'ite as a sect opposed to Arab domination and more willing to submit to both spiritual authorities and hereditary rule.

Two tendencies in teaching about the Islamic world should be guarded against. The first is to suggest that a fragmentation of the culture went hand in hand with the declining authority of the Abbasid Caliphate. While political unity did not outlast the Caliphate, Islam remained culturally vigorous, unified, and strong. Geographically, the largest expansion of Islam came after the Caliphates. Indeed, Islam became the only hemisphere-wide culture of the period.

A second tendency in teaching about the Islamic world is to portray Islamic culture only as an archival service for Western Europe. The importance of the efforts of Islamic scholars to retain, translate, and elaborate on classical Greco-Roman culture can hardly be overstated. These scholars and the Crusades affected Europe more than Europeans affected Islam, but the Islamic world was more than a stepping-stone for later European development. Islamic history and power continue well beyond the first stirrings of Europeans on the world stage.

THE WORLD OF SOUTH AND SOUTHEAST ASIA (500–1500). Two important cultural and political developments occurred within South and Southeast Asia during this period. The first is the spread of classical Indian culture; the second is the Islamic conquest of the subcontinent after 711.

Both Indian Hinduism and Buddhism spread throughout Southeast Asia in the first half of this period. From Balinese Ramayana dances to the monuments of Borobudur in Central Java, from the Khmer temples of Angkor Wat to the Burmese temples of Pagan, the impact of Indian religion and culture is apparent.

The Mogul Empire, which arose after the Delhi Sultanate, made much of India part of the Moslem world. The Mogul civilization could be studied as part of the expansion of the Islamic world or as one of the great civilizations of the period. In looking at the Mogul Empire, students should examine Muslim-Hindu relations and Indian traditions of toleration and syncretism.

THE WORLD OF EAST ASIA (500–1750). During this period Chinese civilization was probably the greatest in the world. The reunification of China under the Sui Dynasty (589–618) was as short-lived as Justinian's reunification of the Roman Empire, but the T'ang Dynasty (618–907) made the achievement permanent. The T'ang redistributed agricultural land, developed the state examination system, and established prosperity and good government. Printing and gunpowder were developed at this time.

It was during the Sung Dynasty (960–1279), however, that China underwent a commercial revolution. Advances in the iron and coal industries helped make the Sung economy the most productive in the world. In the process the Sung might well have initiated an industrial revolution if developments had not been interrupted by the Mongol invasions.

The Chinese dynasty that replaced the Mongols, the Ming (1368–1644), was far more successful in expanding Chinese frontiers than in reviving pre-Mongol prosperity. Ming rulers sent naval expeditions as far as the Persian Gulf and East Africa. Ming armies extracted tribute from Vietnam, Korea, and central Asia, but the Ming suddenly withdrew from overseas navigation in 1433 and increased their attention to land defenses. The completeness and rapidity of the withdrawal says something about the strength of the steppe cavalries, who had recently adopted the religion of Islam.

The Manchu conquest brought the Ch'ing Dynasty (1644–1912) to power. Although culturally Chinese, this alien dynasty oversaw the opening of China to the West.

The history of Japan during this period is best told in relation to other areas. Students should know that the Japanese assimilated many key aspects of Chinese culture, although they managed to avoid Chinese political and cultural domination. The Chinese ideal of centralized absolutism has had a particularly great impact on Japanese political history. However, the history of Japan may best be told with an eye toward Europe. Both Japan and Europe escaped the Mongol onslaught but cultivated militaristic cultures. Both experienced feudalism but successfully encouraged the development of towns. Both struggled to gain their independence from stronger, more orthodox cultures. Both created maritime and commercial institutions that aided future industrialization.

THE CIVILIZATIONS OF AFRICA (500–1750). In looking at civilization in Africa, concentration should be placed on cultures south of the Sahara. However, introductions to African civilization should remind students that ancient Egypt was an African civilization and that North Africa, along with parts of West and East Africa, are part of Islamic civilization.

Geography is as important to African as it is to Indian history. The Sahara Desert helps to explain African isolation from many of the crises that influenced European and Asian history. The Atlantic winds and currents made travel from the Gulf of Guinea to the Mediterranean extremely treacherous, and the malarial mosquito and the tsetse fly made travel within much of Africa hazardous.

Yet students should appreciate that despite these geographic barriers, considerable movement and trade developed. In the classical world Ethiopia was a pivotal stop on trade routes between Rome and India. After A.D. 750 both the Indian Ocean coast and West Africa were integrated into world trade. The gold and salt trade across the Sahara had been important as early as Roman times. It took on enormous significance during European commercial development. Europeans first came for gold and later took slaves.

A key point in studying African history and geography is to dispel stereotypes. Students should see that Africa is more than deserts and tropical rain forests; they should see the variety of political institutions that developed in

Africa. The kingdoms of the Sudan demonstrate that complex state structures developed in Africa, and the cities of East Africa demonstrate the complexity of some African societies. Students should also be introduced to the stateless societies of places like coastal West Africa.

The slave trade is an important subject in world history. Its legacy still shapes the relations of the Americas and Africa, as well as the internal history of both continents. Traditional African slavery should be differentiated in terms of its motivations and impact from the type of slavery that existed in the mines and plantations of the Americas. The human toll taken by Western slavery can hardly be overemphasized. Some West African societies suffered significant population declines as a result of the slave trade. In transit, three Africans died for each one that reached the Americas. Once there, more died than were born. Half the European merchants and soldiers who arrived at African trading posts died in their first year.

THE CIVILIZATIONS OF THE AMERICAS (500–1500).   Geographic isolation shaped and probably hindered American cultural development even more than African. Even the Neolithic Revolution in the Americas occurred without benefit of contact with Eurasia. Perhaps the most important consequence of American isolation was the difference in immunological systems, which resulted in a massive population decline when Eurasian diseases were finally introduced after 1492.

American agriculture began around 5000 B.C., with the cultivation of corn in Central America. Urban civilization developed around 900 B.C. in Central America, and later in the Andes.

The civilizations of the Americas tell us much about the parameters of "civilization." On the one hand, we can stress the similarity with Eurasian civilizations by comparing the highly centralized, sun-worshipping Incan Empire of Peru to that of ancient Egypt. In general terms the priest-dominated, irrigated cities and kingdoms of Mexico are similar to Mesopotamia. On the other hand, we can stress the differences between American and Eurasian civilizations by focusing on the limited use of draft animals, the more rudimentary technology as reflected in building tools and the absence of the wheel, the absence of iron or bronze metallurgy, and the limitations of Mexican pictographic writing and Peruvian knotted cords for communication and recordkeeping. By focusing on these types of comparisons, the study of American civilizations can show students the richness of these civilizations and avoid unduly emphasizing the exotica of Aztec sacrifice, Mayan "astronomy," and lost temples overgrown by jungle.

Part IV: The rise of the West

EUROPEAN RENAISSANCE, REFORMATION, AND REORGANIZATION (1400–1650).   The "rise of the West" is probably the most important historical development in the history of the last millennium. The period from 1400 to 1650 is the era in which Western Europe differentiated itself from the post-Mongol absolutism that reigned elsewhere in Eurasia. The Europeans created a vigorous series of independent nation-states with competing economies, religions, and ambitions.

The dynamism of the West can be seen in its pluralism. A unique competition arose between the secular worldview of Greece and Rome and the sacred worldview of the Judeo-Christian tradition. Politically, a new type of territorial state arose, larger than the city-state but smaller than an empire. Independent of church or ruling orthodoxies, and relatively homogeneous in ethnicity, language, and culture, these new states competed relentlessly with each other for power, bullion, resources, and markets. The competition ensured immediate outlets and ever-growing opportunities for new technologies of war, transport, and production.

The Renaissance and the Reformation take on global significance precisely because these great social movements prevented the creation of a single empire or orthodoxy, despite the intentions of the people involved in them.

EUROPEAN EXPANSION AND A NEW WORLD (1400–1800). The European expansion and unification of the world that began in 1400 irrevocably changed the course of world history.

The focus of this period should be on the elements of European expansion. These include the development of such new technologies and institutions as ocean-going ships, cannon, compasses, national monarchies, sailing schools, merchant adventurers, joint stock companies, and an independent middle class. It also includes the efforts undertaken by the Portuguese under Prince Henry, Columbus, and the first "explorers." The problems of ocean exploration, such as the contrary winds and currents of the Atlantic, or the patterns of global currents and winds could be examined. Whether we follow the currents or conquistadors, this is an excellent opportunity for lessons in global geography.

The integration of the eastern and western hemispheres, the Atlantic and Pacific rims, is also crucial. For the first time in human history, the globe became a single place. The exchange of flora and fauna, as well as microbes, permanently altered the world. The period raises innumerable questions about ecology, peace, and even the exploration of other planets.

SCIENCE, COMMERCE, AND THE MODERN WORLD (1600–1800). A world history course should explore differing assumptions about science, reason, experiment, and truth in Western and non-Western cultures. Rather than a recitation of scientific inventions as in a history of science, this section should help students understand the impact of scientific ways of looking at the world and the changing assumptions that accompanied modern science.

Modern science and modern commerce were both inducements to and the results of Western expansion. As such, they demonstrate the same universalism, rationality, practicality, attention to detail, and middle-class asceticism. Yet, here too, comparisons can place Europe into a new perspective. During this period the Indian subcontinent also enjoyed a vigorous economy. Merchants played important, if not always socially esteemed, roles in the Islamic world, China, and Japan. Southeast Asia had its pirate-merchants, and the transition of samurai from warrior to bureaucrat to capitalist in Tokugawa and Meiji Japan was a politico-economic transformation that rivaled Europe's.

THE WESTERN DEMOCRATIC REVOLUTION (1640–1850). A world history should treat the Enlightenment and "the age of democratic revolutions" as an opportunity to teach the meaning of citizenship in modern democratic society. The English Civil War as well as the American and French Revolutions can be used to show the evolution of parliamentary democracy.

The treatment should focus on the development of middle-class parliamentary states, constitutions, parties and the rule of law. Both the universalistic principles and the class interests that underlay these institutions should be examined. These revolutions should also be portrayed as laying the foundation for the rapid economic development that occurred subsequently as a result of bourgeois ascendancy and the industrial revolution.

THE INDUSTRIAL REVOLUTION (1750–1914). If one had to designate the three most important turning points in world history, they would be the agricultural, urban, and industrial revolutions. Initially English, industrialization rapidly became a European, an Atlantic, and finally a Western phenomenon. More than anything else it has become the defining characteristic of "the West." Yet the industrial revolution was probably a global event from the start. It might not have occurred without slavery in the Caribbean, British control of India, and the world markets and raw materials available through the British Empire.

It is a mistake to exclude North America from a survey of the industrial revolution. While England should take precedence, North America continued to be an important part of the British economic empire well into the nineteenth century.

The industrial revolution should not be treated simply as a catalogue of inventions. More important characteristics include the displacement of farmers and farm laborers, the growth of an impoverished class of urban workers, and the replacement of household industry by factories. Also important are the explosion of mass-produced products at fiercely competitive prices, the periodic collapse of markets, and the central roles played first by cotton and later by railroads in economic growth.

The historical debate regarding the consequences of the industrial revolution should also occupy a key place in a world history course. One need only read some of the literature of the period, Tory and socialist, to understand current debates over industrialization within the Third World. The issue may not be whether the industrial revolution improved or reduced the quality of life. The question being asked in Egypt, India, and even Iran is how to industrialize without losing traditional values and identity. The study of Western industrialization can help in this search by asking what was necessary for industrialization and what was not.

NATIONALISM AND INTERNATIONALISM (1815–1914). In the Western civilization survey this period focuses on the struggle of poets for a national voice under Napoleonic occupation, the tensions between nationalist, liberal, and socialist aspirations in 1848, and the unification of Italy and Germany. These are themes of global significance as well, because the forces that European society was creating in this period would transform the world.

From a global perspective, however, the most significant story during this period involves the deep tensions between the emerging ideologies of nationalism and internationalism. The key to these tensions, and the single most important event of this period, is the enormous population transfer that accompanied industrialization. The peopling of the United States, Canada, Argentina, Brazil, Australia, and South Africa is part of this story.

Students should see the mass migrations of the period in the context of world labor markets and the age of European imperialism. They should see the continuation of these tensions in current debates over immigration policy in the United States.

Part V: The world in the shadow of the West

WESTERN DOMINANCE (1800–1945). Having explored the factors underlying the "rise of the West," students are in a position to understand how the West exerted power over the rest of the world. Part of this story is technological, and part is political and economic. Students should understand that imperial control over territory can be exerted short of occupation. This was, in fact, the mode of European dominance before 1800.

The "New Imperialism" is usually dated from 1880 to 1914. This is the highpoint of military occupation, territorial acquisition, and imperial dominion. Students should see this as a "stage" in European ascendancy and global integration. They should also understand that imperialism did not end with World War I; it merely abated or changed its form. Students might look at current foreign policy issues in this light. How might United States activities in Latin America and other areas of the Third World be interpreted in the context of this history?

The larger question is the relationship between imperialism and "underdevelopment." Has underdevelopment resulted from the political and economic dominance that began in the age of imperialism? Is it the result of continuing systematic exploitation of global "peripheries" by "core" areas in the world economy? Or is underdevelopment simply a reflection of the Western world's head start in industrialization? Will it become a meaningless concept as Third World nations educate their people and add to their industrial capacity?

COLONIAL WORLDS (1800–1945). Students should be encouraged to understand Western domination from the perspective of the various colonial worlds. They should understand the brutality and the philanthropy of imperialism. They should understand the seductiveness of Western material life and culture and the appeal of traditional ways of life, as well as the implicit contradiction in the argument that imperialism represented "improvement" by the overseer in "preparation" for self-government.

To understand all of this, students must see the conflicts between Western and traditional values in particular and specific settings. The choice of which colonial areas to stress should depend on the need for continuity with what has come before and what will follow. It should also depend on the different themes that emerge from the different experiences with imperialism.

A study of Latin America, for example, would stress the impact of Third World elites, especially landed aristocrats and clergy. The lessons of Latin America have much to do with things that failed, but repeated revolutions, caudillos, coups, and dictators all involved at their root a class struggle between a rich landed aristocracy and an impoverished and disenfranchised peasantry. It is also in this context that the development of single-product export economies and the intrusion of foreign companies and governments should be presented. How have the implicit and sometimes explicit alliances between Latin American elites and foreign interests affected the history and the development of Latin American nations?

North Africa and the Middle East can be used to explore Third World efforts to adopt and adapt Western culture and technology in response to imperialism. Turkey attempted to adopt Western ways under the direction of Sultan Selim III, the Young Turks, and Kemal Ataturk. The case of Iran is important in its own right. It shows the role that Russia played as a secondary modernizer. The example of Reza Shah in Iran is very similar to that of Ataturk but with, it would seem, very different results. One might ask how permanent Westernization is. Finally, French policy toward Algeria and the Algerian independence movement set the stage for discussing Third World revolution in the contemporary world.

Sub-Saharan Africa may be one of the best arenas within which to look at imperialism, because of its diversity and impact. The differences between British indirect rule and French direct rule may not have seemed all that critical to Africans, but they have left different legacies. The settler states of East and South Africa also experienced somewhat different histories than colonies more sparsely occupied by Europeans. The wrenching experience of imperialism for individuals can in some ways be better shown in Africa than elsewhere. Western penetration had a more direct impact on everyday life in Africa than in places like Turkey or China, which escaped direct colonial rule. In African cities at least, European tongues, religion, money, and manners became the media for communicating with other Africans as well as the Europeans in authority.

Finally, in Asia a comparison of the experiences of India, China, and Japan reinforces the idea that different forms of colonialism had largely equivalent consequences. The brutal and insensitive policy of the British in China, as represented by the Opium Wars, was ultimately no more effective in preserving Western prerogatives than the liberal and paternalistic policies often pursued in India, as represented by British education for Indians. Both forms of domination undermined themselves. Indeed, as British policy became more aggressively "protective" of Indian interests and committed to "Westernizing" India, the grievances of Indians mounted. Japanese success at modernizing and fending off Western control provides an important contrast.

The study of Third World experiences with imperialism provides an important opportunity to introduce students to non-Western heros, as well as to look at the nature and legacy of Western domination. In this regard Mahatma Gandhi may be one of the most important individuals for students to study. Gandhi's impact on the Indian independence movement was critical, and his philosophy of nonviolence and nonalignment are still important today. Students might ask whether Gandhi's policy can work in places like South Africa.

Part VI: The world in conflict

WORLD WAR I AND THE RUSSIAN REVOLUTION (1914–1921). World War I and the Russian Revolution were global events. The war was fought in Africa and Asia as well as Europe. The commitment of colonial troops involved an implicit promise of and prelude to independence. The Russian Revolution and subsequent industrialization, especially under Stalin, gave the Marxist-Leninist ideology practical appeal to the leaders of emerging nations in Asia and Africa.

Both the war and the revolution should be seen within the context of European history. Students do not need a recounting of the battles of the war, but they should understand the momentous loss of lives it involved. They should also understand the crisis of confidence and lost hope that the war inspired throughout Europe.

The events of the Russian Revolution might usefully be recounted in some detail. Students should know about the conflicts between the Bolsheviks and other parties and about the role of such individuals as Lenin, Trotsky, and Stalin. They should understand the impact of the revolution on European socialism, liberalism, and democracy. American students should know about the Allied Expeditionary Force in Russia and about the early enthusiasm for the revolution expressed by people like John Reed and Henry Ford.

DEPRESSION, TOTALITARIANISM, AND WORLD WAR (1922–1945). Students should see the economic crisis of the 1920s and 1930s, the rise of totalitarianism, and World War II as part of an interrelated set of forces that arose in the aftermath of World War I.

The image of Germans using wheelbarrows to carry the money needed to buy a loaf of bread in the early 1920s may help students understand the subsequent political upheaval. They should understand that both Mussolini and Hitler had genuine and widespread popular support. Their decisiveness, commitment, and sense of renewal contrasted sharply with the floundering political elites they replaced. Students should also understand that American society in the 1930s experienced the same hunger for leadership and quest for community.

Stalin's regime and Japanese militarization should also be included in a survey of totalitarianism during this period, but students should understand the differences among the three manifestations of authoritarian rule. While fascism sought community plus inequality, for example, communism sought community plus equality. Even Stalin's brutal excesses should be seen in this light; despite them, Russians fought harder and died in greater numbers for Stalin than for any Czar.

One theme from this era that is often stressed is the issue of preparedness and war. Munich and Pearl Harbor seem to teach the need for continued alertness, military readiness, and international distrust. At the same time, American leaders of the time believed that the war demonstrated the need for closer economic and political cooperation internationally. Students should be asked what they can learn from the experience of World War II. They should also ask about the lessons of Hiroshima and Nagasaki. Were the bombings justified, or were they avoidable? How have these events changed the world militarily and politically?

Part VII: Problems of the interdependent world

One of the most important functions of a world history course is to teach students to think historically about the problems of their own world. They should be encouraged to explore these problems in the broadest historical view. Which of the vast array of contemporary problems merit attention? The answer becomes less easy without the perspective of future developments. What follows is a suggestive guide to the current problems that seem most important in light of the past.

THE SOVIET-AMERICAN CONFLICT. One of the key tasks is clearly an exploration of the origins and nature of the Cold War. American and Soviet actions in the United Nations and in the nuclear arms race offer opportunities to gauge Soviet and American sincerity, manipulation, disagreement, and common interests. The conflicts in Korea, Hungary, Cuba, and Afghanistan, along with the various efforts to normalize relations, raise questions about whether the relationship has changed over time and where it might be heading.

Changes in the Soviet Union since Stalin and the role of the United States as a world power are also relevant. What changes have taken place in Soviet political and economic life? Have these changes affected Soviet involvement in world affairs? How has the United States used its power in the United Nations and elsewhere? The war in Vietnam should enter into this discussion, as should American efforts to create and maintain economic institutions based on the principles of competition and free trade since World War II.

SOCIAL AND ECONOMIC CHANGE IN THE INDUSTRIALIZED WORLD: WESTERN EUROPE AND JAPAN. A study of social and economic change in the industrialized world since 1945 could focus on Western Europe or Japan.

In Europe, current problems of industrial competition, the need for "re-industrialization," and the limitations of the "welfare state" should be understood in the context of European social and economic development since the war. Students should understand the enormous devastation inflicted on Europe, the remarkable rebuilding of those societies and economies, and the great importance of the Common Market, the Marshall Plan, the World Bank, and an international economy based on free trade in that recovery. Current problems should also be seen in light of competition from the newly industrializing areas of the world.

For geographic and cultural reasons Japan tends to be treated as part of Asia. Yet in the decades since World War II Japan has become a part of the industrialized world, socially and politically as well as economically. In most respects developments in Japan since World War II have more in common with Germany than with other Asian countries.

Students should know about Japan's economic "miracle," but they should also learn about the social revolution that was set in motion by the American occupation. The new Japanese constitution called for sexual equality, collective bargaining, and radical land reform. Article Nine renounced war forever, allowing the Japanese to concentrate their resources on industrial expansion rather than defense. Yet even Japan has not escaped the social and economic problems of the industrialized world. Japan's economic success has not only caused tensions with its trading partners; greater wealth has also led most Japanese to expect higher standards of living. Success has furthered the social revolution begun by the Americans and in certain respects made the Japanese less competitive in comparison with the newly industrializing nations of the Pacific Rim.

THE BURDEN OF COLONIALISM: SUB-SAHARAN AFRICA. The colonial heritage represents an important perspective on events within the contemporary world. No region offers a better arena for looking at the burden of colonialism than Africa.

There were only two independent states on the African continent in 1945: Liberia and Ethiopia. Today all but South Africa and Namibia are independent of European rule or the political domination of European descendants. In some cases, independence was achieved at great cost. The revolutions in the Belgian Congo, Angola, Mozambique, and Zimbabwe are prime examples. In other cases, such as Ghana, Nigeria, the Ivory Coast, and Senegal, independence was attained relatively peacefully.

No matter how political independence was achieved, however, the burden of colonialism remained. Boundaries had no rhyme nor reason. They were carved out on the basis of European *realpolitik*, not on the basis of African ethnic or geographic boundaries. In most cases colonialism either destroyed or compromised indigenous political institutions. As a result independence usually meant that Western-style governments were established without benefit of a functioning political community. By 1980 only Gambia, Botswana, and the offshore island of Mauritius had reasonably stable, functioning democracies. Few African societies were successfully dealing with rapid population growth and urbanization. Food production was falling behind population virtually everywhere. Urbanization was proceeding faster than economic growth, leading to widespread unemployment and other problems.

On the other hand, pan-African movements have been more effective than similar movements in Asia or the Americas. The philosophy of African socialism has had continental appeal, even if different African leaders have defined it differently. Also, the religious and family values of traditional African village life have remained deeply felt parts of African cultures. Few urban inhabitants, for example, lose contact with their villages or relatives.

South Africa represents a special case in terms of the impact of the colonial heritage. The white domination of South Africa increased after 1948 with the victory of the Afrikaner-dominated Nationalist Party. Students should understand what apartheid is and how it influences South African society, both white and black. They should know about the various groups struggling for change and accommodation within the country, including groups at the heart of the unrest in the "black townships."

THE DIFFICULTY OF DEVELOPMENT: CENTRAL AND SOUTH AMERICA. The history of Central and South America since 1945 provides a good, if idiosyncratic, opportunity to look at the problems of economic development within the

Third World. This region holds within it great disparities, from oil-rich Venezuela and the middle-income countries of Brazil and Argentina to the poverty-ridden nations of Haiti and Bolivia. Since many of these states are plural societies, with descendants of Europeans in the majority or at least in control of key political, economic, and social institutions, they should be compared with the United States, Canada, and Australia.

The continuation of the Spanish tradition of autocratic and bureaucratic government is an important theme. So is the traditionally conservative role of the church and the military. Students should understand the importance of these traditional elites and their ties to the international economy as forces for continuity, as well as the role of peasants and urban underclasses as forces for change. The ways in which the military in Peru and the church in Nicaragua and El Salvador have become agents of change should also be noted.

Examining particular revolutions can make these relationships more meaningful. The "frozen revolution" of Mexico, the Cuban revolution, the Allende period in Chile, and the Sandinista revolution in Nicaragua demonstrate these relationships, but so do Peron's fascism in Argentina, the Vargas regime in Brazil, and the Chilean counterrevolution that toppled Allende.

SOCIAL REVOLUTION AND DEVELOPMENT: EAST AND SOUTH ASIA. The theme of social revolution and development is even more starkly posed in a comparison of China and India.

Both the radical nature of the Chinese Revolution and its chaotic swings should be stressed. Students should know that one of the key targets of Chinese communist attacks after 1949 were the traditional Chinese intellectuals. They should understand the enormity of the economic reorganization represented by the "Great Leap Forward," when 88 percent of Chinese farm families were organized into communes. They should know about the shifts in power between radicals and moderates that took place between 1959 and 1972. In particular they should see the turmoil of Mao's "Great Proletarian Cultural Revolution" and the subsequent reassertion of moderate, technocratic policies. Students should try to understand the impact of social revolution on Chinese life and on Chinese efforts to forge a modern economy. They should ask how confident the West can be in the current direction of Chinese policy, given this history.

Indian society has not experienced the radical social revolution of China, although it has experienced some of the turmoil. India inherited a British parliamentary system and is often called "the world's largest democracy." At the same time Indian independence brought enormous social upheaval as a result of the cultural and religious conflict between Muslims and Hindus. The creation of Pakistan involved the movement of 20 million people and the death of many hundreds of thousands. India's democratic aspirations and mixed economy have resulted in greater extremes of wealth and poverty than in China, but they have also created more opportunity for improving one's status and freedom of behavior. Students should ask whether democracy, a mixed economy, and relatively greater political stability have made India more successful than China in terms of achieving political and economic independence and promoting economic development.

NATIONALISM AND CULTURAL IDENTITY: NORTH AFRICA AND THE MIDDLE EAST. The Middle East and North Africa, the heart of the Islamic world, provide an ideal opportunity to look at reactions against imperialism that have stressed cultural identity and integrity of tradition.

In Turkey, Iran, Egypt, and elsewhere in this region, the first response to Western dominance had been the adoption of Western secularism. In Turkey, state judges replaced clergy; piety became a personal matter. Throughout the region, military officers such as Reza Palavi in Iran and Nassar in Egypt led the way, since the military was usually the first Western-ized sector of society. The secularization of life represented a fundamental transformation of the social base of Islamic societies and a direct attack on the social and political role of organized religion. The emergence of Islamic fundamentalism as a force for reasserting an indigenous cultural identity should not be surprising in this light. While the fundamentalist movement has not been successful in Turkey, it has had a marked impact on the politics and economics of the region well beyond Iran.

The contrast between the reassertion of Islamic cultural identity and the power of nationalism in this region is more than a little ironic, given Islam's internationalism and tribalism. Yet various attempts at pan-Arabism and at creating an Arab Union have been defeated. It is similarly ironic that the Zionist movement, a nationalist strain of an internationalist faith, has forged the two most extreme nationalisms in the world: Palestinian and Israeli.

4. Annotated bibliography

Allardyce, Gilbert. "The Rise and Fall of the Western Civilization Course," in *The American Historical Review* (87:3), June 1982, pp. 695–743, including responses. An excellent review of the "rise and fall" of the college course from its beginnings at Columbia College. Also views models developed at Harvard, Chicago, and Stanford. Points to need for a world history course.

Barraclough, Geoffrey. *An Introduction to Contemporary History.* New York: Penguin, 1967. One of the first and best histories of the twentieth-century world.

————. *The Times Atlas of World History.* London: Times, 1978. A superb historical atlas, also available in a shorter, abridged form from Hammond. The basis for a TV series on world history.

————. *Turning Points in World History.* London: Thames & Hudson, 1977. Very short summary of major "turning points" in world history.

Braudel, Fernand. *The Structures of Everyday Life.* New York: Harper & Row, 1981.
————. *The Wheels of Commerce.* New York: Harper & Row, 1981.
————. *The Perspective of the World.* New York: Harper & Row, 1984. Three-volume set that extends and deepens earlier *Capitalism and Material Civilization, 1500–1800.* A wide-ranging history that covers everything from food and clothing to political alliances. Rich use of data, photos, and anecdotes. Mediterranean Europe is best represented, but global insights abound.
Crosby, Alfred. *The Columbian Exchange.* Greenwood Press, 1972. The effects of the Columbian "discovery" and unification of the Eastern and Western hemispheres. Details flora and fauna of both areas, the Spanish response to differences, and the debate over syphilis.
Curtin, Philip D. *Cross Cultural Trade in World History.* Cambridge University Press, 1984. Excellent study of trade in global perspective.
Hodgson, Marshall G.S. *The Venture of Islam,* 3 vols. University of Chicago Press, 1974. Challenging, extensive study of Islam. A lot, but all one needs. Also the outline of a world history approach.
Jones, E.L. *The European Miracle.* Cambridge University Press, 1981. Rich, thoughtful economic history. Explains the bases for the European economic development since 1000 against the background of Asian and Islamic economy and society.
McEvedy, Colin, and Jones, Richard. *Atlas of World Population History.* New York: Penguin, 1980. A basic, short reference containing graphs for population growth in all major countries and areas of the globe since the Neolithic. Also provides narrative explanation of changes.
McNeill, William H. *Plagues and People.* New York: Doubleday, 1976. Global study of epidemic disease in modern history.
————. *The Pursuit of Power.* University of Chicago Press, 1982. The technological-military pursuit of modern Western society.
————. *The Rise of the West.* University of Chicago Press, 1970. The best world history written.
————. *A World History.* Oxford University Press, 1971. An adaptation of the above for college students.
————, et al., eds. *Readings in World History,* 10 vols. Oxford University Press, 1968. Excellent collection of primary source materials.
Moore, Barrington, Jr. *Social Origins of Dictatorship and Democracy.* Boston: Beacon, 1966. Interesting comparative study of the way in which relative power of peasantry and aristocracy leads to fascism, communism, or democracy in modern Europe, U.S., and Japan.
Reilly, Kevin. *The West and the World.* New York: Harper & Row, 1980. A topical history of civilization. Essays to make college students think historically.
————, ed. *World History: Selected Readings and Course Outlines from American Colleges and Universities.* New York: Markus Wiener, 1985. Wide variety of world history syllabi.
Roberts, J.M. *The Pelican History of the World.* New York: Penguin, 1980. Good, thorough survey.
Stavrianos, L.S. *A Global History.* Englewood Cliffs, N.J.: Prentice-Hall, 1983. Very good college text. Especially strong on effects of Western imperialism and colonialism on the Third World.
————. *Global Rift.* New York: William Morrow, 1981. Excellent global history since 1500; argues that development of West engendered underdevelopment of Third World. Written with passion; well-chosen quotes.

Wallerstein, Immanuel. *The Modern World-System*, 2 vols. New York: Academic Press, 1974, 1980. More detailed, scholarly presentation of the dependency thesis, with more attention to intricacies of debate.

Willis, F. Roy. *World Civilizations*. New York: D.C. Heath, 1986. A good college text, centered on urban history with particular cities representing each civilization.

Wolf, Eric R. *Europe and the People without History*. Berkeley, Calif.: University of California Press, 1982. A great anthropologist's world history since 1400. Quirky, telling, and controversial.

5. Content outline for a world history course

UNIT I: HUMAN BEGINNINGS AND FIRST CIVILIZATIONS (to 500 B.C.)

1. Human origins and the agriculture revolution (to 4000 B.C.)
   1.1 Early human development was marked by important technical revolutions
   Fire and speech
   Hunting and gathering tools
   1.2 The agricultural revolution transformed humanity
   Tools and inventors of agriculture
   Farm and pasture
   Neolithic culture
2. Early civilizations in the Middle East and North Africa (4000 B.C.–500 B.C.)
   2.1 Civilization was the product of the urban revolution
   Towns and cities
   Impact of urban revolution
   2.2 The civilizations of Mesopotamia and Egypt were similar and different
   Similarity of river civilizations
   Difference of rivers
   Parallel achievements and problems
3. Early civilizations in South and East Asia (2500 B.C.–500 B.C.)
   3.1 Ancient Indus Valley civilizations were very sophisticated
   Highly centralized and comfortable
   Evidence of caste
   3.2 Ancient Chinese civilization was unique
   Different written script
   Continuous cultural traditions

UNIT II: CLASSICAL EURASIAN CIVILIZATION (2000 B.C.–A.D. 500)

1. The Greek and Hellenistic worlds (2000 B.C.–31 B.C.)
   1.1 The Greek civilization had roots in Minoan Crete and Mycenean civilization
   The civilization of Minoan Crete
   Mycenean civilization and Dorian invasions
   1.2 The uniqueness of Greek civilization was the territorial polity of the city-state
   Importance of *polis* in Greece
   Territory and law (vs. caste)
   Athens and Sparta

1.3 Hellenistic civilization was imperial and cosmopolitan
    Alexander the Great
    Hellenistic empire and culture
2. The Roman world (1000 B.C.–A.D. 476)
  2.1 The Roman Republic replaced Etruscan civilization with Greek colonies
    Etruscans and Greeks
    Republican Rome
  2.2 Roman expansion changed Roman society
    Spread of Roman Empire
    Militarization and civil war
  2.3 The Roman Empire transformed traditional Roman culture
    Augustan Age culture
    Rise and spread of Christianity
    Culture and heritage of Rome
3. The Indian world (500 B.C.–A.D. 500)
  3.1 Classical India produced great religions and religious reformers
    Brahmanism, Jainism, and Buddhism
    Mauryan Empire
  3.2 The Gupta Empire was a golden age
    Spread of Buddhism and Hindu revival
    Indian trade and the Eurasian connection
    Scientific and cultural contributions
    Spread of Indian religions to Southeast Asia
4. The Chinese world (500 B.C.–A.D. 500)
  4.1 The main pattern of Chinese history is steppe invasions followed by dynasties
    Chin Dynasty and Great Wall
    Chou feudalism
  4.2 Confucian thought shaped Chinese culture
    Confucius and Mencius
    Importance of family
  4.3 The Han Dynasty was much like the Roman Empire
    Similar expansion against barbarians
    Bureaucracy and civil service exam
    Role of scholars different

UNIT III: TRADITIONAL CIVILIZATIONS (A.D. 500–1750)

1. The world of Byzantium (500–1453)
  1.1 Byzantine civilization began as a continuation of Roman civilization
    Justinian and Roman law
    Seventh-century invasions and Greek influence
  1.2 The military, church, emperor, and city were important institutions
    Armored cavalry and stirrups
    Monasticism and iconoclasm
    Caesaro-papism
    Constantinople
2. The world of Western Europe (500–1500)
  2.1 Western Rome was fragmented by barbarian invasions

Mayan, Aztec and Inca civilizations
Science and religions
Culture of stateless societies

UNIT IV: THE RISE OF THE WEST (1400–1914)

1. European Renaissance, Reformation and reorganization (1400–1650)
    1.1 Europe changed culturally
        Renaissance and Reformation
        Individualism and secularism
        Printing and nationalism
        Declining influence of the church
    1.2 Europe changed socially and politically
        Pluralism of small nation-states
        Middle classes and merchants
        Kings and constitutions
2. European expansion and a new world (1400–1800)
    2.1 Europe expanded for internal and external reasons
        Chinese maritime withdrawal and Muslim disunity
        European navigation technology
        Political leadership and interest
    2.2 Columbus forged a single, ecological world
        "The Columbian exchange" of plants, animals and diseases
        Destruction of Amerindians
    2.3 Northern Europe took over the early lead of the Spanish and Portuguese
        Different social and political structures
        Mercantilism
        British defeat French
3. Science and commerce in the world (1600–1800)
    3.1 Europe underwent a scientific revolution
        Meaning of science in traditional society
        Observation, objectivity, and experimental method
        Science and technology
        The Enlightenment: Science of society
    3.2 Europe underwent a commercial revolution
        Economics and markets in traditional society
        Commercialization of land and labor
        Alliance of merchants and kings
        Merchant independence
4. The Western democratic revolution (1640–1815)
    4.1 Europe underwent a political revolution
        The English Civil War
        The Glorious Revolution
        The American Revolution
        The French Revolution
    4.2 This revolution established modern democracy
        Political parties and parliaments
        Constitutions and rule of law

Middle-class nation-states
Separation of state and government, state and religion, office and individual
5. The industrial revolution (1750–1914)
    5.1 Europe underwent a technological revolution
        Preconditions of an industrial revolution
        British Empire well suited
        Importance of sugar, slavery, and cotton
    5.2 Industrialization had mixed effects elsewhere
        Imitated in North America and Western Europe
        Increased dependence of many other areas
    5.3 Industrialization ultimately transformed the world
        Mechanical production and interchangeable parts
        Factories replaced handicraft
        Products became much more plentiful and cheap
        Work became highly organized
6. Nationalism and internationalism (1815–1914)
    6.1 Nation-states encouraged national feeling
        Nationalism in European thought
        Ecumenical vs. exclusivist nationalism after 1848
        Nationalist conflict before 1914
    6.2 Nation-states encouraged colonial possessions and international markets
        Free trade empires
        The new imperialism
        International labor migrations
    6.3 Citizens and workers felt conflicting demands
        Nationalist citizenship vs. immigrant ties
        Socialist internationalism vs. national patriotism

UNIT V: THE WORLD IN THE SHADOW OF EUROPE (1750–1945)

1. Latin America (1500–1945)
    1.1 Latin America was the first European colony
        Spanish and Portuguese colonial policy
        Africans and Indians
        European settlers
    1.2 Latin America remained dependent
        Monroe Doctrine
        Monocultures and export economies
        Landed aristocracies and the church
2. North Africa and the Middle East (1750–1945)
    2.1 Westernization was sometimes voluntary and sometimes forced
        Balkan merchants and Turkish soldiers
        Egypt and Persia
    2.2 Russia was first Westernized and then became a Westernizer
        Peter the Great and Westernization
        Russian expansion in Asia and Middle East
3. Sub-Saharan Africa (1750–1945)
    3.1 Colonialism created secondary colonial empires

Ethiopia and Egyptian Sudan
Boer Republic
3.2 New imperialism ignored African society and culture
Boundaries irrelevant
Colonial pawns of European conflict
Entire assault on culture and personality
4. European colonial empires in Asia (1750–1945)
4.1 Private trading company empires became government empires
East India Company in India
Tea and opium
The Raj in India
4.2 Imperial control destroyed colonies
British enlightened policy self-defeating
China insulted
Chinese national revolution and war
4.3 Japanese self-Westernization was the most successful adaptation
Meiji Restoration
Controlled change

UNIT VI: THE WORLD IN CONFLICT (1914–1945)

1. World War I and the Russian Revolution (1914–1921)
1.1 World War I was a European civil war and a global conflict
Causes of the war
Effect on the colonies
1.2 World War I led to the Russian Revolution
The Russian Revolution
Its global impact
2. Depression, totalitarianism, and war (1922–1945)
2.1 The Great Depression changed Western societies
Economic collapse
Italian Fascism
German Nazism
Japanese militarization
2.2 World War II ended an era
The good fight
Liberalism and human brutality
Soviet allies
Total war

UNIT VII: PROBLEMS OF THE INTERDEPENDENT WORLD

1. The United States and the Soviet Union (1945–present)
1.1 North America underwent economic, social, and cultural changes
Economic integration and competition
New immigrants
Social and political tensions

Chapter 3
A Western Civilization Approach

Michael Gordon

1. Rationale

INTRODUCTION

For nearly a hundred years, the most prevalent world studies course in American high schools has been a survey of Western civilization. That course has been organized around two principles. First, it has been historical—more often than not, strictly chronological. It has looked to the past to understand how our world came to be what it is. Second, the course has centered on the Western experience. It has sought primarily (often exclusively) to teach students about the development of the values and institutions that were formulated in the Mediterranean world, took root in Europe, and eventually spread throughout Northern Eurasia, much of the Americas, and even parts of Oceania.

This time-honored course on the history of Western civilization has received renewed attention of late. Its advocates believe that American schools must do a better job of imparting to students an appreciation of Western values and institutions. Their defense of the approach comes as a response to the criticism that the traditional Western civilization course has been too ethnocentric. To survive in an increasingly interdependent and less Western-dominated world, critics argue, Americans must learn to view history in more global terms. What both the advocates and critics assume is that a choice must be made between two mutually exclusive ways of teaching history: an ethnocentric "Western" approach and a cosmopolitan "world" approach.

The approach suggested in this chapter rejects the premise that a "Western civilization" course must be ethnocentric and parochial. The approach suggested here does concentrate on the history of Western civilization. Its purpose is to help students understand the contemporary world through a historical explanation of the evolution of the West. The structure of the course is primarily chronological; it begins with the origins of Western civilization in the Middle East and Greece and concludes with the present. Course content is highly selective. Emphasis is placed on those institutions and values that have been critical in the development of Western society and culture.

However, the course suggested here also endeavors to avoid the ethnocentric or parochial bias that has beset past Western civilization courses. The selection of a Western civilization approach need not imply a value judgement concerning the intrinsic merits of Western civilization. Rather, it acknowledges that for Western students taught by Western teachers, Western civilization will unavoidably, and probably not undesirably, occupy a major role in the world studies course. Indeed, the role played by the West in world history over the past 500 years makes an understanding of its values and institutions of global, not just Western, importance.

Likewise, while the approach emphasizes the history of Western civilization, it does not ignore the existence or integrity of other civilizations. The history of the West is best seen through a "global perspective." Contacts with other parts of the world have played a major role in the history of the West. Comparison and contrast with other areas of the world are needed to explain Western society fully. Indeed, Western history becomes more meaningful and important when viewed from a global perspective. An ethnocentric and parochial focus on the West neglects one of the prime rationales for a world studies course of any kind: helping students understand how their lives are simultaneously and inextricably involved in both their own society and its global context. The idea of a global perspective thus becomes more than a mere label: It becomes an organizing principle that informs, influences, and affects our understanding of both Western and world history.

WESTERN CIVILIZATION AND WORLD HISTORY

Students currently in the tenth grade will live most of their lives in the twenty-first century. This realization, which tends to be mildly shocking to those of an older generation, should guide those responsible for education. The key goal of the high school world studies course is to help students understand the world they will face as adults. Only with such an understanding will they be able to function as informed citizens and make the reasoned decisions and judgments upon which the future of our society depends.

Appreciating the historical foundations of our world is critical to this goal. Western society has traditionally explained itself historically. An historical perspective (that is, an awareness of where we are coming from) is crucial to understanding where we are and where we may be going. While history does not pretend to predict the future, it does contribute to an understanding of the present. By isolating the threads of change and continuity in the past, history clarifies the significant issues and dynamics of the present. Armed with this understanding, it becomes possible to extrapolate likely images of the future, albeit with neither certainty nor precision.

Appreciating the role of Western civilization in the world is equally critical. It is well known that the world of the late twentieth century, and probably that of the twenty-first century as well, is characterized by interaction across and throughout the globe. The expression "global village" has become almost hackneyed. Awareness of our membership and role in this global community is one of the most central goals of the high school world studies course. What, then, are the characteristics of this global community? What are its dynamics? Any realistic answer to these questions will highlight the role of the West in the world. A complete answer will also highlight the problem of focusing the high school world studies course exclusively on the West rather than approaching Western civilization from a global perspective.

The twin dynamics of the contemporary world

Two key dynamics seem to operate simultaneously in today's world. The first is a tension between East and West, more specifically between the Soviet Union and the United States. Often described as a conflict between communism and capitalism, or between democracy and authoritarianism, this dynamic seems to dominate perceptions of the world in contemporary American society. The second dynamic is a tension between North and South, between the "more developed" or "imperialist" countries of the North and the "less developed" or "Third World" countries of the South. While less influential in American perspectives on the world today, this dynamic is likely to be of at least equal significance to our future.

The existence and importance of an East-West dynamic within the contemporary world is indisputable. Equally obvious is its importance to the world in which today's students will grow up. Short of Armageddon, it is difficult to imagine any changes in the global community that would render this dynamic obsolete. Whether in its current form or in some other one, it seems certain to persist.

A global studies course must try to explain the origins, development, and nature of this East-West dynamic. Since this has been essentially a conflict between different versions of Western civilization, explaining it requires an understanding of the origins, development, and nature of Western civilization itself. Indeed, this dynamic might be adequately explained within the context of a course concentrating solely on Western history.

However, the second dynamic, the tension between North and South, cannot be genuinely understood within the context of a parochial approach to Western history. The origins, the nature, and (most significantly) the future of this dynamic require an understanding of the West in relation to the rest of the world and of the integrity of other civilizations.

Like the East-West dynamic, this "North-South" dynamic is a major factor in the world of today and in all probability will continue its importance in the world of tomorrow. It is precisely here that the validity of a course concentrating exclusively on Western history becomes questionable.

THE SOURCE OF WESTERN HEGEMONY. Growing Western domination ("hegemony") over the rest of the world was the dominant fact of the last century. The capability of the West to achieve such domination is without parallel in human history. The West has not only been able to dominate the world; it has also been able to shape the reactions to its domination. Western technology and Western ideologies have been the primary means by which the non-Western areas of the world have sought to understand and escape from Western hegemony. This too is without precedent.

In these capabilities to dominate and to shape reactions to its domination, the West has exhibited a uniqueness. While other countries and civilizations have been able to dominate other societies, the hegemony of the West is both quantitatively and qualitatively different. The ability of the West to mobilize resources and to undergo self-transformations is truly exceptional. The development of the characteristics that have given Western civilization this ability, along with the consequences of Western hegemony, should be the focus of a course on the history of Western civilization.

What are the origins of the West's uniqueness? One approach to understanding it would be to begin in the years around A.D. 1500. Developments such as the Renaissance and the Reformation, the discoveries and the scientific revolution, are often regarded as the beginnings of the "modern" world. Recent scholarship, however, would tend to give less significance to these events and to date the origins of Western "modernity" much earlier. By 1500, Western society was a mature civilization whose defining characteristics were already centuries old. Indeed, the broad similarities among the classical civilizations of Eurasia suggest that a real understanding of the uniqueness of the West must begin with an understanding of the classical world.

REACTIONS TO WESTERN HEGEMONY. While reactions to Western hegemony have been characterized by the adoption of Western political, economic, and cultural structures, there has also existed a reluctance outside the West to adopt these structures. Non-Western cultures have retained their vitality and their appeal. It is critically important that students learn to acknowledge, even appreciate, this vitality. The basic but difficult realization is that "not everyone wants to be like us."

Appreciation of the vitality of non-Western civilizations, then, is also a goal of a Western civilization course. Although this topic will necessarily receive less emphasis than that given to the West, it has a vital role to play. It is essential to be aware of these civilizations and of the appeal they hold for millions of people today. Only with such an awareness can a balanced understanding of the place of the West in today's world be achieved.

Once again, 1500 A.D. is too late a beginning for the study of non-Western civilizations. These societies need to be introduced before they came into extensive contact with the West. Only then can students truly appreciate their complexity and sophistication. Here too, we must begin with classical origins.

Characteristics of a Western civilization approach

A world studies course emphasizing the history of Western civilization, then, should be characterized by the following:

1. A chronological treatment of history, beginning with the classical origins of the major civilizations of Eurasia
2. A focus on the history of the West, with particular attention given to the development of those distinctive characteristics that give rise to its ability to mobilize resources and engage in self-transformation
3. Selective attention to other civilizations, aimed at providing a basis for comparisons and an understanding of the broader context within which key changes in Western civilization occurred

ADVANTAGES OF THE APPROACH

The advantages of focusing specifically on the Western experience are several.

First, a focus on the history of the West anticipates and answers the often-repeated charge that a primary responsibility of the tenth-grade social studies course is to enable students to understand their own culture. How, the argument often goes, can students be expected to understand Chinese civilization when they do not even understand the classical origins of their own culture? How can they appreciate the contributions and values of other societies when they are unacquainted with those of their own? The focus of the Western civilization approach is to provide students with a solid historical understanding of the dominant culture of their own society.

A second advantage of focusing specifically on the Western experience is that teachers responsible for the course are likely to be familiar with the core material to be covered. Both formal training in school and subsequent reading have given the great majority of educated Americans at least a passing knowledge of the major events of Western history. Classical Greece, the French Revolution, Charlemagne, and Napoleon are concepts and names that most people recognize, however superficially. A course based on such familiar landmarks will generally not be as alien (and, indeed, frightening) as one based on political units such as the Abbasid and Mogul Empires and names such as Sargon and Tokugawa Ieyasu.

Similarly, by focusing on the Western experience the approach provides some relatively unambiguous criteria for selecting course content from the overwhelming array of factual material clamoring for inclusion in the course. While it is possible to become bogged down in detail even in a Western civilization approach, at least some initial criteria for excluding content are available to the curriculum planner.

A fourth advantage of the Western civilization approach lies in the ready availability of student materials at varying ability levels. The past dominance of this approach in American education has ensured a large pool of resources upon which teachers can draw. There may be fewer resources for imparting a global perspective to the course, but these represent gaps to be filled— not a whole course in need of materials development.

Finally, a Western civilization approach will in many cases be more consistent with traditional community expectations. Thus this approach may represent a "least effort" path toward introducing world studies into the core curriculum.

DISADVANTAGES OF THE APPROACH

However strong the advantages, there remain clear disadvantages and pitfalls to a course focused on Western history.

One set of problems emerges from the emphasis on the Western experience. Precisely because it is focused on the West, teachers familiar with European history may be tempted to ignore the global components of the approach. If the purpose of the course is seen primarily as helping students understand the Western experience, rather than helping them to understand the contemporary world through the Western experience, the approach can easily become nothing more than the traditional "Western-oriented" course. As such it is open not only to a charge of "false advertising" but also to one of distortion. A parochial emphasis on the West distorts the history of both the world and the West. Western history can be clearly seen only if placed in a global context. To persist in seeing Western history without reference to the rest of the world only reinforces cultural blindness. The Western civilization approach thus presents a unique and perhaps difficult challenge for staff development. It requires that teachers learn to see an apparently familiar course in a new light.

Even if approached from a global perspective, the emphasis the approach gives to the dominant "high culture" of Western Europe and the United States may tend to neglect relevant parts of Western civilization. It may tend, for example, to exclude women, to neglect the contributions of minorities, and to overlook the cultures of Southern and Eastern Europe.

Similarly, emphasis on one civilization necessarily detracts from others. In the course proposed here, traditional African, Indian, and Meso-American societies receive little attention. While the dominant culture of the United States lies within the Western tradition, there are many places in which the histories of these or similar cultures are salient. A course that focuses on the Western experiences may not be able to meet the needs of those communities.

A second set of pitfalls may face educators who genuinely attempt to implement a Western civilization course from a global perspective. The effort to concentrate on Western culture and at the same time include material on other civilizations may itself lead to various distortions and problems.

Most importantly, the concentration on Western civilization can result in a course that regards other civilizations as important only to the degree that they contribute to or affect the West. Seeing such societies as mere conduits of change for the West can undermine students' appreciation for the vitality and integrity of those societies.

Finally, the effort to add a global perspective to the traditional survey of Western history, if combined with a reluctance to eliminate traditional subjects, will simply lead to the chronic "content coverage" problem. The material covered will inevitably overwhelm both teacher and student. Implementing an academically sound Western civilization course requires teachers to look at their content in new ways and to sacrifice some beloved topics in the interest of curriculum improvement.

All of these pitfalls are possible, but they should primarily serve to remind curriculum planners that even a "least effort" path to curriculum change and improvement is not "effortless." Nonetheless, sensitive and skillful teachers, along with a structured and coherent syllabus, can overcome these pitfalls.

2. Goals for students

A course on the history of Western civilization should prepare students for citizenship in the "global village" of the twenty-first century. It assumes that to be good citizens, especially citizens within an interdependent world, students must understand their own civilization as well as how it interacts with other societies of the world. It also assumes that knowledgeable citizenship requires that students understand how the past has given rise to the present and thus gives shape to the future.

MAJOR KNOWLEDGE GOALS

In a Western civilization approach to the high school world studies course, the main knowledge goals should be to help students:

1. Realize that the values and institutions that characterize our society have their origins in the past
2. Understand that historical and social change are complex processes that result from many factors, often including contact with other cultures and civilizations
3. See the relationship between a culture's values and its social and physical environment
4. Understand the nature of civilization as a complex social organization that is dependent on functional specialization
5. Deepen their understanding of the values and institutions that characterize Western civilization and the contemporary world, including the territorial state, industrial capitalism, democratic norms, and science-based ways of understanding reality
6. Recognize the basic similarities as well as the many differences between the classical Eurasian civilizations
7. Understand how the Western experience and Western civilization became unique in comparison to other civilizations
8. Deepen their appreciation of the fact that key differences exist between Western and non-Western civilizations
9. Appreciate the validity of cultural traditions and values other than their own and understand that not everyone wants to be like them
10. Understand the critical role played by the industrial and democratic revolutions in the rise of Western hegemony
11. Understand how non-Western societies reacted to Western hegemony and how Western imperialism affects relations among states today
12. Understand how the East-West and North-South dynamics developed historically and why these two dynamics continue to be important today
13. Deepen their appreciation of the ways in which historical processes contribute to our understanding of the world today

MAJOR SKILL OUTCOMES

A Western civilization course can and should enhance a variety of student skills, including geographic skills, reading, and communication skills. However, history is particularly valuable in helping students develop a range of analytical competencies that fall within the domain of critical thinking. In particular, such a course should help students learn to:

1. Look for complex sets of causes to explain events and historical changes rather than accepting simplistic explanations
2. Examine events and social change analytically by isolating their discrete social, political, economic, and cultural components and exploring the relationships among those components
3. Recognize and generate alternate explanations for events and social change
4. Recognize the need for and dangers of generalization
5. Generate explicit criteria for judging events, decisions, relationships, and historical changes, and make judgments in terms of those criteria
6. Trace change processes through and across historical periods
7. Compare and contrast similar developments in societies that are chronologically and/or geographically distinct

In addition, a Western civilization course should help students learn to:

8. Develop cross-cultural sensitivity and empathy
9. Express their thoughts in clear and precise prose

3. Organization of subject matter

The general framework of a Western civilization approach should be chronological. A chronological organization of the course is most familiar to teachers of the traditional Western civilization course. It also contributes most effectively to students' understanding of the process of historical change.

PERIODIZATION AND CONTENT FOCUS

The familiar progression of events from Mesopotamia and Greece through Rome, from Charlemagne through the Middle Ages, from the Renaissance through the French Revolution, and from the wars of Napoleon to those of the mid-twentieth century will remain basic to the approach outlined here. However, Western history does look somewhat different from a global perspective, so some components of the course will be slightly unfamiliar.

MODIFICATIONS IN PERIODIZATION. The history of Western civilization has traditionally been divided into three major periods: (1) classical, (2) medieval, and (3) modern. The first period is typically seen as beginning sometime between 1000 B.C. and 500 B.C. and ending over a thousand years later. The next millennium, from 500 A.D. to 1500 A.D., comprises the Middle Ages, with the modern world beginning in the sixteenth century and extending to the present. Further subdivisions exist: "classical" is divided into Greek and Roman; "medieval" into early, high, and late; and "modern" into early and recent. This periodization of the course directs attention toward basic changes that occurred as Western society moved from one period to the next. For reasons explained in more detail below, two modifications in this traditional periodization will be suggested in the approach presented here.

The first involves the period from A.D. 200 to 1000. This era has usually been divided between two periods: the late classical and the early medieval. Lately, however, considerable scholarly controversy has arisen over precisely when the ancient world ended and the medieval world began. Also, the traditional periodization may tend to distract attention from important differences in the ways in which the West and other classical civilizations responded to the crisis that enveloped Eurasia in the late classical period. For the course described here, this entire period will be seen as a single and distinct era.

A similar controversy exists over the dating of the end of the Middle Ages and the beginning of the modern world. Here too, a wider perspective suggests a non-traditional periodization. The period from approximately

1000 A.D. to around 1700 A.D. will not be divided into "medieval" and "modern" but rather treated as a single unit. Such a treatment is in conformity with recent scholarship in social and economic history. More importantly, it provides a continuity to the discussion of how those characteristics that are distinctive to modern Western society emerged.

It should be stressed that these changes in periodization are suggestions, not dicta. The structure of existing textbooks and the preference of teachers may recommend the retention of the traditional periodization and the division of Western chronology into ancient, medieval, and modern eras. Such a division could accommodate the new emphases and material that arise from seeing Western history from a global perspective.

MODIFICATIONS IN EMPHASIS. Partly because of the modifications in periodization, and partly because of the perspective of a comparative framework, two critical differences in emphasis will also occur.

Since the nineteenth century, treatment of the classical period in Western history has emphasized the Greek rather than the Roman experience. Without denigrating the contributions of Greek society and culture to Western civilization, a global perspective suggests that Imperial Rome merits relatively more attention. Roman society and history highlight the fundamental similarities between classical Western civilization and the classical civilizations elsewhere in Eurasia. Demonstrating these similarities helps emphasize the subsequent changes that result in the uniqueness of Western civilization.

Similarly, the treatment of the period from 1000 A.D. to 1700 A.D. as a unity also suggests that greater emphasis be placed on the High Middle Ages (1000–1300) and that reduced emphasis be placed on the Renaissance and Reformation (1500–1650). The tendency in most histories of Western civilization is virtually to ignore late medieval society. More recent scholarship, however, has begun to emphasize the critical role of this period in laying the foundation for many of the institutions that characterize the modern West.

These shifts in emphasis will not alter the basic familiarity of the material, nor need they alter its organization. What should be altered, however, is the final picture. The same bricks can build very different structures, and the validity of a given structure depends on how it will be used. The visions of our past elaborated in the late nineteenth and early twentieth centuries may not be the appropriate ones for students who will be living in the twenty-first century.

AN OVERVIEW OF THE APPROACH

How might a Western civilization course, as seen from a global perspective, be organized? Based on the above discussion, the body of the course would have seven major chronological units, conforming to the modified periodization. These chronologically organized units would be preceded by an introductory unit that sets the thematic stage for the remainder of the course. The eight units would thus deal with the following periods, themes, and concepts:

1. An introduction to the contemporary world, outlining basic concepts and themes that will inform the course, such as the idea of Western civilization, the East-West and North-South dynamics, and the issue of Western hegemony
2. The early growth of civilization in the Middle East and the concepts of civilization and urbanization
3. The formation of classical civilizations in Eurasia, with particular attention to the defining characteristics of Greek and Roman societies
4. The disruption of these classical civilizations and the spread of new religions, particularly Christianity
5. The restoration of stability in the "middle period" and the uniqueness of developments in the West
6. The development of Western hegemony, with particular attention to the transformations brought about by the industrial and democratic revolutions
7. The changes in Western society brought on by World War I and the reactions to Western imperialism throughout the globe
8. The contemporary world, with special emphasis on the Cold War, the relationship of industrialized to non-industrialized countries, and the interaction of these two dynamics

All but the first and last units should conclude with a comparative survey of the world, placing developments in the West within a global context.

INTRODUCTION: THE WORLD TODAY

The intent of this unit is to identify themes and perspectives that will be explored in the course. Referral back to these themes throughout the course should keep them, and the final goal of understanding the contemporary world, alive in the minds of both students and teachers.

CHARACTERISTICS OF THE WEST. The idea of Western civilization and some basic differences between Western and non-Western societies should be established at the outset of the course. Students should understand that American society is part of a broader Western civilization. Characteristics peculiar to the West should be identified. These basic characteristics include the existence and importance of the territorial state, industrial capitalism, the reliance upon scientific explanations of the world, and the acceptance of technological and social change. These characteristics can easily be illustrated with references to contemporary popular culture.

Differences among civilizations and the issue of cultural bias should also be addressed in this unit. The idea of Western civilization is only meaningful because there are other, "non-Western" civilizations. Who are these people and how are their civilizations different from the West? To what degree can we "understand" the values and structures of peoples different from us?

INTERDEPENDENCE. A second theme that should be stressed is that of interdependence—the fact that events in any one part of the globe are likely to affect people in other parts. Manifestations of this theme could also be illustrated by examples drawn from contemporary society. How do changes in the price of VCRs or oil affect us? What has been the impact of rising demand for Japanese automobiles?

Having established the reality of interdependence, it would be appropriate to characterize and assess it. Is the interaction between the West and the rest of the world a "good thing," a "bad thing," or is it more ambiguous? What are the differing views about this relationship?

These themes—the defining characteristics of Western civilization, the fact of interdependence between the West and the world, and the ambiguity concerning the value of this interdependence—constitute both key topics to be explored in the course and a basis for subsequently deciding what content is more or less central to the course.

PART I: THE ORIGINS OF CIVILIZATION

This unit should examine the nature of civilization and the origins of civilized societies.

THE NEOLITHIC REVOLUTION. The unit should begin with the Neolithic revolution and a discussion of the division of labor and the transformation of culture that accompanied sedentary life. Emphasis would be on the invention of agriculture in Western Eurasia, though mention should be made of parallel developments in Southeast Asia and the Americas. The debate over diffusion or independent creation might be raised. Was the invention of agriculture a development that occurred once and then spread to other lands and peoples? Or was it a development that happened separately and independently in each place?

THE URBAN REVOLUTION. The urban revolution also raises the problem of whether fundamental historical changes resulted from parallel creation or borrowing, though it now seems evident that developments in China happened independently of those in the Middle East. However, attention should be focused on the nature of civilization and the significance of its invention. Four key points should be stressed: the rise of social stratification and functional specialization, the invention of writing, the development of cities and permanent territorial states, and the dependence of civilization upon the production and collection of an agricultural surplus.

PART II: THE FORMATION OF CLASSICAL CIVILIZATIONS

Although civilized societies everywhere share certain common characteristics that identify them as civilized, significant differences exist as well. This unit should primarily serve to introduce students to the major civilized traditions of Eurasia, with particular emphasis on those traditions from which our society is descended. It should also raise the issue of comparison. When viewed in a comparative perspective, is it the similarities or the differences among these civilized traditions that are most striking?

Certain civilizations are traditionally described as "classical" because subsequent societies looked back to them as their cultural foundation. Attention should be focused on the elaboration of those characteristics that distinguished the classical civilizations that emerged before 200 A.D. Whether these characteristics—which by definition differentiate these civilizations—are more significant than their basic similarities is a critical issue.

MIDDLE EASTERN CIVILIZATION. Because of its continuity with Part I, the examination of classical civilizations should begin with the Middle East.

The succession of larger and larger territorial empires characterizes the history of the Middle East from 1800–300 B.C. Behind these events lies the more important development of certain social and cultural characteristics that were to have a powerful impact on subsequent Western and Middle Eastern history. One of the key characteristics was the emergence of bureaucratic government, which became necessary as increasingly cosmopolitan empires drew together peoples of varying ethnic backgrounds.

It is against this backdrop that the story of the Hebrews, as revealed in the Old Testament, might be viewed. To the degree that they resisted assimilation, the Hebrews were unique, but in the fact that they were confronted with pressure to assimilate, they were typical of Middle Eastern peoples.

The history of the Hebrews also illustrates a second key characteristic that came to define Middle Eastern society: the movement towards monotheism. The transformation of the God of Moses into the God of Isaiah, the efforts of Ikhnaton in Egypt to institutionalize the worship of Aton, and the elaboration of Zoroastrianism as the state religion in Persia are all part of a regional impetus toward monotheism that was unique to Middle Eastern culture. The importance of monotheism to the study of Western civilization is twofold. On the one hand, Middle Eastern monotheism fundamentally shaped the Western experience through Christianity. On the other, the fact that monotheism was conceived and developed in a complex, heterogeneous society suggests a relationship between environment and worldview. The outlook and values of a culture are usually connected to its social structure and physical environment. This relationship merits attention in the course.

CHINESE CIVILIZATION.   Although a Western civilization course will focus on the history of the West, the development of Chinese civilization merits discussion. Fruitful comparisons between the West and China can be made throughout the course. Indeed, the similarities in the development of the West and China and their subsequent divergence dramatically illustrate the origins of Western uniqueness.

While coverage should be brief, mention should be made of the development of China through the Han Empire. Chinese civilization, like other classical civilizations, rested on an agrarian economic base. Politically, it was characterized by a large territorial empire, governed through an elaborate bureaucracy by a class of landed gentry. The formulation of a secular worldview, exemplified by Confucian thought, provided a universal set of values and a code of conduct that helped unify what was in fact a highly heterogeneous society. These elements combined to create a dynamic civilization that proved to be the most enduring of all classical civilizations.

In looking at Chinese civilization, special attention should be given to two characteristics of that culture. The development of a system of ethical values that were not based on religion and the evolution of a society in which warriors were not held in high esteem represent two important points of contrast with the characteristics that define Western society.

INDIAN CIVILIZATION.   In contrast to Chinese civilization, it is probably unnecessary to include material on the development of Indian civilization within a Western civilization course. Although of great intrinsic value, the structures and outlook of Indian cultures are alien to most contemporary American students. Likewise, the caste system is a marvelous tool for comparing social structures, but it may be historically idiosyncratic. Finally, while the elaboration of transcendental thought may have significantly influenced the development of Christianity, the connection is tenuous and problematic. The arguments for the linkage are probably too sophisticated and complex for a high school survey course.

GREEK CIVILIZATION.   Classical civilization in the West may be viewed as the culture that arose in Greece around 800 B.C., spread around the Mediterranean in the next few centuries, reached its fullest extent in the second century A.D. within the Roman Empire, and then dissolved under a series of barbarian invasions around 500 A.D.

Treatment of classical civilization in the West has tended to emphasize the first two centuries of this millennium—that is, the Greek rather than the Roman experience. Since the nineteenth century, Western society has looked back to Athens in the fifth and fourth centuries B.C. as the source from which the Western cultural tradition evolved. The development of a unique political and social environment, the small independent city-state or *polis*, governed by a relatively egalitarian group of yeoman farmers through a democratic system of government, has quite properly attracted our attention. The corresponding cultural flowering, with the invention and elaboration of science and philosophy, drama and prose, art and architecture, has always been seen as the very origin of the culture that still characterizes us today. Indeed, two characteristics that still distinguish Western society— the primacy of the territorial state and the tendency to rely upon scientific explanations of the world—do have their origins in classical Greece.

At the same time the Hellenic experience must be placed in a larger context. The flourishing, indeed the very existence, of a network of small independent cities was an historical anomaly. It ran counter to the historical tradition that had been developing in the neighboring Middle East for almost two millennia: the impetus toward large territorial empires. In reality the victory and escape of the Greeks from the Persian Wars only delayed the inevitable. This accident, a happy and fortunate one for Western society, did not mean that the future would lie with political structures such as the *polis*. The inherent instability and constant warfare that characterized classical Greek life left that society open and vulnerable to attack from outside. In the fourth century, a large territorial empire emerged, enveloping the Greek cities. For the next millennium classical civilization in the West, as elsewhere, was characterized by similar empires.

These Western empires, the Hellenistic and the Roman, can be seen in part as mediums through which Greek culture spread. As the political and social environment changed from that of the *polis* to that of a complex empire governed through a bureaucracy by a landed elite, so too did the culture and worldview of Western civilization. Indeed, for many centuries Western and Middle Eastern society knew Greek culture primarily through Roman and Hellenistic eyes.

THE HELLENISTIC EMPIRES. The Hellenistic world should be included here because it perpetuated some traditional Greek characteristics, such as scientific thought. The confrontation with Middle Eastern society, which occurred with Alexander's conquests, may be viewed on the one hand as a contribution to the cosmopolitanism characteristic of that region, and on the other hand as the imposition of a layer or veneer of Greek culture upon a society that in many ways was otherwise not affected. In the latter sense, a comparison of the Hellenistic world with that of Rome is most instructive. The Romans were "less Greek" in language and culture than the successors of Alexander, but their impact was more lasting.

ROMAN CIVILIZATION. Rome has often been viewed as a society that became the transmission belt through which Greek thought and values were transferred to subsequent Western society. This image of Rome leads one to emphasize the Republic over the Empire and to concentrate on literature and philosophy. However, Rome may also be viewed as a society that made its own contributions to Western society. This perspective leads one to emphasize the Empire and to concentrate on law and government. Both perspectives have validity, and a definitive choice need not be made between them. What is important, however, is the realization that throughout most of its history and to most societies that looked back to the classical world, classical civilization in the West was epitomized by the Roman Empire.

THE WORLD IN 200 A.D.   This second chronological part of the course should end with a brief review of the world in 200 A.D. Although there were clearly significant differences between the civilizations of Eurasia at this time, there were important similarities as well. The West, the Middle East, and China were all governed as large territorial empires by bureaucratic governments staffed by a landed elite. The worldviews of this elite were not that different from one civilization to the next. The outlook and values of a Roman noble family were in many ways more similar to those of a family belonging to the Confucian elite in China than to Roman slaves. Western uniqueness was not yet apparent.

PART III: THE CRISIS OF THE CLASSICAL WORLD

The period from 200 A.D. to 1000 A.D. is a confused one. Indeed, it is this period that has most confounded Western historians. Neither Western civilization nor the other civilizations of Eurasia may be viewed in isolation during this period; they are not self-contained units of historical study. Often neglected because it falls between the end of antiquity and the beginning of the Middle Ages, this period was of critical importance to the subsequent history of the West and ultimately of the world.

Beginning in the second century B.C., the civilizations of Eurasia came into direct contact with one another. This interaction, which took place along several routes, was not merely one in which goods, both luxury and mundane, were exchanged. Also exchanged were diseases and ideas.

These contacts between the classical Eurasian civilizations should be stressed. They provide not only the foundation for understanding the history of this time, but also an opportunity to begin exploring an issue of increasing importance in later historical periods. What happens when peoples of differing civilizations encounter each other? How do they communicate? What things can they share? What things can they not share?

THE FALL OF ROME.   The classic explanation of the collapse of the Roman Empire in the third and fourth centuries A.D.—the "triumph" of barbarism and religion—begs the question of why Rome fell. Rome clearly was conquered, at least in the West, by Germanic peoples. The question is, why was it vulnerable to such conquest? Rome clearly adopted a new religion and experienced a fundamental alteration in its worldview; but why was it susceptible to such a conversion?

The importance of these questions becomes apparent when the experience of Rome is seen in the context of the mingling of ideas, goods, and diseases that took place among the classical empires of this time. Is it a simple coincidence that the classical Han Empire of China was also attacked and overcome by barbarians from the outside? Is it coincidence that the Chinese also experienced the spread and popularity of a new "universal" religion?

Beginning in the late second century A.D., epidemics of disastrous proportions, resulting from increased contact across the Eurasian trade routes, spread across Eurasia. A decline in population accompanied these epidemics. This demographic reversal severely weakened the classical empires from one end of Eurasia to the other. This weakness, in turn, left the empires vulnerable to the attacks of "barbarians" from outside.

In Rome, the combination of a declining population and an increased need for defense against Germanic invaders led to various attempts to reconstitute the empire. In the end it was decided to abandon those areas that were least important—the Western Empire—and to concentrate resources on the East.

THE GROWTH OF CHRISTIANITY.   It is against the background of "decline and fall" that the second component of Eurasian interaction, the exchange of ideas, appears most important. The history of Christianity should be seen in the context of this interaction. The formulation, spread, and acceptance of this new religion are intimately connected to the intercultural interaction that characterized the centuries between 200 B.C. and 500 A.D.

This interaction seems to have contributed to the growth of more than one new world religion during this period. A comparison of them shows the important role that the contacts among civilizations played in their development and spread. Just as Christianity arose in the Near East, an area where Greco-Roman and Middle Eastern cultures encountered each other, Mahayana Buddhism arose in northwestern India, where Indian, Middle Eastern, and Greek cultural influences mingled. A number of characteristics of Christianity were probably shaped by this encounter. Middle Eastern monotheism and Greek philosophy combined to form what became the orthodox Christian faith.

Nor do the basic similarities in the history of Christianity and Buddhism end there. Buddhism spread across the trade routes of Central Asia to China just as Christianity spread across the Mediterranean trade routes throughout the Roman Empire and beyond. Both Mahayana Buddhism and Christianity offered personal salvation to believers through the mediation of an incarnate god. To inhabitants of the increasingly besieged and impoverished empires of China and Rome, such a promise of personal immortality must have been quite compelling.

The discussion of Christianity should concentrate on the issues of its origin and explore the appeal it clearly had to citizens of Rome. Of significance is the fact that the adoption of Christianity by Constantine led to its becoming a "state religion," not unlike traditional Roman religion.

THE GROWTH OF ISLAM.   The rise of another world religion merits some attention in the course. Islam is significant not only for its impact on the contemporary world, but also for its impact on the West. Like Christianity, it arose in areas where differing cultural traditions interacted. Like Christianity, it spread throughout much of the older Middle Eastern and Roman Empires. Unlike Christianity, it should not be viewed as resulting from or combining these cultural traditions. Rather, Islam may best be regarded as an assertion of Middle Eastern culture, an affirmation of monotheism as opposed to trinitarian Christianity.

RECOVERY WITHIN THE CLASSICAL WORLD.   It is not necessary to dwell upon the long-standing controversy over when the Roman Empire ended and the Middle Ages began. In the case of Rome, the lengthy population decline that began around 200 A.D. was of such an intensity and duration that not only were the empire and the civilization it encompassed destroyed, but all attempts to resurrect that classical order also failed.

Here again, a global perspective is useful. By the sixth century, Chinese civilization began its recovery from this period of crisis. By the beginning of the T'ang Empire, Chinese civilization had successfully reconstituted itself on classical patterns and themes. Similarly, by the eighth century, Middle Eastern civilization had achieved renewed stability and equilibrium. In the Islamic Abbasid Empire both classical and innovative structures were combined.

THE CAROLINGIAN EMPIRE.   In the West, however, recovery proved to be illusory at first. Charlemagne has traditionally been regarded as the "father of Europe," and attention has been given to the contribution of his empire and its culture to subsequent European history. Although components of this contribution certainly merit consideration, it is important to realize that insofar as there was a self-conscious direction to Carolingian policies, it looked backward to Rome, not forward to something new. In his cultural priorities and in his religious policies, Charlemagne's intent seems to have been to restore the Roman Empire. Although the result was instead to create something new (feudalism), this was clearly not his intent. In this sense the Carolingian Empire was similar to the T'ang Empire in China. It was an attempt to restore a civilization based on the classical past.

The similarity between the T'ang and the Carolingians goes no further, however. While the T'ang Dynasty was basically successful, the Carolingians were not. It should be stressed that Charlemagne failed not only in his attempt to restore Rome but even in his attempt to construct a lasting political structure. Indeed, in some ways the significance of the Carolingian period lies primarily in its failure rather than its successes.

This failure meant that Western society—when it finally was able to begin the process of recovery—was to start from a very different basis than the societies of the Middle East and of China. In a very real sense, it was beginning anew.

THE WORLD IN 900 A.D.   A survey of the world in 900 A.D. clearly reveals a startling difference between the West and other Eurasian civilizations. While the previous review suggested that similarities seemed more significant than the differences, by 900 A.D. the opposite had become true. China and the Middle East were relatively stable, relatively prosperous, and relatively sophisticated, but the West in the years around 900 A.D. was anarchic, impoverished, and crude. It is here that the origins of Western uniqueness are really first to be found.

PART IV: THE RESTORATION OF STABILITY IN THE WEST

The usual division of the centuries between the eleventh and eighteenth into medieval and early modern seems to make little sense in the light of both current research and a global perspective. The institutions that emerged in the centuries around 1000 A.D. still characterized the West on the eve of the industrial revolution. Between medieval and early modern society there is more continuity than change. Developments such as the rise of capitalism, which once seemed to be new in the sixteenth century, are now seen as having a history stretching back into the medieval period. Whereas modern civilization may trace its values and worldview back to its classical past, the institutions that characterize contemporary Western society have their origin in the Middle Ages.

CONTINUITY AND CHANGE.   The complementary themes of continuity and change may serve to illustrate how unique the West became at this time. Here again, a comparison of the West with the Middle East and China can be useful. Indeed, if at all possible it would be desirable to give Islamic and Chinese society more than a passing review. One of the goals of the world studies course should be to lead students to appreciate the vitality and attractiveness of other civilized traditions. This period may be the best to examine for this purpose.

In this middle period, which extends from the end of the crisis to the eve of the industrial revolution, each of these three civilizations clearly had some continuity with its classical past, and each also exhibited some features that were new. The balance between tradition and innovation, between the old and the new, between continuity and change was significantly different in each society.

CHINA. At one end of the spectrum of continuity and change lies China. Clearly there were some new factors in Chinese civilization. A new religion, Buddhism, had arisen, although it had not entirely displaced older religions or value codes. A new emphasis on technology and trade had also emerged. Yet the elements of continuity were much stronger than those of change. The empire and its complex bureaucracy, the social stature of the landed elite, and the self-conscious attempt to structure society around its traditional past testify to the continuity between China during this period and the classical past. This continuity, which in fact improved upon classical norms in certain respects, resulted in the most prosperous and most sophisticated society of this millennium.

ISLAM. In the middle of the spectrum of continuity and change lies the Middle East. In Islamic civilization, continuity and change seem to have been balanced. The political structure of Islamic society, a bureaucratic territorial empire, was clearly derived from older Persian models. The cosmopolitanism characteristic of classical Middle Eastern society became even more pronounced in this period. At the same time, the predominance of a new religion, Islam, and a new unifying language, Arabic, clearly represent significant innovations. In the Middle East this balance between tradition and innovation combined to form the most expansive and dynamic society of this millennium.

MEDIEVAL AND EARLY MODERN EUROPE. Despite their vitality and sophistication, neither the Chinese nor the Islamic civilization was to achieve global hegemony. Rather, this was to be the role of the civilization at the other end of the spectrum of change and continuity: the West. Paradoxically, the West's lack of continuity with its classical past was responsible not only for its initial weakness in comparison with China and Islam but also for its future capabilities.

In discussing the period between the ninth century, which marks the beginning of the demographic revival of Europe, and the eighteenth, which marks the eve of the industrial and democratic revolutions, emphasis should be given to the development of those institutions that even today characterize Western society. In particular, attention should be given to political and economic developments. Capitalism and the territorial nation-state, which provided the capability for both the production of wealth and the mobilization of resources on an unprecedented scale, were innovative aspects of the new Western civilization that emerged after 1000 A.D. They mark a sharp departure from classical forms of economic and political organization. It is also in these aspects of the new Western civilization that the foundations of subsequent Western hegemony lie.

EUROPEANS ENCOUNTER THE WORLD. The final part of the period, the "age of exploration" that lasted from the fifteenth to the eighteenth centuries, naturally plays a large part in American treatments of European history. It should continue to do so in a course incorporating a global perspective, but it is important that the discoveries be seen in the proper context. To look only at those areas in which Europeans confronted and conquered "primitive" peoples, the Americas and Central Asia, can be highly misleading. European culture did spread during this period of exploration and expansion. The United States and Russia are key examples of the expansion of Western civilization. However, in those parts of the world in which Europeans encountered stronger and more sophisticated societies, the story was quite different.

The European experience in Asia provides a sharp contrast to the Americas. Advancements in naval technology allowed Europeans to dominate the centuries-old trade routes along the eastern and southern coasts of Asia, but the Europeans did not possess the ability to control inland territories. During most of this period the European "empires" in Asia were confined to scattered coastal enclaves that could be protected and supplied by sea. Indeed, in Eastern Europe and the Balkans, the one area where Europe directly confronted another civilization, the Ottoman Empire was clearly the aggressive and dynamic power through most of the seventeenth century.

THE WORLD IN 1700. A look at the world scene in 1600 or 1700 would again be appropriate. It would reveal that considerable changes had occurred in the past eight centuries. Politically and economically, Europe was now clearly out of step with the other major civilizations of the world. Yet if an impartial "outside observer" surveyed the civilizations of Eurasia, he or she might well predict that the civilizations of Eurasia would remain in some kind of equilibrium for the foreseeable future. If told that one civilization would rise to a position of global dominance, the observer might well speculate that it would be the Chinese or perhaps the Ottoman Empire. Western uniqueness had become apparent, but Western hegemony still lay in the future.

PART V: THE RISE OF THE WEST

Beginning in the late eighteenth century, Europe underwent a series of rapid political and economic transformations that were as fundamental as the Neolithic and urban revolutions millennia earlier. Coverage of this period should emphasize these transformations, European reactions to them, and finally their global implications.

THE TRANSFORMATION OF EUROPE AND WESTERN HEGEMONY. The industrial revolution can be seen as culminating an economic process that began centuries earlier with the growth and development of capitalism. The democratic revolutions of the late eighteenth century can be seen as culminating the political process that began with feudalism. The former, through the creation of industrial capitalism, laid the foundation for unparalleled economic growth. The latter, through the creation of democratic liberalism and especially political nationalism, gave the states of Europe the ability to mobilize human resources to a degree also without parallel. The result of these two simultaneous processes was to give the West vast economic and political power.

Europe in the nineteenth century should be approached from two perspectives: internally and externally. Within Europe, the working-out of the industrial and democratic revolutions clearly merits the attention it has traditionally received. Reactions to the industrial revolution such as Marxism, the potency and vigor of nationalism, the growth of the welfare state, and mass democracy all had significant effects both within the West and on the rest of the world.

This transformation of Europe also offers an opportunity to look in depth at the process of social and historical change. Do societies change as a result of external pressures, or is change self-generated? How do changes in technology affect societies? Are ordinary people necessarily aware of large-scale social change? Why do they accept or reject change?

Outside of Europe, the industrial and democratic revolutions combined to give Europe the capability to extend and impose its economic and political power on other civilizations. This process, called "imperialism," can be approached in a variety of ways. Attention can be given to the causes and motives, both explicit and implicit, behind imperialism. Attention can be given to the ways, both political and economic, in which Western power was exercised. Attention can be given to the impact, both positive and negative, which Western rule and penetration had on other societies. Regardless of the emphasis one adopts, it is important to discuss economic as well as political matters. The growth of a world economy and Western economic penetration of the Middle East are as significant as the British Raj in India, which was also based on economic factors.

THE WORLD IN 1900. The survey of the world in 1900, which should end this unit, will necessarily differ from previous reviews. By 1900 the fact of Western uniqueness is well established. A new issue has emerged: Western hegemony. Why did Westerners seek hegemony over other societies? How did they view imperialism? How did other societies view it? What are the ways in which domination occurred and how was it achieved? The discussion of these questions can provide a foundation to help students understand related issues in the contemporary world.

PART VI: THE END OF HEGEMONY

WORLD WAR I. Even from a global perspective, World War I represents a fundamental turning point in the history of the West. The Great War began the process through which the centers of power within the Western world shifted to countries outside Western Europe. It provoked the Russian Revolution and thus set in motion events that would lead to the Cold War. Through its impact on Germany, it launched the West on the path to World War II, and it led to a loss of self-confidence among Europeans that came to be as important outside Europe as within.

REACTIONS TO IMPERIALISM. Outside Europe, the twentieth century has seen a series of reactions to Western imperialism. Key points here include the nature of these reactions and the ways in which the non-Western world used Western technology and ideology to fight imperialism. Students should comprehend the ironic fact that the way to escape Western domination was, at least in part, to become "Westernized." They should also understand the emerging power of nationalism and the ways in which it combined with industrialism in Japan, with liberalism in India, and with Marxism in China, in the effort to shake off Western hegemony.

PART VII: THE GLOBAL VILLAGE

Since 1945, the history of the West and the world have become inseparable. Distinctions between internal and external developments are no longer appropriate. Rather, the appropriate distinction is on the development of two global dynamics.

THE COLD WAR. The first dynamic is, of course, the East-West conflict and the Cold War. The eclipse of Europe and the growth of the superpowers should be examined in the context of World War II, but the East-West conflict should also be seen as the culmination of the forces of capitalism and nationalism unleashed by the industrial and democratic revolutions.

THE TRANSFORMATION OF IMPERIALISM. The second dynamic is the transformation of imperialism. Case studies indicating how imperialism and reactions to it shape events in the global community can be drawn from very recent history. Islamic fundamentalism and the revolution in Iran, for example, represent a "nativist" reaction to Western cultural, political, and economic domination. The Vietnamese struggle represents a "nationalist" response to Western rule. On the other side, French involvement in Algeria and the white minority's efforts to retain their dominance in South Africa represent cases of Western efforts to retain hegemony.

The interaction of these two dynamics should also be stressed. Many reactions against imperialism have become involved in the East-West conflict as the great powers competed for influence in societies escaping from colonial rule. Appropriate cases here would include Cuba and Vietnam.

THE WORLD TODAY. A look at contemporary events in the light of these themes should conclude the course. Brief case studies of conflicts and events in such places as Central America or Iran could be used to point out the existence and interaction of the twin dynamics of the East-West and the North-South conflicts.

These case studies should be developed in such a way that they emphasize the inadequacy of oversimplified generalizations and the complexity of human affairs. In addition to reviewing and explaining the actual situation, attention should be given to the issue of differing perspectives. How, for example, does the situation in Nicaragua appear to different Americans? How does it appear to Nicaraguans? How does it appear to people living in other countries in Central America? To Europeans? To the leaders of the Soviet Union? Helping students achieve such an understanding of the contemporary world is the appropriate end to an historical treatment of Western civilization.

4. Annotated bibliography

The following books would provide excellent resources for teachers preparing or teaching a Western civilization course from a global perspective.

Achebe, C. *Things Fall Apart.* New York: Fawcett, 1978. This novel provides a marvelous view of the impact of imperialism on an African community. It is written by an African, from an African perspective.

Anderson, Perry. *Passages from Antiquity to Feudalism.* New York: Schocken, 1978. A provocative account of the transition from classical to medieval history.

Barraclough, Geoffrey, ed. *The Times Atlas of World History.* London: Times Books, 1979. This atlas is a superb source for both Western and global history.

Braudel, Fernand. *Capitalism and Material Life.* New York: Harper and Row, 1983. Explores the development of capitalism in the West from a global perspective. Much more readable, however, is his *Afterthought on Capitalism and Material Life* (Baltimore, Md.: Johns Hopkins University Press, 1979).

Childe, V. Gordon. *What Happened in History.* New York: Penguin, 1985. This is a fine introduction to the Neolithic and urban revolutions and to the early history of the Middle East.

Cipolla, Carlo. *Before the Industrial Revolution.* New York: Norton, 1980. Demonstrates the continuities within the period from 1000 to 1700.

————. *Guns, Sails and Empires.* Manhattan, Kan.: Sunflower University Press, 1985. Explores the technological factors behind the explorers' discoveries from a global perspective.

Dawood, N.J., ed. *Tales from the Thousand and One Nights.* New York: Penguin, 1973. This is a collection of Middle Eastern folk tales. They demonstrate the rich cosmopolitanism of Islamic life and are fun. In spite of their reputation as "racy," they are rather mild by contemporary standards.

Fieldhouse, D.K. *The Colonial Empires.* New York: Delacorte, 1967. A broad survey of imperialism.

Finley, Moses. *Aspects of Antiquity.* New York: Penguin, 1977. A series of essays on Greek and Roman history. The introduction, "Desperately Foreign," discusses classical civilization as both familiar and alien.

Huttenback, Robert. *The British Imperial Experience.* Westport, Conn.: Greenwood, 1976. Concentrates on British imperialism, particularly in India and Africa, and discusses the ending of the British Empire.

Lopez, Robert S. *The Birth of Europe.* New York: Evans, 1967. This survey of medieval Europe emphasizes the lack of continuity between classical and medieval history.

————. *The Commercial Revolution of the Middle Ages.* New York: Cambridge Press, 1976. Demonstrates the originality of medieval economic and political developments and their influence on subsequent Western history.

McNeill, William H. *The Rise of the West.* University of Chicago Press, 1970. Provides background for both Western and non-Western societies. As a reference, it is preferable to his *A World History* (New York: Oxford, 1979).

Palmer, Robert. *The Age of the Democratic Revolutions* and *The World of the French Revolution.* Princeton, N.J.: Princeton University Press, 1959. This work discusses the late eighteenth century in a comparative perspective.

Strayer, Joseph R. *On the Medieval Origins of the Modern State.* Princeton, N.J.: Princeton University Press, 1972. A look at the impact of medieval political and economic developments on the evolution of the modern West.

Spence, Jonathan. *Emperor of China.* New York: Random House, 1975.

————. *Death of Woman Wang.* New York: Viking, 1978. Both of Spence's works provide an insight into seventeenth-century Chinese civilization.

van Gulik, Robert. *The Chinese Nail Murders.* University of Chicago Press, 1977.

————. *The Chinese Gold Murders.* New York: Random House, 1983. These are detective stories written in the 1950s. They are set in the T'ang period but actually provide an authentic and enjoyable image of life in the Ming period.

Wolf, Eric. *Europe and the Peoples without History.* Berkeley, Calif.: University of California Press, 1982. Views European developments in this period in a truly global context.

5. Content outline for a Western civilization course

UNIT I: THE WORLD TODAY

1. The United States and the West
   1.1 The United States is part of Western civilization

        Political and economic alliances with Europe
        Shared culture
  1.2 Western civilization shares common features
        Patriotism and the state
        Science
        Acceptance of change

2. The West and the world
  2.1 There are other civilized traditions
        Middle Eastern
        East Asian
  2.2 The West interacts with the world
        Politically
        Economically
        Culturally

3. The nature of this interaction
  3.1 The interaction is beneficial
        Benefits of democracy
        Benefits of economic growth
  3.2 The interaction is harmful
        Political control
        Economic domination

UNIT II: THE ORIGINS OF CIVILIZATION

1. The Neolithic revolution
  1.1 Where are the origins of humanity?
        Geographical
        Physiological
  1.2 Agriculture was invented
        Technology
        Geography
  1.3 The agricultural revolution had many effects
        Sedentary lives
        Social structure

2. The urban revolution
  2.1 Cities were created
        Sumer
        Egypt
  2.2 Urban society was necessarily complex
        Dependence on an agricultural surplus
        The evolution of territorial states
  2.3 Civilization needs cities
        Functional specialization
        Social stratification
        Cultural possibilities

UNIT III: THE FORMATION OF CLASSICAL CIVILIZATIONS

1. Middle Eastern civilization
    1.1 There is a growth of empire
        Series of empires
        More governmental sophistication
    1.2 Society is marked by cosmopolitanism
        Heterogeneity
        Commerce
    1.3 The worldview tends towards monotheism
        Hebrews
        Egypt
        Zoroastrianism
2. Chinese civilization
    2.1 There is a growth of empire
        Origins
        Han Empire
    2.2 Who runs this society?
        Landed gentry
        Arms or letters?
    2.3 A secular wordview emerges
        Confucian thought
        Filial piety
3. Greek civilization
    3.1 Western society begins in Greece
        Homeric Greece
        The Dark Ages
        The Persian Wars
    3.2 The Greeks live in independent city-states
        The *polis*
        Democracy
    3.3 The Greeks invent science
        Philosophy
        Physics and astronomy
        History and political science
    3.4 Greek culture has strengths and weaknesses
        Participation
        Instability
    3.5 The Greeks are conquered
        Alexander
        The Hellenistic Empire spreads Greek culture
    3.6 Greek culture changes
        Science
        Religion
4. Roman civilization
    4.1 Rome begins as a city-state
        Etruscans
        The Republic

UNIT IV: THE CRISIS OF THE CLASSICAL WORLD

3.3 What did Christianity offer to Romans?
Personal immortality
Incarnate savior
3.4 Why did Rome become Christian?
Appeal to individuals
Appeal to the government
3.5 Other new religions also emerged in similar circumstances
Mahayana Buddhism
Islam
3.6 Rome and China are similar
Declining empires
Barbarian invasions
New religions
4. Charlemagne and the end of the crises
4.1 In China and the Middle East, empires are reestablished
The T'ang Empire reconstructs classical China
The Abbasid Empire unites the Islamic world
4.2 Charlemagne tries to revive the Roman Empire
Church
Culture
4.3 His empire collapses
Poverty
Treaty of Verdun
4.4 Charlemagne is the "father of Europe"
Through his achievements
Through his failures
5. The world in 900
5.1 A new society is emerging in the West
Europe, not the Mediterranean
Viking invasions
Germanic influences
5.2 The West differs from the Middle East and China
Wealth
Stability
Sophistication

UNIT V: THE RESTORATION OF STABILITY

1. Continuity and change
1.1 A sophisticated China returns to old patterns
Classical traditions
Technological innovation
1.2 A dynamic Middle East combines the old and the new
Middle Eastern continuity
Islamic innovation
1.3 Europe creates new forms of states
Feudalism
Nation-states

1.4 Europe creates new forms of economic organization
Trade and commerce
Capitalism and city-states
1.5 Continuity with its past unifies Europe
Christianity
The Renaissance
2. The age of discoveries
2.1 Why and how did they happen?
Economic motivations
Religious motivations
Political motivations
Technological changes
2.2 What happened when Europe encountered less-sophisticated peoples?
North and South America
Central Asia
2.3 What happened when Europe encountered mature civilizations?
India
China
3. The world in 1700
3.1 The West is still unique
Politically
Economically
3.2 What suggests that the West will dominate?
Economic organization
Technological innovation
3.3 What suggests that the West will not dominate?
Wealth
Sophistication

UNIT VI: THE RISE OF THE WEST

1. The economic transformation of Europe
1.1 What was the industrial revolution?
Mass production
Technology
1.2 Why did it occur in Europe?
Social and economic factors
Political and cultural factors
1.3 What is an industrial economy?
Raw materials
Markets
1.4 Industrial capitalism changes society
Cities
Workers
2. The political transformation of Europe
2.1 Democratic revolutions occurred throughout the West
France
United States

    2.2 The democratic revolutions created new ideologies
        Liberalism
        Nationalism
    2.3 These economic and political changes revolutionized Europe in the nineteenth century
        England
        Germany
    2.4 These economic and political changes provoked strong reactions in Europe
        Marxism
        Welfare state
        Mass democracy
3. The age of imperialism
    3.1 The industrial and democratic revolutions gave European states vast new powers
        Economic
        Political
    3.2 European states came to dominate the world
        Britain
        France
    3.3 This domination could be political
        India
        Africa
    3.4 This domination could be economic
        China
        The Middle East
        Latin America
4. The world in 1900
    4.1 A world economy had been created
        Need for materials and markets
        Financial interdependence
    4.2 Imperialism could be defended
        Britain and the "white man's burden"
        The United States and "manifest destiny"
    4.3 Imperialism could be criticized
        The destruction of native societies in Africa
        The humiliation of China

UNIT VII: THE END OF HEGEMONY

1. World War I
    1.1 The war had many causes
        Nationalism
        Germany's place in Europe
    1.2 The war did not solve these problems
        Nationalism
        Germany
    1.3 The war led to a crisis in European confidence
        Doubts about benefits of technology
        Skepticism concerning governments

UNIT VIII: THE GLOBAL VILLAGE

Chapter 4
An Historical Cultures Approach

Paul Bohannan

1. Rationale

INTRODUCTION

To live successfully in today's complex world society, people must learn that they can simultaneously be individuals true to themselves, patriots true to their country and nation, and world citizens true to the human species. They can do this only if they truly understand who they are and where they fit in the modern world. The best way to discover who we are is to look at other people who are recognizably like ourselves in some ways and yet very different in others. Looking at differences in the context of similarity throws our uniqueness into relief, as well as exposing the common underlying humanity.

The history of humankind was created largely by peoples very different from ourselves. Some of those strange and different peoples were our ancestors. An historical cultures approach to the high school world studies course uses the historical development of the human species to discover who and where we are. It does so by looking self-consciously at the variety of cultural forms that have emerged throughout history. It helps students understand that they, like all people, are subject to both the glories and the limitations of culture.

LOOKING AT CULTURE WITHIN HISTORY

The approach described in this chapter has been labeled an "historical cultures" approach because it draws upon both anthropology and history in its quest to understand the world. While the approach attends largely to the questions and interests of the anthropologist, it does so using historical data and insights.

CULTURAL CHANGE AS HISTORY. A major substantive focus of the approach is an examination of the processes through which today's regional cultures came into being. It looks at the major values and achievements of such regional civilizations as the Chinese, the Indian, the African, the European, the Inca, and the Meso-American.

In looking at different cultures, the approach presented here is not interested in merely cataloguing the complexity of human institutions and values. Rather, it is interested in looking at the dynamics of cultural change within history. The main focus is on the ways in which people throughout history have responded to the changing challenges of their environment. Thus for each of the cultures and cultural areas studied, the approach examines three major topics.

First, the approach looks at the achievements of different cultures in meeting the historical challenges they faced. What premises or assumptions about the world lay behind successful responses to these challenges? What ideas allowed people to find new and adaptive answers to difficult questions?

Second, the approach looks at situations in which societies have faltered. What ideas or premises kept those societies from finding successful solutions to problems? In this regard the approach stresses that a society is seldom undone by one single incapacity to adapt. When analyzing societies, historians and anthropologists must take great care not to oversimplify. Students will also learn to examine the many, complex, interlinking difficulties facing a society.

Finally, this approach addresses the question: What might have been a good solution to a problem that a society failed to solve? What have other societies invented that allowed them not to fail in a similar situation? Such questions lead naturally to a consideration of the question: What are our primary problems today? What premises cloud our eyes so we cannot see adequate solutions? Will the available solutions work? If not, what can we do about it?

THE EMERGENCE OF CONTEMPORARY WORLDWIDE CULTURES. The approach also makes students aware of the forces and processes that determine the way they themselves live. It looks at the processes through which worldwide civilization has emerged since the fourteenth and fifteenth centuries. It helps students see that these processes have completely altered the way in which the world regions interact, and that they have led to a newly urgent need for cross-cultural understanding.

The approach helps students use insights from past cultural adaptation to understand current problems—and to realize when those insights are inadequate. The world today is in the throes of extensive technological change. People perceive a variety of social, cultural, and ecological challenges. In order to "improve" their adjustment to their environment, to lead easier and more pleasant lives—indeed, just to survive—they innovate. Every innovation seems to lead to a new set of challenges. The constant progression of challenges and responses places most social arrangements in a constant state of flux. By looking at history from an anthropological point of view, students can better deal with the contemporary dilemma. They see history as the story of how various social groups have responded to the challenges they faced. At the same time, they develop the ability to think about present challenges in ways that help them to identify appropriate responses.

HISTORY AND ANTHROPOLOGY. There are critical differences between the worldviews of the historian and the anthropologist, yet the integration of history and anthropology in this approach has a long-standing tradition. Historians and anthropologists have much in common. Most importantly, they face the same basic problem. Both endeavor to learn about one place or time in order to better understand another place and time.

An old saw assures us that history has to be rewritten for each generation. Because history happened in the past but is communicated and re-experienced in the present, it embodies a built-in challenge. How do we bridge differences in values or viewpoint between past and present? Only if we succeed at that can we "learn the lessons of history."

Anthropologists obviously face the same challenge. They study life within one culture but try to communicate and recreate the experience within another. They too must bridge the differences in values or viewpoint between the two cultures. They too must find a way to transform an "exotic experience" into a lesson to be learned.

The historical cultures approach is designed to help students learn to look at events from two angles at once. They learn to see it from the perspective of the place and time when the events occurred and from the perspective of the time and place in which they now stand. Thus the course is intended to help students develop an ability to see social realities in three dimensions— not unlike the stereoscopic vision that gives us our excellent eye-hand coordination.

ADVANTAGES OF AN HISTORICAL CULTURES APPROACH

The advantages of the historical cultures approach emerge from its simultaneous and explicit concern for both culture and history.

PROVIDING A CULTURAL PERSPECTIVE. The historical cultures approach emphasizes as no other approach can that there is both a basic similarity among peoples and an infinite variety of ways to be human.

The approach does not merely look at other peoples; it focuses explicitly on culture as a basic human trait. Students learn the relationship between environment and culture. Just as importantly, they learn that specific cultures are shaped by the ways in which past generations have responded to the challenges they faced.

By looking at cultures and cultural change, students become keenly aware of the hierarchy of human needs. They come to understand that only when basic subsistence needs are met can people turn to their social needs. And only when those social needs are at least minimally met can people turn to the intricacies of cultural growth and to their own fuller self-realization.

The approach also allows students to understand their place in the world in a special way. The course will address the following questions. Who are we culturally? How did we get this way? What were the problems to which today's culture is an answer? How will our solutions affect tomorrow—that is, what problems will our solutions create for our descendants?

Students will come to understand their place in the world better by learning to examine the premises behind other people's actions. Anthropologists recognize that all of our actions, values, and reasoning are based on premises in the same way that geometry is undergirded by its axioms. The difference, however, is that premises are seldom spelled out; we may even hold several conflicting premises about any particular set of issues.

The ability to express and assess the premises of a culture is critical, because societies are likely to falter if their citizens get trapped in the cultural premises of the past. Societies die if their premises do not allow them even to contemplate the next step to growth, much less take it. While people always find it difficult to discover their premises, by learning how premises have affected motives and events in the past and in other cultures, students can begin the process of uncovering their own.

As they explore their premises and those of other cultures, students will come to understand that their own place and time do not provide a good platform from which to evaluate other places and times. They will see that their own values and ideas can get in the way of seeing the views of others.

PROVIDING AN HISTORICAL PERSPECTIVE.   In relation to other social science approaches to world studies, including a strictly anthropological one, the historical perspective of this approach has many of the advantages inherent in historical approaches.

The approach allows much of the subject matter to be taught in terms of the "story" of the past. Thus it can be more intrinsically interesting to students than a more conceptual social science approach.

Similarly, the approach allows students to see the sweep of human cultural history. Like a chronological history course, it gives them a sense of the series of historical changes through which the contemporary world has emerged. It gives students a sense of how cultures change, not just over the short run, but over vast historical eras.

Finally, the combination of historical and cultural perspectives can also give students a powerful foundation for looking at the future. By having students examine how the actions of one generation have affected the problems encountered by the next, this approach makes students keenly aware of the necessity for planning the future. Through its analysis of past cultural change, it gives them the skills to think about how to make their future a better one. In this sense an historical cultures approach prepares students for citizenship in its richest sense.

DISADVANTAGES OF AN HISTORICAL CULTURES APPROACH

There are at least four disadvantages to an historical cultures approach to the high school world studies course. They emerge from its focus on "culture" and its presentation of cultural change within an historical framework.

THE PROBLEM OF BREADTH. Culture includes everything human: from language to getting a living, from tools to music. History, especially if one adopts a "world" history approach, as one must within a multicultural perspective, is equally all-encompassing. Thus curriculum planners who would adopt an historical cultures approach encounter a radical form of the problem of selecting course content.

From one point of view the problem of breadth is primarily a question of selectivity. The scope of material relevant to this approach is indeed broad. Any course that would try to encompass it all would result in confusion rather than education. Anthropologists—like historians but unlike economists or political scientists—like to focus on a wide variety of topics. They look for the small scale and the "homey"—kinship, family, and household—but they also look for the intricate and complex—the meanings of religion and myth, or the impact of political practices or trade on community. In any case, the point must be insisted on: They do focus.

On what, then, should an historical cultures approach focus? The reasoning behind the focus presented here can best be seen through an analogy between "culture" and "life." What culture is to the social sciences and history, life is to the biological sciences. Like culture, life can be studied in various ways: by examining its chemistry, by investigating its modes of reproduction, or by cataloguing the many forms it takes. Some anthropologists have wanted to catalogue the various forms of culture, much as Linnaeus catalogued the various forms of life. This can be an interesting and for some purposes valuable exercise, but it misses the key question: How does life work? This approach focuses on two key questions. How does culture work? More importantly, how does culture change?

THE PROBLEM OF ABSTRACTION. From a very different point of view, the problem of breadth is not one of selectivity but rather one of abstraction.

When dealing with a great wealth of material, we must extract broad concepts that make the "babble" intelligible. However, this can easily cause us to pass over important historical events too quickly. What seem to be significant contemporary problems—no matter what history may make of them—may not be given adequate consideration. Or the attempt to teach "concepts"—even historical concepts—can lead us to leave out the detail that gives the concepts meaning and vitality.

The anthropological method itself provides a strategy for responding to this dilemma. The secret to encompassing great breadth and yet attending to more concrete details lies in a systematic change in focus. As a first step, we must focus on some details of data (say, the family in classical China or in ancient Greece) and exhaustively examine the way it is organized. Only then do we change the "focal length" of our attention so that we can see more of the context of the original topic. After some practice, it becomes possible to see distinct reverberations and relationships between the "foreground" and the context.

PERSONALIZING HISTORY. As suggested above, by integrating historical and cultural materials, this approach has a clear advantage over more conceptual social-science-based approaches to world studies. By the same token, however, the effort to use the story of history creates a clear temptation to overemphasize personalities.

People, particularly tenth graders, tend to remember history in terms of stories and specific images of individuals rather than in terms of general concepts. They remember concrete images because of their psychological identification with these historical figures. Yet the more one inserts "real" people into historical analysis, the greater the chance that students will understand history in terms of some version of the "great man" theory. That result is not entirely inappropriate. Queen Elizabeth I of England and Shaka Zulu were personalities who clearly affected the course of history, but, as we know today, overdoing the "great-man theory" leads to one-sided interpretations of the past. It may be especially distorting when the focus of investigation is cultural change.

The challenge is thus to find a form in which the story of the growth and evolution of social and cultural forms can take on the same kind of immediacy that stories about individuals can command. How can we teach the story of the species so that students will get involved? How do we show them that the most thrilling of all stories is the cultural conquest of environment and animality?

THE PROBLEM OF PROGRESS. There is, finally, still a tendency in the Western world to confuse our capacity to meet new challenges with an idea we call "progress." This tendency does not stem from within the social sciences but rather from traditional views of our ancestors and their activities. The natural tendency to view cultural change in terms of "progress" is a problem for any cultural or historical approach. It becomes a more tenacious problem when cultural change is portrayed within the context of world history.

"Progress" is a Western notion that must be examined carefully within the course. It is a notion that may quite appropriately be applied to our view of ourselves. We find it in our view of economics, in our view of technology, and even in our view of people and whether they are getting better or getting worse. However, the notion of progress is not something we can apply cross-culturally. The point must be made firmly that history and cultural evolution are not progress toward some goal. Rather, they are almost always an accidental result of our short-term solutions to the problems that beset us. The problem, simply stated, is to recognize that cultural change may or may not represent "progress." "Progress" is a value judgment from the narrow standpoint of our own values.

2. Goals for students

Citizenship in a democracy requires that people be educated to look for the roots of problems. An historical cultures approach does this in a unique way. It enhances the capacity of young people to see the problems and convictions of our society in comparison with those of other peoples in other eras. This approach contributes to the development of citizens who understand that the precise customs and ideas that served our forefathers may not serve us if the conditions we face are different. At the same time, it helps develop citizens who can display the kind of energy and creativity our forefathers displayed in arriving at novel solutions to real problems in the real world. Such people are essential in today's world, if democracy is to continue succeeding.

Specifically, this approach should teach young people to analyze historical situations in terms of their component parts and to examine the relationship among these parts. It should teach them to distinguish between their values and their self-interest. It should also help them to appreciate that, just by living today, they are creating the future in which they and their children will be living tomorrow.

MAJOR KNOWLEDGE GOALS

In an historical cultures approach to a high school world studies course, the major knowledge goals should be to help students:

1. Know the meaning of culture and its fundamental importance for understanding human history

2. Deepen their understanding that all human thought is based on cultural premises, many of which are hidden from people's awareness
3. Examine the dynamics by which cultures develop, grow, change, and disappear
4. Understand the principal characteristics and meaning of civilization
5. Know the major historical culture crests through which fundamentally new cultural patterns have arisen
6. Apply the concepts of chaining and back-chaining to the examination of cultural change in major historical periods, including the present and the future
7. Apply basic social principles like hierarchy, kinship, and specialization to analyzing different cultures in different historical periods
8. Comprehend more fully that their "place in the world" is different from others' places
9. Deepen their understanding that they cannot expect everybody to think or behave as they themselves do

MAJOR SKILL GOALS

In an historical cultures approach to a high school world studies course, the major skill goals should be to help students:

1. Systematically compare and contrast cultures in different times and places with each other and with their own culture
2. Use critical thinking skills and basic social science concepts to analyze cultural development and adaptation in different historical eras
3. Make reasoned judgments about the efficacy of various cultural adaptations in different periods of history
4. Develop "stereoscopic vision," an ability to see simultaneously their own culture's point (or points) of view and the point of view of other cultures

3. Organization of subject matter

A high school course taking an historical cultures approach must weave together two distinct ways of thinking and studying about the world. These must be carefully distinguished and yet brought together into a sensible whole. The first way of thinking is drawn from the discipline of history; it includes not only historical material but, more importantly, the image of world studies as a story of change. The second way of thinking is drawn from the social sciences, especially anthropology. It includes the conceptual focus and search for patterns and generalizations that are the heart of the social sciences.

History courses are "linear," in the sense that they are best taught chronologically. The story of history has a beginning, a middle, and presumably an end. Events and changes build on each other through causation over time. Social science courses are not "linear" in this sense; there is no necessarily "right" place to begin and no unquestionably "right" road to follow. At the same time there is a rationality: Concepts do build on each other and fit together into larger patterns of meaning. The approach described here is based on the idea that one can simultaneously teach the chronology of history and the concepts of social science.

This section first describes the major concepts and social principles from anthropology and other social sciences that should be woven throughout an historical cultures approach. These include culture, civilization, chaining, and back-chaining. It then considers the chronological organization and historical material through which these concepts can be taught.

CULTURE AND CIVILIZATION

This course is about human culture and that subset of human cultures known as civilization. It runs a vast gamut. It begins with prehistoric cultures that discovered the cultural techniques for working stone, bone, leather, feathers, and wood, leading to what we call the "Stone Age." It extends all the way to today's culture and the discoveries that are leading to the "Space Age." The course deals with the ways culture has developed and grown in all parts of the world and highlights the astonishing similarity among different geographical areas and historical eras.

The subject matter of an historical cultures approach should be selected and organized around three questions:

1. How and why have human beings developed culture? Why do they constantly refine it?
2. How is culture passed from one generation to the next? How does it change over time?
3. How have similarities and differences among the cultures of different groups appeared? Why?

THE MEANING OF CULTURE.   Culture is the core organizing principle of this course. The content of the course should be chosen to convey clearly the idea that culture is as basic to human affairs as energy and matter are to physics. Culture is the "stuff" that makes people of different times and places different from one another. The birth, development, and death of different cultures is the very substance of human history.

Since it was first tried in the 1870s, defining culture has proven to be unyieldingly difficult. It is, indeed, as difficult as defining "life" or "matter." We can best understand what culture is by seeing the two ways in which it can be manifested. First, culture appears as "artifact." Artifacts are things in the real world that people can see, hear, or touch, including speech and other behavior as well as tools. Second, culture appears as "mentifact." Mentifacts are our concepts, values, logic, premises, and techniques. We are often unaware of mentifacts, simply because they are so basic to the way we live or to our understanding of ourselves and our world.

For culture to exist, both the artifact and the mentifact must be present. In other words, in one way or another culture traits must be simultaneously in the environment and in people's heads. Students should understand that external culture (artifacts) gets into people's heads through learning. They should understand that internal culture (mentifacts) gets expressed in the external world through everyday activity as well as through discovery and invention.

CULTURE CHANGES AND GROWS. Culture can be changed ("improved," in the sight of its users) by three means:

1. *Innovation.* When people are faced with new problems, they can invent new ways of dealing with them.
2. *Reinterpretation.* People can use old ideas or tools in new ways or to solve new problems.
3. *Diffusion.* People can learn how others have solved problems and adopt ways that are new to them.

Cultures can grow in these ways simply as a result of people looking for easier, more pleasant ways of carrying on their lives. However, cultural growth most often occurs as a result of a process of "adaptation." Like all other creatures, people must use their environment to provide what they need to live. They join together into social groups and invent and use culture precisely in order to get a living. Thus culture and social systems must change with changes in the environment or changes in the technology used to carry out basic activities. This process of reconciling culture to changes in environment or technology is called "adaptation."

Whether societies face the need for adaptation or not, cultural growth can only take place when people can question their values and premises. Only then can they make room for new ideas and improvements. Culture cannot progress if values forbid inquiry, or if premises cannot be made overt so that they can be openly questioned.

A CULTURE CAN WANE AND DISAPPEAR. When cultures cannot question their values and premises, and thus cannot change with new insights, they may fail to make the adaptations necessary to survive.

Societies in which values and premises cannot be questioned tend to settle into repetitive cycles. This may not always be a disadvantage; some cultures have continued for centuries with little or no innovation. The inability to change becomes a disadvantage whenever there is a significant change in the ecological situation. Ecological challenges to a group can take many forms, including a changing climate, rapid growth in population, or the sudden appearance of another social group with a radically different culture. If conditions change and people keep doing what they have done traditionally, the results may not come out as expected—certainly not as they have in the past. Then an inability to adjust the culture can become destructive.

Even societies that can question the premises of their culture may fail to adapt in critical situations. Students should be encouraged to think about societies that may have difficulty adapting. Dictatorial regimes with totalitarian control over their people could be a prime example; such a society is crippled because people cannot make their own choices. Colonialism probably poses a similar (if not as stark) example: When a culture is forced on a group, that group may have good and rational reasons for resenting and resisting it—that is, for questioning its values and premises. However, a "colonized" people usually cannot make all the adaptations they may want to make. Thus their system of cultural institutions becomes lopsided and their society disadvantaged.

THE MEANING OF "CIVILIZATION." A second key concept that runs throughout the course is "civilization." The idea of civilization is important because both the word and the condition imply the best kind of life human beings have been able to devise. Yet the task of defining "civilization" should be one to which students return again and again as the year proceeds.

The great anthropologist, V. Gordon Childe, defined civilization by the presence of the following traits:

1. Food production instead of food gathering
2. A specialization of social roles beyond a simple sexual division of labor—including specialized farmers who can produce a surplus; skilled craftspeople and traders who can produce and exchange goods; and the roles encompassed by a formal political system such as governors, the governed, and an army for enforcing rules
3. Science, writing, and mathematics
4. Urban settlements—that is, cities with developed hinterland trade
5. Metallurgy
6. Monumental architecture

Whether these particular traits actually define civilization has been questioned by other scholars, however. The Inca in Peru, for example, did not have a highly elaborated system of writing. Similarly, the urban settlement patterns of the Maya of Central America were somewhat different from those found elsewhere. Yet, despite these different traits, historians and anthropologists alike would call the Inca and Maya "civilizations."

An historical cultures approach should encourage students to question whether the traits on Childe's list are essential to civilization. Indeed, they should question our very premises about what civilization is. Should civilization be defined in terms of certain types of cultural traits, as Childe did? Should all civilizations be expected to share these same types of traits? What are the essential components of "civilization?" Do civilizations necessarily have to be "civilized," given that the latter term attributes certain kinds of moral values to a society in addition to a certain sophistication in social structure and technology?

A civilization, however defined, can only continue to prosper as long as people continue to solve the problems they confront. Harsh problems present stark challenges. Indeed, history is littered with civilizations that faced life-and-death challenges. Only with immense creativity can civilizations rise to those challenges—and that necessarily implies culture change.

In examining past civilizations, an historical cultures approach should focus on the challenges they faced and on their success or failure to adapt. The criterion for selecting specific civilizations should be the relevance of the challenges and of the inventions, changes, and solutions to the understanding of all civilization. The course should examine problems successfully solved by those civilizations, but it should examine just as closely the problems that were not solved and therefore spelled the doom of particular civilizations. In the process, students should learn that a society's finest values sometimes lead it to untenable situations. They should see that if the people of such societies cannot find new values that will allow solution of new problems, and cannot find new answers to old problems, they will perish or be conquered.

CULTURE CRESTS

The idea of a "culture crest" provides the primary foundation for organizing the wide-ranging material in an historical cultures course. A culture crest implies a fundamental cultural turning point: a situation in which small cultural changes have multiplied to such an extent within a society that the "old ways" become irrelevant, even unintelligible.

To understand the idea of culture crests and how they occur, students must first understand the systemic nature of culture. A system is a group of discrete "parts" that work together to accomplish some purpose. Every social group is a system. Its "parts" include its people. They also include the cultural traits and premises of the group—that is, the artifacts and mentifacts that allow the people to operate together as a group.

The parts of a system must work closely together; they must be compatible with each other. When one part changes, incompatibilities are almost certain to result. If one part is changed, the rest of the system feels pressures that are likely to lead to still other changes in order to reduce contradictions.

Changes in cultural elements can come about through people's efforts to make their lives easier or more rewarding. They can also occur as a result of adaptation to some change in the ecology of the group. For the most part the necessary adaptations are likely to be small and comfortable, although still easily recognizable. In this sense they are likely to represent additions or subtractions from the cultural core rather than the creation of a whole new one. Nonetheless, changes in one cultural trait may represent "challenges" for the rest of the cultural system. The system must then respond in some way to restore compatibility. That response will involve some cultural change, initiating a new set of challenges that requires a new set of responses.

In this way, even small cultural changes can eventually stack up into major changes. At some point the cumulative change will become so great that it will be evident that a people's overall pattern of using and adapting to the real world has changed. It is even likely to be evident to the people themselves. In many respects the "old" ways will no longer work. Indeed, the old ways may no longer even be intelligible.

A dramatic example of a culture crest set in motion by ecological change occurred about 12,000 years ago at the end of the Ice Ages. The desiccation of the Afro-Asian steppes presented a formidable challenge to the Paleolithic peoples of the area. Their response was a whole series of readjustments that eventually led to the first civilizations.

Technological changes can also lead to culture crests. In several parts of the world, improvements in sailing ships and navigational procedures resulted from the strong desire to trade with other civilizations and to explore new lands. In Europe after the fourteenth century these technological improvements led to the voyages of discovery and a whole new set of challenges. As Europeans responded to the challenges that trade and empire created, they eventually created the global mercantile empires that changed the world.

Thus, with a culture crest, the culture core itself changes. People's expectations change. The activities that fill their daily lives become vastly different from those of their ancestors. The kind of social relations they create and live with are altered. By such changes are the ages of history differentiated.

Contemporary civilization may itself be in the throes of a culture crest of which students should be aware. Our need for resources and excitement, among other things, are driving us into space. The new technologies, discoveries, and opportunities that result from space exploration are likely to induce social changes as great as those produced by the agricultural or the industrial revolution.

Students need to see the contemporary world in this light. They should ask whether we are any better prepared to face this culture crest than people have been in the past. Are we thinking any more systematically about the changes we face than Queen Isabella thought about the far-reaching changes that would surely follow the discovery of new worlds? Are we any more self-conscious about the impact of our technological innovations than was John Watt as he introduced his new steam engine? Most natural scientists and engineers acknowledge the need for this self-consciousness, but few of us have been prepared to examine in detail the possibilities for cultural change in human society.

CHAINING AND BACK-CHAINING

The idea of "chaining" represents a way of thinking about and explaining why particular culture crests occur. It is a process that can help students answer questions about why historical processes occur or do not occur when we expect them or why events sometimes lead to unforeseen results.

When we examine large historical movements like the agricultural revolution or the aerospace revolution, we have to examine the necessary conditions for each step of the revolution to occur at all. Unless certain conditions are satisfied, these events cannot occur. What are those conditions? As we search the historical record, we find that events fit into a pattern or "chain." Each event creates conditions that allow the next major step to occur. Any solution to a challenge facing a civilization can be seen as a set of interconnected links in one or more chains. The solution itself leads to new links in the chain, and ultimately to new challenges.

The idea of chaining is used here in preference to the idea of causation. The cause of events is too often seen in simplistic terms. We tend to look for causes only in temporally proximate events rather than seeing the "chain" of events that make up the historical story. We also tend to look for only one or two "causes." Finally, we tend to treat causes as if a particular cause must inevitably lead to the same specific results. The idea of chaining avoids many of these problems by implicitly building in a historical perspective, an assumption of multicausality, and an open-ended perspective on the future. Chains reach far into the past; they are made up of many links; and they do not assume that you can predict the next link to be added to the chain.

An historical cultures approach should present examples of chaining throughout the course. It should give special attention to using the idea of chaining toward the end of the year.

Students should also be introduced to the idea of "back-chaining." Back-chaining can be thought of as identifying a desired future condition or goal and then working backward in time to the present to determine what conditions (links in the chain) must be met before the desired goal can be attained. Those necessary conditions can be compared to what currently exists to identify the changes that must be made to reach the desired goal. In short, back-chaining represents a way for students to think about alternative futures. It asks how you get there from here. In the process of back-chaining, students will learn about the difficulties of controlling multiply caused situations. They will also come to appreciate better the principles of multicausation and multifinality.

SOCIAL PRINCIPLES

A final set of concepts that should be woven into an historical cultures approach can be called "social principles." The word "principle" is used here in the same way that it is in the phrase "principles of geometry." The principles of society are the sets of rules that explain how people behave socially. Thus they are the means or devices that allow people to live together in groups. Social principles are not in themselves culture; in fact, a few of them occur among animal species as well. Human beings, however, always "culturize" whatever social principles they use. In other words, in human society all social principles are perceived and revered as part of the culture, even if they stem from innate urges and behavior.

Seven basic social principles

There are seven social principles that appear to have been basic to human societies since the first culture crests. Three of them—hierarchy, kinship, and specialization—are so basic that they can be seen in most mammals and some other animals as well. Four others—ranking, office, common cause, and contract—are unique to human groups.

HIERARCHY. This refers to a differentiation among people that gives one power over another. It is based ultimately on threat of force. In the animal world examples of hierarchy run from the simple pecking order of chickens to the complex associations among baboons and chimpanzees. As anyone who has ever served on a committee knows, human culture may lead to excruciatingly complex forms of hierarchy.

KINSHIP. This is a relationship among people that is ultimately based on shared genes. There are two natural types of kinship. Vertical kinship exists between donors and receivers of genes—that is, between parents and children. Horizontal kinship exists between creatures who share genes— for example, among siblings or among cousins. Human culture adds a third type of kinship: "affinal kinship," the kinship of affinity. This is the fictive relationship between the kinsmen of spouses. Human culture adds many affective and social perspectives to basic kinship relationships.

SPECIALIZATION. This is the division of the activities of a group among two or more different categories of animals or people. Social insects like ants have an involved specialization of tasks, even though they have no culture (their artifacts are not accompanied by mentifacts). Among humans the innate bases of specialization are sex and age, but specialization becomes vastly more complex as culture and civilization develop. That is, human beings, in addition to culturizing social principles, also tend to expand the number of criteria upon which specialization can occur.

Human culture can also create social principles that are not innate. Four of these—ranking, office, common cause, and contract—further complicate the patterns of specialization within human cultures.

RANKING. This involves placing one thing above another. Many things can be ranked: culture items, individual people, social groups. Such rankings may be used to determine or constrain human rights and privileges.

OFFICE OR ROLE. This is a familiar concept today. We recognize that with specialization people play particular roles within the social group. More importantly, human groups also come to make a distinction between an individual and the roles or offices he or she plays. Thus offices can be ranked without reference to the particular people who fill them. Likewise, competition among different individuals for particular offices can lead to fierce struggles.

COMMON CAUSE OR COOPERATION. This is one of two kinds of social agreement. It is based on the idea that people who are not already connected by kinship or some other linkage can band together to achieve shared goals that they cannot achieve alone.

CONTRACT. Contract is a second basic form of social agreement. It underlies many social relationships, even those that are based on hierarchy or kinship. The basic idea of contract is summed up in the phrase, "you do something for me, I do something for you, and we both prosper." As is evident in Western society today, the law can add formalization and, perhaps more important, sanctions to enforce contracts among people. Contracts are most often made by people who have no other basis for relationship.

Elaborating social principles

Within human groups basic social principles like hierarchy can become highly complex and varied when they are combined with other principles or when secondary criteria are established. For example, if we recognize that authority, which is the result of hierarchy, may inhere in roles (the principle of office) instead of merely in a powerful individual, we have laid the foundation of many human social forms. In many small groups, chiefship is the recognition that authority may abide in a role. The chiefship, as opposed to the chief, is often protected and expressed in terms of religious doctrine. With growth in the size of society and the complexity of its units, chiefship may grow to be kingship. It may ultimately become a center of "empire," itself a hierarchal organization of states.

The elaboration of social principles in this way results in the wide diversity of cultural patterns any one social principle can take. It can also lead to important cultural traits and norms that are not necessarily social principles in the sense used here. For example, anthropologists do not regard property as a social principle. Rather, it is a Western idea that can be used in connection with many principles to identify different people's rights with respect to some good. Thus an individual or group that has "property rights" over a parcel of land deprives others of at least some rights over that land.

Emerging social principles

In recent years there have emerged two new social principles that are likely to have a tremendous impact on the future: the principles of network and audience. Both are in fact older principles, but they have generally remained unimportant, even unrecognized, until recent decades. They have emerged as specialization of work and rapid communication have reduced the influence of other social principles. Thus, as kinship groups have grown smaller and cities and firms grown more impersonal, the principles of network and audience have taken on added significance.

NETWORK. Every person is a node in a social network. The people with whom we talk and interact are themselves connected with others we may not even know. These networks of social connections stretch throughout the society, providing it with a loose structure. Often these networks remain unrecognized. Some of the people represented on a kinship chart, for example, may form a social network because they associate with one another on a voluntary basis, not just because of kinship bonds. The fact that these people form a network may be of little relevance if attention is focused on the kinship between them.

As the scale of society expands and as specialization increases, awareness of networks eventually becomes overpowering. In today's world networks hold together large numbers of people who have at least one common interest but no other ties. The resulting "single-interest groups" become more important as the cultures of the world become internally more varied and as the training of individuals becomes more and more specialized.

AUDIENCE. The second principle that has become prominent in the contemporary world is "audience." Audiences are as old as storytellers, but mass audiences have been with us only since the 1920s. The precursors of the mass audience were all the individuals who read a particular book or all the participants in a specific ritual. Such people rarely became an important social force, because of the limited size of the audience or their lack of structures for organizing their efforts. Exceptions did occur. The way in which the readers of *Uncle Tom's Cabin* subsequently became abolitionists provides a case in point.

With the mass audiences created by modern communications media, new possibilities for relating people and dealing with large-scale social structures have emerged. So have new ways of controlling people. Today, many observers are concerned that "passivity" induced in the audience is dangerous for individuals and may be antisocial. Others are concerned that when all information is turned into "entertainment," the audience is more and more subject to social manipulation. Students taking an historical cultures approach should be aware of the emergence of audience as a social principle.

Through this example, they should also come to see how apparently benign elements of a culture can also create challenges for it.

COMPARING CULTURES

Intuitively, the comparison of cultures and civilizations should be a central feature of an historical cultures approach to world studies. As fundamental as comparison is to the approach outlined here, it must also be acknowledged how difficult genuine efforts to compare cultures can be. Despite our best intentions, both cultural and historical approaches to civilization tend to produce individually interesting catalogues or portrayals of different civilizations. They rarely, however, make comparisons among those civilizations or even produce comparable profiles of them.

Comparison is the way we come to understand the differences and similarities among cultures. Studying and knowing about any culture enriches our understanding of all the others. In addition, knowing other cultures gives us "a place to stand" as we examine our own. Thus one major value of comparing cultures is to appreciate our own culture better.

One of the most important lessons that comparison of cultures should impart to students is the realization that some aspects of regional cultures are more resistant to change than others. Today technology is often the first part of our worldwide culture to invade regional cultures. Economic efficiencies often take longer to be adopted, but ultimately even the economies of "developing" countries come to participate more and more in the world economy. Those aspects of regional cultures that seem most resistant to change, on the other hand, are religion and family life.

HISTORICAL CONTENT

The historical content of this approach should begin with the earliest known facts about humankind. It can proceed chronologically, with different periods and cultures defined by historical culture crests. As is always the case, the selection of the key culture crests upon which to base this organization requires interpretation. The historical anthropologist must make decisions, preferably on the basis of overt principles.

The primary criterion for determining historical eras, and thus identifying culture crests, will be technological. Using cultural technology, human beings have proceeded along a clear route from the socially and technologically simple toward the complex. The overview of historical content and the course outline presented later will follow this route as well. The exact number of culture crests is a matter of definition—indeed, of taste to some extent. However, some are undeniable and will be clearly recognized as critical turning points in human history.

It is important to emphasize (also to students during the course) that this organization does not assume that human history has been dictated by technology. Technological change has been one extremely important dimension of cultural change, but it should never be considered the prime mover. Ideas and beliefs are equally important. The difference is that ideas do not chain historically with the same ease as technological advances do.

THE OLD STONE AGE. The first culture crest, represented by the culture of the Paleolithic period, was ushered in over vast millennia. Starting from something like the simple proto-culture exhibited by today's chimpanzees, human beings gradually created tools and weapons from stone, wood, and other readily available resources. This step allowed human beings to move beyond gathering vegetable food, supplemented by occasional animal protein. Now they could also hunt large animals.

Culturally, the Old Stone Age was the age of the hunting and gathering band. The social techniques of these human groups were simple. They recognized kinship and almost surely were organized into families. They recognized and used simple hierarchies. Strong and prestigious people held some authority over younger or less able people. They divided the social labor between men and women and between adults and children.

Old Stone Age culture, based as it was on hunting and gathering, encouraged human beings to spread to most parts of the globe. As they moved, people altered details of their culture to deal with local conditions better. As new environments posed new challenges, human invention transformed more and more of the features of the environment into resources, leading to more and more complex culture.

THE NEW STONE AGE. This culture crest, the Neolithic period, was marked by the use of far larger numbers of species for food and by increasingly small and fine stone tools—scrapers, awls, arrow points. Improved diets allowed populations to grow more dense. The beginnings of metallurgy are also to be found in this period.

THE AGRICULTURAL REVOLUTION. Taking up agriculture as a way of life represented one of the most profoundly important culture crests in history. The agricultural revolution occurred independently in several parts of the world when population pressures or ecological changes accumulated, making it impossible for people to make a living by hunting and gathering.

Agriculture required people to settle down to tend their crops and domesticated animals, so it led to the first sedentary human settlements. Within these settlements, specialization of tasks became more complex because sedentary people, even when all remain basically farmers, can specialize their economic activities. Thus trade increased and became more complex.

Agriculture also allowed far larger numbers of people to live together. Whereas a hunting band contained from thirty to fifty members, an agricultural village could contain several hundred. This increased population meant that more people were in daily contact, and that one could not know or trust all of them equally. In this situation, innovative governmental roles began to appear. Chiefs and headmen, who were often the same people as the priests, could adjudicate disputes among people and enforce contracts between them. With these new governmental roles came a new social principle: the principle of office. A "chiefship" is an office held by an individual called the "chief." The chief and his office are not the same.

THE URBAN REVOLUTION. When the population grew even further, when specialization of tasks reached genuine complexity, then what is called an "urban revolution" occurred. The resulting changes in the way people lived and worked certainly qualifies as a major cultural crest.

Larger populations and greater specialization of tasks both enabled and necessitated wider-scale trade and government. Thus, as large settlements resembling cities arose, they created new challenges leading to further specialization.

In the urban settlement, a considerable proportion of people were no longer directly involved with subsistence production. To ensure their livelihood, people who specialized in farming and craft production were needed. So were the traders who specialized in carrying goods among them. To feed a larger non-farming population required advanced agricultural techniques. Along river valleys, irrigation emerged as a response. Irrigation schemes are complex and must be managed, so they translated back into greater governmental specialization and power.

A key response to the challenge of city life involved the emergence of a variety of new government roles for recordkeeping, tax collection, and community management. Just as it is possible to arrange individuals into a hierarchy, it is possible to arrange offices hierarchically. The hierarchy of offices became of the utmost importance in the emergence of the bureaucracies needed to run the increasingly complex governments of these city-states.

As urban settlements led to city-states, people's loyalties became fixed on those areas and the officials and kings who represented them. The city-states, however, were likely to battle furiously with the people of adjoining city-states. Indeed, one of the major reasons that the golden age of the Greek city-states did not last longer was the constant and destructive warfare among them. Permanent, professional armies emerged as a response to the need for trained people to do battle against adversaries.

When one king defeated another and began to rule both kingdoms, empire came into being. The increasing complexity and opportunities inherent in empires further elaborated the specialization of urban cultures. Professional armies became even more important, as did long-distance traders. Bureaucracies grew even larger in response to the challenge of governing large, heterogeneous populations.

In the urban revolution, religion also underwent profound change. Religion among hunters and gatherers focused on the abundance of game and the health of the plant species. A religious or magical association between people's activities and the plentitude of food resources made people see their gods in terms of environmental riches and in terms of what they could do (morally and ritually) to encourage the forces of nature to be beneficent. Among agriculturalists, religious concern turned to the fertility of crops and to the weather conditions that allowed them to prosper. In both periods, ancestors and spirits may be postulated either as forces in themselves or as go-betweens linking man to the gods.

With the arrival of urban settlement, religion became more affected by emerging scientific discoveries—usually beginning with astronomy—and its priests came to be seen as officeholders, who could be ranked just like bureaucrats. Learning and writing were also associated with religion, so priests gained more power. In many places priests and kings were the same people. In virtually all places, the priests initially controlled formal education and scientific information.

THE FIRST ENERGY CREST.   An important link in the chain leading to various culture crests routinely involves the development of new techniques for utilizing energy. The first energy crest occurred during the New Stone Age. People discovered how to harness animal power and, more importantly in the long run, the kinetic energy of the winds. These new sources of energy increased agricultural productivity and laid a basis for specialization by expanding the possibilities for long-distance trade.

Following the urban revolution, societies built on this energy crest in various ways. During this period the basic principles of mechanics were discovered and put to use. Principles such as the use of rollers to move huge objects, the lever, and the inclined plane allowed people to build the ziggurats and pyramids so often associated with civilization. Principles for turning the potential energy of wind and flowing water into mechanical energy were also discovered and brought into cultural use. As methods of manufacture became more advanced, demands were created for new and better machines; that reinforced the search for scientific understanding.

The first energy crest set in motion an immensely important chain of technological, scientific, political, and economic challenges and responses throughout all parts of the world. Among the most important achievements that grew out of the first energy crest were those associated with sailing and navigation. By the 1400s the Chinese, the Mediterranean, and the

European peoples had made huge advances in shipping. As early as A.D. 100 the entire Eurasian world was tied together by water-borne trade. In the 1300s the Chinese lanuched voyages of discovery that took immense fleets as far West as Africa and Arabia. However, it was the revolution in sailing and navigation technology that occurred in Europe that led to the next culture crest.

THE SECOND ENERGY CREST AND THE INDUSTRIAL REVOLUTION. In the year 1400, each hemisphere of our planet was crisscrossed by trade routes. Each hemisphere, however, operated in isolation from the other.

The voyages of Columbus and the other European mariners brought the two hemispheres together. As traders, missionaries, and conquerors responded to the challenges and opportunities posed by the discoveries, the planet would in fact become "one world." Only the most remote corners of the world would remain outside the global system. At the same time, as other Europeans—especially the Dutch and the English—became involved in trade between the hemispheres, yet another social form emerged: capitalism. Capitalism is a unique form of economic organization in the sense that land, labor, know-how, and resources all entered the same market as agricultural produce and manufactured goods.

It was in this context that the second energy crest erupted, with the invention of the steam engine. It would soon be followed by the discovery and harnessing of electricity. Within the next century and a half, this second energy crest had led to the industrial revolution and changed the way of living of almost all the peoples of the world.

Technologically, the second energy revolution represented a means for turning the energy contained in wood and other fossil fuels into mechanical energy. The discovery of electricity significantly extended the ways in which this energy source could be used by providing a means for turning the mechanical energy into a form that could be "shipped" along lines or "stored" in batteries. The discovery of atomic power, in which the immense energy of the atom could similarly be turned into heat energy, mechanical energy, and electricity, represented a further fundamental advance.

With each new energy source or energy principle, new vistas opened up. The changes that followed quickly in the wake of the discovery of steam power are called the "industrial revolution." At that time and in the decades following, people completely changed their way of living. Work was no longer geared to the seasons or to the needs of plants and animals, but rather to the clock and the needs of machines. Thus demands made on people by industrial work dictated different activities and different rhythms from those dictated by agricultural work. Utterly new lifestyles resulted. New kinds of community and new social differentiations, based on the new relationships of the workplace, also emerged. Societies faced new technical and social problems as a result.

Some scholars argue that the atomic revolution should be treated separately from the earlier manifestations of the fossil-fuel-based industrial revolution. It is unquestionable that the Atomic Age has brought a situation of maximum danger that mankind has never before faced. Yet it is probably more meaningful to see it as a late and deadly manifestation of the industrial revolution rather than as the harbinger of a new age.

THE "POST-INDUSTRIAL" ERA. Historically, the World War II era represents the most recent culture crest. Although some parts of the world did not participate in the war itself, none remained unaffected by it. Some of the major new components of the post-World War II cultural lifestyle include atomic energy, instant communication throughout the world, and computers.

A hallmark of the postwar culture is the growth of worldwide cultures, as represented by transnational corporations, the Red Cross, the Club of Rome, and the antinuclear movement. However, these worldwide cultures have not replaced or even necessarily interfered with the continued prosperity of regional cultures. The world is not becoming "homogenized" just because regional cultures are changing and worldwide cultures are growing. Indeed, worldwide cultures could serve to make the world "safe" for regional cultures. As we interact with other cultures and come to understand them, we should realize that human beings have a wide variety of choices and that there are many rewarding ways of being human.

However, this type of learning is not always apparent. Although every people in the world is now part of a single great social system, ideas and values remain disparate. For the most part our ability to deal with differences among regional cultures remains locked in thought patterns characterized by such dichotomies as "good and bad," "right and wrong," "ours and theirs."

It is in this context that contemporary society must deal with the challenges of the contemporary era. Among these challenges is the division of the world between the industrialized nations and those countries that have come to be known as the "developing" world. The social and ethical problems inherent in this economic division are only beginning to emerge.

Contemporary society must also deal with the challenge posed by past reactions to industrial capitalism. Various kinds of socialism arose in response to the social evils that accompanied rapid industrialization. Since industrialization and capitalism grew up together, these evils have often been blamed on the latter. The growth of socialism has, in fact, strengthened capitalism. Now the political division between the two has been made more difficult and frightening by the threat of nuclear war.

The post-World War II culture crest is truly novel in one critical respect. A radically accelerated rate of culture change has become characteristic of contemporary society. Acceptance of rapid change has itself become a culture trait in some parts of the world. This has not only produced new challenges for adaptation, as people find themselves awash in a fluid cultural sea; it has actually made the process and risks of adaptation more challenging. The time available to respond to challenges has become ever shorter.

THE AEROSPACE REVOLUTION. It is in this light that the aerospace revolution needs to be considered. From one perspective the aerospace revolution has been a part of the culture crest that has produced contemporary society. From another, it represents a chain of events that is likely to launch human society into yet another culture crest within the lifetimes of our students.

The aerospace revolution began in the late nineteenth century and got off the ground, as it were, in the late twentieth. We have already seen significant changes in social organization as a result. The airplane has changed travel and migration patterns. Linked with the communication revolution, air travel has fostered the development of far-flung social networks of a size and range the world has never before seen.

Of more far-reaching significance, however, is the challenge the aerospace revolution is creating by making outer space accessible to human societies. Resources in space are complete and unlimited. Everything we need is there, although it is not in a condition that makes it particularly easy to use. Unless our collective responses to the challenges of history change abruptly, it is almost certain that we will soon do manufacturing in space. Not long thereafter, we may get energy from space as well. Ultimately, people will live beyond the earth's atmosphere. Life in moon colonies and space stations will be very demanding and will require people to make changes that will be vast in comparison with any adaptation our ancestors have had to make.

Students today should be studying and preparing for the changes that will be made in our behavior and our societies by space mining, space manufacturing, space exploration, and space living. It is here that the study of back-chaining becomes important. Throughout an historical cultures approach, students should have been learning that special conditions and ideas are essential for the next step in human adaptation to occur. Perhaps as a society all of us are now ready to take the next step forward by doing things right without the need for experience. The course might conclude by having students consider the "ideal cultural traits" of a future space settlement. Then, by "back-chaining" to our present social situation, they can identify what would have to occur to make their plan genuinely possible.

4. Annotated bibliography

Adams, Robert M. "Urban Revolution: Introduction." In *Encyclopedia of the Social Sciences*, edited by David L. Sills. New York: Macmillan, 1968. Reviews the criteria of civilization in terms of specialists and rulers, mechanisms for redistributing wealth, monumental public buildings, predictive sciences, foreign trade, and political organization based on residence.

_____. *The Evolution of Urban Society: Early Mesopotamia and Prehispanic Mexico.* Chicago: Aldine, 1966. Gives a detailed and informative comparison of the way similar patterns of civilization emerged in two quite different world areas. Provides an excellent resource for special units and projects.

Braidwood, Robert J., and Willey, Gordon R. *Courses Toward Urban Life.* Chicago: Aldine, 1962. A series of essays providing good source materials for detailed classroom units.

Curtin, Philip D. *Cross-Cultural Trade in World History.* Cambridge University Press, 1984. An excellent study. Examines trade diasporas in which traders spread out from their homelands and established a permanent presence in foreign lands. Beginning with the agricultural revolution, these processes were responsible for much of the interconnection within each hemisphere and for the early history of the colonial era.

Daniel, Glyn. *The First Civilizations: The Archaeology of Their Origins.* London: Thames and Hudson, 1968. A popular account of the culture and the archaeology used in discovering the cultures of Sumer, Egypt, China, and American civilizations. Well written.

Deane, Phyllis. *The First Industrial Revolution.* Cambridge University Press, 2nd ed., 1979 (1st ed., 1965). Explains the history and economics of the industrial revolution in England in the eighteenth and early nineteenth centuries. If one reads only one book on the industrial revolution, this short book should be it.

Freeman, Kathleen, *Greek City-States.* New York: W.W. Norton, 1950. The introduction and conclusion make a clear case for the difficulties that led to the demise of the Greek city-states. Contains histories of ten individual states, on which specific projects could be based. Heavily editorialized, the book states British values about what the Greeks might have done better.

Langer, William L. *An Encyclopedia of World History: Ancient, Medieval and Modern, Chronologically Arranged,* 5th ed. Boston: Houghton Mifflin, 1972. An excellent source of dates. Can help to keep complex chronologies straight.

McNeill, William H. *The Rise of the West: A History of the Human Community.*
_____. *A World History,* 2nd ed. New York: Oxford University Press, 1971. Excellent accounts. The second is a college text based on the first. It provides good background to world history.

Ribeiro, Darcy. *The Civilizational Process.* Translated from the Portuguese by Betty J. Meggers. Washington D.C.: Smithsonian Institute Press, 1968. The best book available on the growth and spread of world cultures from the earliest times until the present era. It has the advantage of being a short book, but it is not easy, because it is so densely packed. The chart at the beginning provides an excellent summary of world history as a series of concentric circles.

Toynbee, Arnold J. *A Study of History.* Abridgement by D.C. Somervell. New York and London: Oxford University Press, Vol. I, 1946; Vol. II, 1957. A book that is outdated in many respects. Still a classic and valuable for its analysis of the patterns that appear and reappear in history. The most important single idea is that civilizations arise because people respond to challenges. Toynbee was among the first to grasp the immense importance of the social environment to history. Toynbee is himself challenging because he assumes that his reader knows a great deal, including how to read Greek words in the Greek alphabet. Nonetheless a classic that should not be ignored.

Wolf, Eric R. *Europe and the People without History.* Berkeley, Calif.: University of

California Press, 1982. A brilliant explanation of the interconnections among world societies before the year 1400 and what happened in the years after 1400 to change them.

5. Content outline for an historical cultures approach

UNIT I: PEOPLE AND CULTURE

1. Why human beings are different from other creatures
   1.1 Human beings adapt to their environment and to each other by using culture
       Culture as a tool
       People versus chimpanzees
   1.2 Culture is associated with language
       Learning to speak
       Words as symbols
       The ability to cooperate efficiently
       Tools and language
   1.3 Human beings share basic social arrangements with the great apes but there are differences
       Paternity
       The human family
       Positions of power separate from individuals
2. People learn their culture
   2.1 People depend more on what they learn than on their biological endowments
       Learning culture from other people
       Learning language
       Know-how
       Learning from parents, age-mates, schools, books, and television
   2.2 "Creativity" means adding something new and different to one's culture
       How and why
       Creativity as a tool

UNIT II: THE ORIGINS AND GROWTH OF CULTURE

1. Hunting and gathering
   1.1 Hunters and gatherers live by gathering seeds and roots and hunting animals
       First major culture crest
       The tools—use of fire
       Organization—family and band
   1.2 Hunters and gatherers move in response to the availability of food
       Drought and other climatic conditions
       Presence of enemies
       Bushmen and Australian Aborigines
   1.3 Sometimes a band gets too large to be supported by its current culture in its current environment
       The band splits
       In search of a new place
       The Aboriginal settling of Australia

The Amerindian settlement of the New World
1.4 As culture grows more efficient or as the environment grows easier to exploit, the size of the band increases
Fishing groups in Africa
The northwest coast of North America
2. Local cultures develop in the Paleolithic period
2.1 Different cultures arose in response to different environments and climates
Adapting through culture
The limiting factor of adequate culture
2.2 As people moved farther apart, they stopped learning each others' cultures
The globe filled up
Eskimo and desert peoples
Growth and change of language
2.3 When early human beings began to make stone tools, the results of their work lasted
Archaeologists' finds
Earliest recoverable human cultures
Earliest tools in Africa
Early tools in Asia and Europe
3. The Neolithic (New Stone Age) revolution
3.1 Ecological changes of various sorts posed a challenge for hunting and gathering groups
Demographic pressure
Changes in climate
Growth of the deserts
3.2 As the desert dried up, peoples of the Sahara had several responses available to them, all of which involved radical cultural change
Stay and perish
Stay and become nomads
Go south to Africa
Go north and become farmers
Go into the swamps along the Nile
Take to the sea
4. The agricultural revolutions
4.1 The agricultural revolution has occurred several times in the history of the world
Food production replaces food collecting
The earliest agricultural revolution—Mesopotamia
Subsequent revolutions in China, India, Andean highlands, Middle America, West Africa, and New Guinea
4.2 Agriculture became a way of life
Knowledge of the function of seeds
Discovering "how" to do agriculture
4.3 Each time agriculture was discovered, a different group of plants was used
Grains in the Middle East
Other grains in West Africa and China
Corn, squash, peppers, and tomatoes in Middle America
4.4 Agricultural communities required new social and political forms
The social challenges posed by the agricultural lifestyle

New political and social forms
Chiefship and kingship
4.5 Agricultural lifestyles require other adaptations as well
Pressures on the kinship system
Larger extended families
Differences in attitude toward work and one's neighbors

UNIT III: THE CULTURE OF EARLY CIVILIZATIONS

1. The urbanization culture crest
    1.1 Ancient cities grew up as specialization and trade grew
    Decrease of subsistence farmers
    Increase of craft specialties
    Trade specialists
    Agricultural specialists
    1.2 The challenge of the "specialist revolution" led to new social principles, skills, and knowledge
    New social principles
    Ranking and holding office
    Metallurgy, science, and writing
    1.3 City-states emerged
    Athens and other Greek city-states
    City-states in India and Africa
    Bureaucracies and further specialization
2. Ancient empires
    2.1 Ancient empires grew as the areas of trade and political hegemony expanded
    Conquest empires (Alexander the Great)
    Bureaucratic empires (Iran, China, and the Aztecs)
    Colonial empires (Rome and India)
    2.2 The complexity of empire posed new challenges that led to new social forms
    The creation of professional armies
    Bureaucracy and law
    The rise of universalist religions and philosophies

UNIT IV: THE FIRST ENERGY CREST AND THE EXPANSION OF CULTURE

1. Early energy sources
    1.1 Human beings learn to use fire
    Discovery of the use of fire
    Wood as most important fuel
    Uses of fire—warmth, cooking, hardening pottery, melting metal
    1.2 Wind power was used after 3200 B.C.
    Egyptians invented sails around 3200 B.C.
    Windmills
    1.3 Water wheels were developed in the first century B.C.
    Early functions of a water wheel

Early manufacturing and the industrial revolution
2. The expansion of trade
    2.1 Use of animals and wind power permitted long-distance trade
        Overland caravan trade
        Coastal trade
    2.2 Expansion of trade eventually led to "two worlds"
        Increased contact and spread of culture
        Contacts within Afro-Eurasia and within the Americas
        Separation of the two hemispheres
3. European voyages of discovery and the initial adaptations of Spain and Portugal
    3.1 The revolution in sailing and other technologies created "one world"
        Seafaring revolution in the Mediterranean
        Lateen sails and long-distance sailing
    3.2 Portuguese and Spanish missions are launched to enhance trade
        Sea routes to the Indies
        Portuguese explorers found a way around Africa
        The unification of Spain and Muslim knowledge
        Columbus' discoveries
    3.4 Spanish and Portuguese expansion produced great wealth, but the response
        of both to the challenge of expansion was a failure
        Portuguese and Spanish colonies around the world
        Vicious cycle—increase supply for an unlimited demand
        A failed response—new wealth not invested in productive ways
4. The successful adaptation of France, Holland, and England
    4.1 France and Holland establish trading and settler colonies
        French and Dutch colonies
        Did not develop fully into capitalism
        Did not exhaust country or colonies for money
    4.2 England develops capitalism and a capitalist empire
        Traded and colonized in India and America
        First country with a full-fledged capitalist system
5. Capitalism
    5.1 Capitalism is based on processes that invest wealth to produce wealth
        Land, labor, resources and know-how (entrepreneurialism) and the market
        Prices and the market
    5.2 Capitalism is a system controlled by two factors
        National income is reinvested in future production
        Factors of production enter the same market as consumer goods
6. The challenges of the colonial system
    6.1 All colonial systems have built-in problems
        Capitalist colonies as competitors
        Precapitalist empire colonies and exhaustion without development
        Trading colonies and differing cultures
        Heavy immigration and capitalist colonies
    6.2 In the colonial form of government, decisions about the operation and welfare
        of the colony are made in the metropolitan country
        Limited information
        Colonies' welfare ranks second
        Revolution and the cost of empire

UNIT V: THE SECOND ENERGY CREST AND THE INDUSTRIAL REVOLUTION

1. The second energy crest
   1.1 The second energy crest allowed manufacturing processes to be developed and centralized
   Watt's steam engine—transforming heat into mechanical energy
   New power-driven machinery
   Increasing use of energy
   1.2 The steam engine changed transportation and trade
   Steamships
   First steps to the railroad
   1.3 The electric generator brought new changes
   Water wheels, windmills, and steam turbines
   The electric motor and the internal combustion engine
   New developments and inventions
   Wood as a fuel becomes scarce
   1.4 Coal becomes the most widespread fuel for generating electricity
   Coal use in China and Europe before the sixteenth century
   English factories and coal mines
   A coal-fed industrial revolution in the United States
   1.5 Growing use of petroleum creates an age of oil
   Gaslights and social adjustment
   Gasoline and the automobile-based society
   A global petroleum industry
   Petroleum and world politics
2. The industrial revolution
   2.1 The industrial revolution was a new way of adapting to the environment
   Changes in the environment to meet the needs of human beings
   Supports a much larger population at a much higher level of consumption
   2.2 Technological changes make new demands on individuals and on their social institutions
   Life is organized around machines
   New demands and questionable improvements
   Social results
   Prosperity and increased population
   The spiral of consumption and resource use
   2.3 Increasing use of resources has caused several world reactions
   Resource use by developed vs. developing countries
   The location of resources and the structure of the world economy
   Increasing cost of energy
   Air and water pollution
   The search for alternative energy sources (solar, nuclear fusion, hydrogen)
3. Capitalism and capitalist society
   3.1 Capitalism requires large segments of the population to enter the market
   Changes in activities and relationship to nature and society
   Growth in class differentiation
   Working classes at a disadvantage
   Social forces vs. natural forces

3.2 Some believe that capitalist society is unfair and destructive
Industrial society vs. peasant society
The socialist critique of capitalism
4. Socialism and communism
4.1 Socialism responds to the ills of society by turning to government ownership and planning
Robert Owen—harmony vs. competition
Socialism in Sweden and Great Britain
National Socialism—the Nazis and Fascists
African Socialism
4.2 Communism responds to the ills of the industrial world through "communal" ownership of the means of production, along with central government planning
Karl Marx and Friedrich Engels—grand theoreticians of communism
Lenin and the role of the party after the revolution in Russia
Changes in Soviet communism under Stalin
Communism as a political system
5. Totalitarianism
5.1 Totalitarianism or dictatorship is a very old form of government
Roman—Julius Caesar
Chinese—Shih Huang-ti
5.2 It reemerged after World War I in response to political and economic ills
Hitler, Mussolini, and Stalin
Neo-Nazi groups today

UNIT VI: THE POST-INDUSTRIAL PERIOD—CULTURE CREST?

1. The communication revolution
1.1 Movable type and Gutenberg begin the revolution
Democratization of education
Inexpensive printing and widespread education
Mass audience
1.2 Radio and television in the early twentieth century create "instant communication"
Telegraph, telephone, radio, and TV
Information independent of social relationships
Technical information requiring special education
Instant global problems but not solutions
1.3 Modern technology encourages international networks of people who have only one major interest in common
Communicating agendas
Decentralization of people responding
Single issues and democratic government
2. The aerospace revolution
2.1 The dream of conquering the air is ancient
Angels, winged animals, and Icarus

Early lighter-than-air craft

The gasoline engine, hooked to a winged kite, revolutionized flight

2.2 Advances in airplane technology, combined with communication, have altered the ways we live

From Kitty Hawk to the jumbo jet

Increased trade and travel internationally

Juxtaposition of the world's cultures

Contact speeds culture change

2.3 Rockets made space accessible to human groups with enough culture

Chinese rockets in the 1200s

The use of rockets in war

3. Nuclear power and nuclear war

3.1 Atomic power emerged from new discoveries in physics

Early theories of atomic energy

World War II and the nuclear bomb

3.2 Atomic energy was used as another source of power

Types of nuclear reactors: fission and fusion

Benefits of nuclear power: predicted and real

Problems of nuclear power: scarcity of fuel, wastes, accidents, terrorism

The global spread of nuclear technology and the challenge it poses

Anti-nuclear forces as a single-issue group

3.3 Nuclear power and advances in rockets created a new challenge for security and survival

The arms race

International anti-nuclear movements

3.4 Peace in a nuclear age means more than the absence of war

The search to discover what types of societies, social organizations, cultures, and technologies maintain world peace

Understanding conflict

A dyad or interlinked dyads

The social system and conflict or potential conflict

UNIT VII: UNIVERSAL CIVILIZATION—CULTURE TODAY AND TOMORROW

1. Toward a new culture crest: The space age

1.1 Competition and cooperation between the U.S. and U.S.S.R. sped the development of new space technologies

The political and military importance of space

Sputnik and the early Soviet lead

The Apollo program and the race to the moon

Soviet and American programs today

Enter the Europeans and the Japanese

1.2 Space technology has affected science and everyday life

New knowledge in physics, chemistry, and astronomy

Space medicine and the biological sciences

Commercialization of space satellites and new space technologies

2. Practical uses of space
   2.1 New aerospace technology may allow us to create permanent settlements in space
      Laboratories in space
      Manufacturing in space
      Mining in space
      Space tourism
   2.2 Space medicine today concentrates on studying the physical and psychological problems of living and working in space
      Effects of weightlessness on injuries and diseases
      The future
   2.3 Communication and weather satellites will be improved
      Meteorology
      Navigation satellites
3. Space-age culture
   3.1 Human beings can live anywhere if they have enough culture, but there are many problems to overcome
      The "gravity well"
      Space hazards
      Greater cultural manipulation of space's infinite resources
   3.2 New social contexts will emerge that will demand new kinds of social structure
      Governments of space settlements
      Moon and Mars bases
      Effects of space manufacturing on Earth societies
      Impact of medicine, recreation, and nationalism
   3.3 Regional cultures may disappear or become more "regional"
      World cultures
      A world safe for differences
   3.4 Known social principles will need to be newly institutionalized in new contexts
      Designing social groups
      Maximize rewards
   3.5 The nature of work will change
      Changes throughout history
      Work as an element of self-identity and self-fulfillment
   3.6 The nature of communities will change
      Continuation of the trend toward "special-purpose communities"
      Growth of specialization
   3.7 International corporations will become more powerful
      Corporations as powerful as nations
      Global problems instead of national problems
   3.8 The importance of being women and men will change
      Improved technology reduces the need for physical strength
      Families change
      Longer life spans
4. The new role of audiences
   4.1 Audience has become a newly important social form
      One-way communication
      Advertising and propaganda and the issue of control
      Effect on modern society

Changes in artistic statement and social commentary
4.2 We need to find ways to "back-chain" from desired goals to the present
Non-haphazard cultural growth and change
The future culture crest

Chapter 5
A World Geography Approach

W. Randy Smith

1. Rationale

INTRODUCTION

Hardly a day passes when we are not exposed to some manifestation of the geographic complexity and diversity of the world. Television reports on famine in Africa are juxtaposed with images of surplus grain in North America. Newspapers discuss future oil shortages in Europe and Japan despite vast surpluses in the Middle East. Devastating monsoon rains in India are contrasted with a decade-long drought in Africa. Yet despite this routine exposure to the world's geographic diversity and complexity, most students are unable to describe or explain even the most basic aspects of world geography.

In the United States, unlike most other countries, geography is not a well-defined academic subject. In elementary schools geography is almost never a separate course. When geography is taught, teachers often concentrate on map skills or physical geography. In secondary schools geography is typically relegated to a secondary status, behind history and government. As a result, when most students complete high school, they are not aware of what the study of geography is or how it can help them understand the world around them. Many students, including those who have completed several history courses, never learn where the world's major political units are located, why they hold prominence, or how they are related to the United States.

This chapter outlines a world geography approach for a high school world studies course. It has been designed with two thoughts in mind. First, it recognizes that such a course would represent most students' first exposure to geography as a subject. Therefore it emphasizes basic geographic concepts and skills. Second, the chapter takes into account that many teachers will be unfamiliar with the concepts and assumptions inherent in the discipline of geography, so it clearly describes what is distinctive about a geographic approach to world studies.

THE DISTINCTIVENESS OF THE GEOGRAPHIC APPROACH

Stated simply, geography studies the ways in which physical and human phenomena are distributed on the Earth's surface. It also studies the forces that bring about those distributions. There are two main branches of geography today: physical geography and human geography. They should both be included in a world geography approach. Physical geography looks at natural characteristics of the Earth's surface, such as landforms (mountains and plains), climate (temperature and precipitation), and vegetation (forest and grassland). Human geography studies the distribution and characteristics of the populations living on the Earth.

Literally, geography means writing about the Earth, but it is best interpreted as a way of thinking about the Earth. Geography approaches the study of the contemporary world from a different perspective than the other social and physical sciences. Both physical and human geographers ask two basic questions. Where are phenomena located on the Earth's surface? Why are they located where they are?

In answering the question of where phenomena are located, maps remain the basic tool of the geographer. Whether they detail a nation, a continent, or the world, maps identify variations from one place to another. For example, in physical geography, world maps might show the tremendous variation in temperature or rainfall levels across the Earth. They might reveal complex landscapes in which landforms vary from rugged, heavily mountainous areas to flat plains crossed by major rivers. In human geography, world maps might show the uneven distribution of the Earth's 5 billion people, or the complex pattern of world trade in petroleum. Another map might identify the range of economic activities, from those parts of the Earth that are primarily rural and agricultural to those parts that are urban and industrial.

Once geographic variations are identified on a map, an explanation of the pattern of variation is necessary. Thus geographers are also concerned with explaining those processes or forces that have produced the observed variations. For example, understanding variations in landscapes requires some understanding of both geological and meteorological forces. The physical landscape results in part from the activity of volcanoes and earthquakes. The surface is continuously being altered as forces inside the Earth place pressure on the Earth's outer edge and crust. At the same time, the landscape is continuously being eroded or worn down by atmospheric forces such as heating/cooling, wind, and rain. Together these two forces help explain why the landscape looks the way it does, where it does. They also show the dynamic nature of the physical environment.

In human geography, understanding why variations across places have occurred is also complex. For example, to understand why population is unevenly distributed on the Earth's surface, we need to know something about historical settlement trends, types of economic system, and the extent to which cultural characteristics influence where people settle. The impact of physical characteristics would also have to be considered. For much of human history the physical geography of the Earth strongly influenced where people could settle and what they could do. Early human settlement was concentrated geographically in lowland areas with adequate water supply, such as the Nile River valley in Africa, the Fertile Crescent region of the Middle East, and the Indus River valley in South Asia. Today the physical environment does not exert as strong an influence. Technology now permits humans to alter the physical geography. We can create needed transport routes by rerouting rivers or tunneling through mountains. We can make arid regions more livable by seeding clouds or transporting water hundreds of miles through aqueducts.

THE IMPORTANCE OF WORLD GEOGRAPHY

Geography is not just a distinctive way of thinking about the world—it is a critical foundation for understanding how and why the world functions as it does.

All parts of the world are becoming increasingly interdependent; no part of the Earth's surface functions independently of the others. We see evidence of our interdependence on the labels of the products we buy, in the newspapers and magazines we read, and through the people we meet. Students need to acknowledge and understand this interdependence. The idea that this has become a small world needs to be made clear. Students need to grapple with questions such as the following. What parts of the world are involved in our lives and why? How do we interact with other parts of the world? What are the consequences of those interactions?

World geography is important to understanding the world because interdependence is inherently geographic in its origins. Stated simply, variations across different places provide the basis for interactions among those places. In addition, changes within a particular place are likely to cause the pattern of its interactions to change.

Consider North America. Several areas in western North America and along the north slope of Alaska were endowed with rich petroleum reserves. These resources are located in those places for reasons explained by physical geography. In the past those petroleum reserves provided the basis for extensive transfers of oil from the southwest to those parts of North America that lacked petroleum resources but still depended on the automobile for transportation and fuel oil for heating. This oil trade provided a foundation for the economy throughout much of the southwest. When oil prices were good and demand outside the region high, the economies of Texas and Oklahoma boomed. Populations grew as new economic opportunities were created with money from the oil trade.

In the late 1960s, however, the petroleum resources of the American southwest "topped out." New discoveries did not replace the petroleum being used. As a result the oil-poor parts of North America turned to other places around the world which geologic history had endowed with rich oil reserves. Chief among these were Nigeria, Venezuela, and Mexico—places whose proximity and resource base (that is, whose physical and human geography) enabled them to provide oil at relatively low costs.

The implications of this changing pattern of oil trade for the American southwest was disguised at first by high prices for oil. When the price of oil fell in the 1980s, however, the combination of fewer resources, lower oil exports to other regions, and lower prices led to radically lower economic and population growth.

The new pattern of petroleum trade between the American northeast to West Africa and the Caribbean Basin will also change someday. Possibly by the next century the petroleum resources of Nigeria and Venezuela will begin to decline. At that point, North American dependence on the oil resources of the Persian Gulf Basin or the East China Sea may grow.

This example demonstrates how one geographic pattern can produce one set of interdependencies and how changes in that pattern result in a new set of interdependencies. It also demonstrates the importance of geography and geographic concepts to the very way we think and talk about the world. It is impossible to ignore place and variations among places, whether we are talking about international economies, foreign policy, global issues, other cultures, or any other aspect of world studies.

ADVANTAGES OF A WORLD GEOGRAPHY APPROACH

Adopting a world geography approach to a world studies course has several important advantages.

First, stressing explicitly and continuously where phenomena are located impresses visually on students the complexity of the contemporary world. At present most students are not aware of such complexity. They cannot appreciate just how much their community and their country differ from other parts of the world in both physical and human terms. Through their study of history most students learn to appreciate variation over time. In geography they learn to appreciate variation over space.

Second, because geography examines both physical and human

phenomena, it naturally integrates the physical and social sciences. As geographers attempt to understand the complex patterns that make up the earth's surface, they synthesize work from such natural sciences as geology, meteorology, and botany with such social sciences as economics, sociology, and history. Thus students are exposed to a variety of physical and human processes as they study geography. They also develop a more holistic approach to understanding their world.

Third, a world geography approach explicitly promotes a stronger appreciation of "place." In part this relates to knowledge of locational specifics. Recent studies have revealed a basic geographic illiteracy among American students. Many cannot locate such political units as South Africa, China, and Nicaragua, even though they hear about them daily in the news. They cannot locate major cities or physical features on a world map or even identify the states of their own country. A world geography course addresses the issue of geographic illiteracy more directly and explicitly than any other approach can.

Similarly, geography shows that all human activities occur in places. We reside in a place; we typically work in another place. Why are residential and commercial/industrial activities located where they are? Why do agricultural activities predominate in some areas and industrial activities in others? The reasons for locating activities in one place or another are rooted in the characteristics of the place. A world geography approach helps students develop the understandings and skills to explain these differences.

Fourth, because it helps students understand the world in terms of places, a world geography course represents a building block for subsequent learning. It will help students understand world events better as they occur. For students who go on to college, it will provide a foundation for subsequent courses in geography, international studies, political science, and history.

Finally, because of geography's emphasis on the characteristics of places and the differences among places, students receive an important foundation for citizenship in two respects. First, they are exposed to differences that exist within their own country or region. They can describe and explain areas that are rich or poor in resources and areas that are growing rapidly or slowly. In this way they become sensitized to the plurality of their own society. They are better prepared to define problems and develop solutions for different areas.

Second, a geographic approach exposes students to the linkages among places that result from physical and human differences. They learn where our major trading partners, allies, or adversaries are located and why we depend on them. This type of understanding is crucial for making decisions and judgments about world affairs. Knowing about the physical and human characteristics of Japan can help us understand our relationship with that country and the international economic policies it pursues. Similar knowledge about Nicaragua helps us understand the economic and political nature of that country. It helps us to consider alternative policies in our relations with it.

DISADVANTAGES OF A WORLD GEOGRAPHY APPROACH

There are disadvantages as well as advantages to adopting a world geography approach.

First, the approach does not lend itself to a strong historical perspective. No attention will be given to important historical epochs or to individuals who have played a major role in the historical development of particular regions. A world geography approach examines the world as it is structured today. The interpretation of current patterns may require some discussion of changes over time, but only more proximate time periods are likely to be considered.

Second, the approach presented here does not concentrate on a detailed examination of the internal cultural, political, economic, or social characteristics of a particular region or society. It is in this sense a rather different concept of world geography than many curriculum planners may assume. For example, little attention will be given to describing how the Chinese political system operates. No emphasis will be placed on such things as family relationships and social structures associated with a particular cultural group. Cultural groups and political systems will be considered, but primarily within the context of the impact they have on the geographic distribution of physical and human phenomena.

A third disadvantage of this approach stems from the current status of geography education. Many teachers may not be familiar with geography as a way of thinking about the world. They may have had little if any real training in geography themselves, so they may be uncomfortable with developing and teaching a world geography course, especially in the terms presented here. It should be stressed, however, that many teaching resources are available to help teachers in this regard. A course could be developed and offered with a "mutual learning" philosophy in mind.

Nonetheless, teachers' lack of training in geography can produce problems. It may result in a course that overemphasizes the physical environment. As an integral part of the social studies curriculum, a world geography course should emphasize human geography. This includes human relationships with the physical environment, but it does not imply an "environmental deter-minist" viewpoint, in which physical geography characteristics take precedence over, or are seen as controlling, human activity.

Lack of geographic training may also result in the temptation to teach geography in an "inventory" manner. Modern geography must not be equated with locational specifics. It should not be seen primarily in terms of the definitions of terms, map location exercises, or lists of countries with their major agricultural, mineral, or industrial products. These are elements of a world geography course, but they are not the main thrust of it. Locational specifics serve as a point of departure. They allow students to "fix" places as reference points on a map so that a broader discussion or analysis of differences among parts of the world can be accomplished. The main aim is to draw geographic generalizations.

2. Goals for students

A world geography approach should introduce students to a new, distinctive way of thinking about the Earth and help them overcome basic geographic illiteracy. Such an approach should teach students to subdivide the world into areas with distinctive physical or human characteristics. In so doing it should give them a better appreciation of how different parts of the world function and interact. Accomplishing these ends will help students understand and interpret day-to-day events in the contemporary world, the role that their country plays in the world, and their place as citizens in their country.

Recently, there has been a growing acceptance, by state legislatures and individual school districts, of the need for geography education in both elementary and secondary schools. There have been efforts to develop geography curricula at both levels. In 1984, the National Council for Geographic Education and the Association of American Geographers prepared *Guidelines for Geographic Education*. This publication identifies and discusses learning outcomes and student skills that should result from high school geography courses. The knowledge and skill goals listed below are derived from those guidelines.

MAJOR KNOWLEDGE GOALS

Knowledge goals for the course described here are organized around five fundamental themes of modern geography: location, place, relationships within places, linkages between places, and regions. In a world geography approach to a high school world studies course, the main knowledge goals should be to help students:

1. Deepen their understanding of the importance of location and position on the Earth's surface
2. Learn basic locational specifics: the Earth's major continental regions and bodies of water, the parts of the world that share certain cultural and economic characteristics, and the exact locations of political units about which they hear regularly in current events
3. Understand that position on the Earth's surface influences the type and nature of physical processes occurring there

4. Deepen their understanding of the ways in which places are distinctive in terms of their physical and human makeup
5. Know that places with similar physical characteristics may have different human or cultural characteristics
6. Know that the importance and characteristics of places change over time
7. Comprehend more fully that within any place—city, state, or country—tremendous geographic diversity exists
8. Understand that relationships within places change and that people modify and adapt to natural settings in ways that reveal their cultural values, economic and political circumstances, and technological abilities
9. Understand that as a result of geographic differences in resource base, food supply, or population characteristics, all parts of the world are interconnected
10. Divide the world into regions with distinctive physical and human characteristics
11. Learn some geographic details about specific regions for which they have little understanding
12. Use the concepts of location, place, and interdependence to understand how large regions such as North America, Asia, or Africa function internally and how they are linked to other regions

MAJOR SKILL GOALS

A world geography course should also enhance students' capacities to process the geographical information needed to understand and analyze important issues. Such a course should help students:

1. Learn how to ask geographic questions about a particular place, region, or national/international problem—that is, ask where phenomena are located and why they are located there
2. Acquire basic geographic information through the use of atlases, maps, census data, and the like
3. Evaluate and select the best sources of information possible for answering a particular geographic question
4. Read and interpret tables, graphs, and maps presenting geographic information
5. Develop and test geographic generalizations about general distributions of physical and human phenomena

3. Organization of subject matter

What is the basic subject matter of a world geography approach? How can it best be organized over a two-semester high school course?

The first semester should begin by introducing students to the notion of "thinking geographically." Students should be shown that they already think in geographic terms. In other words, they have an image of different places, of the differences and similarities among those places, and of the spatial relationships among them. They should further develop their ability to think geographically using information about the local community and the nation.

Students should begin to think about interactions that link different places; they can even begin to ask why these patterns exist. The goal, however, is to help students learn to think self-consciously about location and place.

As students develop their ability to think geographically, they can begin to examine geographic variations at the continental scale (that is, across different regions on a world map). They should also examine how the different regions interact with each other. By the end of the first semester students should be able to take a world map, identify the different continental areas and give some basic physical and human distinctions among them. Moreover, they should display some understanding of which regions have the highest levels of interaction.

The second semester should focus on the variations within the major continental regions in a way that builds on the first semester's work. This study of internal regional variations should be used to help students understand the functioning of the contemporary world. In particular, this part of the course should stress the concept of "uneven development," an idea with which students may already be superficially familiar in terms of the distinction between developed and less developed countries. When the second semester is complete, students should understand more fully how individual regions are organized geographically and why the different regions interact as they do with each other. This will provide a needed perspective for understanding contemporary international relations, in particular the role of the United States in world affairs.

THINKING GEOGRAPHICALLY: INTRODUCING LOCATION AND PLACE

All students think geographically, although most are probably unaware that they do so. All students have a "mental map"—a mental image—of the geographic pattern of their part of town, or perhaps even their whole community. These mental maps may not be completely accurate, but most are detailed enough that students can distinguish the key characteristics of different areas.

Thus, if a stranger were to ask where the principal shopping areas in town were, a student could visualize those areas and name them. Indeed, many students could probably subdivide their mental map of the whole community to distinguish "shopping areas," "residential areas," and "industrial areas." Whenever students distinguish one location from another on the basis of some set of characteristics, they are thinking geographically.

A second way of thinking geographically involves understanding the spatial relationship among different places. A student traveling from home to school, or from school to work, usually takes a particular route. It is likely that the route was chosen after the student consulted his or her mental map of the area many times to determine the most efficient way of moving from one place to the other. If one day the route were obstructed, the student would automatically consult his or her mental map and identify an alternative route.

In this example, the city or town or county is not subdivided into areas with distinctive characteristics. Rather, it appears as a set of places or locations associated with various activities, such as home, school, and work. The mental map includes not only the places but the spatial linkages or relationships among them.

Thus students come to the study of geography with a more or less detailed mental map of the local area. They also come with practical experience in thinking geographically. Even in a course that focuses on the global arena, it is useful to begin with local examples. As students develop greater skill, confidence, and understanding, the scale can be increased to the national and continental levels—a process that primarily involves increasing the degree of generalization. In this way studying world geography becomes a more personal and cumulative learning process.

GEOGRAPHIC VARIATION

Organizing a world geography course is to some extent a matter of keeping in mind that geography asks two key questions. First it asks, "Where?" It does this primarily by describing differences from location to location. Second, it asks, "Why?" It does this by explaining differences among locations.

Variations on the local scale

The course can formally introduce the discussions of "where" and "why" by using a county map depicting the nearest metropolitan area or a topographical map of the locality.

The modern metropolitan area has a distinctive geography that students should be able to describe and discuss. Every metropolitan area is composed of areas of different land use. The centers of cities, for example, are given over to commercial land uses. This is an area with retail shops, office towers, hotels, and government buildings. The activities of the city center generate jobs and economic wealth far out of proportion to the relative size of the area. Students should understand why these activities are located where they are. They should see that those who provide goods and services to the population as a whole want a central location, to serve people more easily. They are also willing to pay more to have a central location.

Surrounding the commercial areas of a city are areas of residential land use. These areas extend for miles, virtually to the edge of the city. There is usually a distinctive geography to residential land use. Closer to the city center are smaller homes, packed densely together on small pieces of land. Rooming houses and high-rise units are often found there. At the outer edge of the city, homes are larger and located on larger lots. Students should understand that this pattern is associated with the social and economic characteristics of the population. Inner-city areas are often populated by lower-income workers who need easy access to central city employment and less expensive housing. At the edge of the city are middle- and upper-income families. They can afford both the cost of commuting longer distances to work and the cost of larger homes and lots. This pattern dates to the period when immigrants moved to large American cities and settled in the inner-city areas. Higher-income families in turn moved farther and farther out, generally settling along the transportation lines that radiated out from the center city.

Topographic maps are also useful in this type of discussion. They are particularly helpful in showing relationships among places. The distributions of towns and activities can be interpreted in terms of the physical characteristics of the landscape. Settlement is heavier on flat landscapes; mining and resort activities tend to be located near more rugged landform areas. It can be shown that transportation routes make some places more accessible than others. As a result, those places become larger in size and have a greater variety of activities associated with them.

It is useful to set the discussion of geographic patterns in a temporal context. How would the map of the city or county have looked ten, twenty, or fifty years ago? How have the current distributions of land use and population come about? Indeed, what geographic changes are taking place right now, and what changes might be expected in the years ahead? In the past fifty years, most American cities have changed from having a single node, the center city, to having multiple nodes or centers of activity. Students should be able to describe and explain these changes. Moreover, they should be able to begin thinking about their implications. What will happen as more and more agricultural land is used for urban development? What happens to cities if their inner-city areas deteriorate as people move outward to the suburbs?

Looking at the local area in this way establishes the context for thinking about geographic patterns and why they exist. Once students begin thinking in these terms, the scale of analysis can change.

Variations on the national scale

Students should be able to distinguish the characteristics of different parts of their country just as they can distinguish different areas locally.

One of the key characteristics of human geography that should be considered on the national scale is population. Three important dimensions of population are geographic distribution, racial/ethnic makeup, and religious distinctions. Where, for example, is the majority of the population concentrated, and why? Students should be aware of the heavy concentration of population in the northeast and north-central parts of the United States. They should also understand its relationship to the physical characteristics of these areas and historical settlement trends.

Students should also consider variations in the ethnic and racial makeup of the country. Historically, immigration has been dominated by Europeans, who settled in the northeast and north-central states. More recently it has become dominated by Latin Americans, especially Mexicans, who settle in the south and southwest, and by Asians, who locate primarily along the west coast. Why are today's immigrants coming from different places? Why are they settling in different places? What impact do these immigrants have on those parts of the country in which they are settling?

Economic variations on the national scale are also important. What types of economic activities are carried out in different parts of the country? For example, where are the main agricultural parts of the United States? Where are the major manufacturing areas, and why are they concentrated so heavily where they are? The complex pattern of economic differences that emerges provides a foundation for discussing the reasons for interactions among the different areas.

Indicating variations in population and economic characteristics on maps of the United States will give students a visual image of the human complexity of their nation. Interpreting the variations in these human characteristics is likely to lead to a discussion of variation in physical characteristics.

The United States can easily be subdivided into areas with distinctive physical characteristics. The two most important types of physical characteristics are landforms and climate. Students can probably identify many of these variations in a rudimentary way, and the course can build on this foundation. Regarding landforms, for example, students are likely to be aware of the Appalachians, the Great Plains, and the Rocky Mountains. They know that each can be distinguished by certain characteristics. The Appalachians, for example, have low mountains; the Rockies have high mountains; the Great Plains have no mountains. Similarly, they can probably classify different parts of the country climatically. The southeast has a warm and wet climate; the southwest is warm and dry; the northeast cool and wet.

Although they may not realize it, as they subdivide their country in this way, they are in the first phase of geographic analysis. Indeed, by trying to link the physical and human characteristics they identify, they are beginning to learn why the Wheat Belt is where it is and why it produces what it does. They will begin to understand that steel manufacturing became concentrated in areas with local coal and iron ore resources. They will begin to understand the terms "Sunbelt" and "Snowbelt."

When they have completed their consideration of how to think geographically on the national scale, students should be able to identify geographic variations nationally for the key physical and human characteristics. They should understand how these physical and human characteristics are inter-related, and also what impact these variations have on the different parts of the country and on their linkages to each other.

Variation on the global scale

Identifying geographic variations globally is usually difficult, because students are less likely to have readily accessible mental maps of the world as a whole. Still, students may have some sense of the broad variations in cultural and economic characteristics. These may provide a basis for beginning to work on the global scale even if students cannot locate specific places or areas on the world map.

For example, most students will know that the Middle East is an area on the earth's surface with more or less distinct boundaries, and that the area is associated with oil and with religious and political conflict. They may further know that the Middle East can be associated with a distinctive language, Arabic, and a distinctive religion, Islam. They may have similar images of such areas as tropical Africa or Southeast Asia. By being able to associate particular parts of the world with specific sets of characteristics, students are thinking geographically on the global scale.

Teachers can build on this first level of geographic generalization by taking a world map and asking the students for their impressions of geographic variations. Broad regional names or titles such as the Amazon Basin or the Himalayan Mountains can be located on a map. They can be discussed in terms of the characteristics that make the area distinctive, in both physical and human terms. This type of exercise can demonstrate to students that distinguishing one area from another on the global scale is no different from distinguishing one place from another on the local scale.

VARIATIONS AND INTERACTIONS ON THE GLOBAL SCALE

Geography involves the study of physical and human variation on the Earth's surface. As maps of both types of phenomena reveal, the world is made up of a complex pattern of physical and human features, which differ from one place to another. These differences are labeled "spatial variations," because physical and human features vary across the space that makes up the Earth's surface. Maps reveal spatial variations in climate, landform, population distribution, economic activities, and political systems, among many other characteristics.

As a first, basic step to geographic understanding on the global scale, students need to undertake a systematic identification of the spatial variations in physical and human phenomena around the globe. This may be done by introducing them to the concept of a region and highlighting differences within and among those spatial units.

Regionalization

A "region" is a part of the Earth's surface with distinctive characteristics. The process of identifying and locating regions on the earth's surface is called "regionalization."

It is important for students to understand that the process of identifying a particular region is basically arbitrary. In other words, we create regions to help us talk about differences and similarities across places on the Earth's surface. When students identified residential and commercial areas within the local community, they were regionalizing. When they distinguished between the Sunbelt and the Snowbelt, they were regionalizing. In both cases they were identifying one characteristic in which they were interested (principal land use and climate) and labeling a particular area on the Earth's surface in terms of that characteristic.

Indeed, it is possible to regionalize simply by specifying the "absolute location" of an area. Absolute location refers to the latitude and longitude of a place or area. We can create a region simply by identifying an area bounded by two lines of longitude and two lines of latitude. We can then explore variations in characteristics between that region and others or variations in characteristics within the region.

Defining regions in terms of absolute location brings home the ultimately arbitrary nature of the process; other ways of identifying regions are more useful. There are two basic approaches that are important. The first is based on relative location, the second on areal content.

"Relative location" refers to the position of one place with respect to other places. Regions are often defined on the basis of proximity to some key physical feature on the Earth's surface. For example, the Amazon Basin is a region defined on the basis of relative location. It singles out a part of the earth's surface adjacent to the Amazon River. No discussion of the region's formal boundaries is implied or needed.

The relative location approach to identifying regions does say something about how places fit together, at least spatially. However, it says little about the characteristics of the region, how it functions, or how it is likely to interact with other regions.

The most useful approach to regionalization is based on areal content. "Areal content" refers to the characteristics of an area that allow it to be differentiated from other areas. In general terms, three types of regions can be identified on the basis of areal content: formal physical regions, formal human regions, and functional regions.

Formal regions are generally defined by some similarity in characteristics throughout their area. Formal physical regions are defined by some characteristic of physical geography. For example, areas like the Arctic Zone or the Great Plains, which have a similar climate and landform type, respectively, are formal physical regions. Similarly, a formal human region is defined by some characteristic of human geography. Thus an area that has the same dominant religion or language can be considered a formal human region. The key point is that throughout its area a formal region manifests a sameness in terms of some characteristic or set of characteristics. Typically, no concern is placed on the exact boundaries of formal regions. In the case of formal human regions in particular, it may be impossible to find a clearly defined boundary. The emphasis instead is on what characteristics permit us to define the area as a region.

The third type of region based on areal content is the functional region, which is composed of points (usually cities) and the linkages among them. A functional region is thus similar to the local area defined by a student's home, school, work, and other points of daily activity. On the global scale the best examples of functional regions are the global transportation and communication linkages joining cities together. (See Figure 1.) No interest is shown in the areas between the points, only in the nature of the linkages among them. Functional regions can be used to show trade patterns among countries or the flow of people through international migration. Functional regions can even be defined on the basis of political linkages such as membership in a particular international organization.

FORMAL PHYSICAL REGIONS.   A high school world geography course should highlight one component of physical geography. It should show students the formal physical regions that appear on the Earth's surface. Students should be introduced to physical regions defined on the basis of both climate and landform, but climatic regions are probably the more important to consider.

There exists tremendous variation in climatic regions on the Earth. Several detailed classifications have been produced by geographers, but for simplicity a high school course should focus on the three broad climatic zones or regions shown in Figure 2. These regions are the Tropical Zone, the Temperate Zone, and the Arctic/Antarctic Zone. The boundaries of each are defined in terms of latitude.

The Tropical Zone, or "low latitudes," extends from the Equator northward to about 23 degrees (Tropic of Cancer) and southward to about 23 degrees (Tropic of Capricorn). This is a formal climatic region whose distinctive characteristic is its warm temperature throughout the year. This region receives the most intense and consistent solar radiation of any part of the Earth's surface. Thus for the most part it has a year-long growing season. It has also been heavily settled throughout human history.

In terms of precipitation, another climatic characteristic, the Tropical Zone varies from being too wet to being too dry. The world's largest rainforests and its largest deserts are located in the Tropical Zone. As a result, this region, which includes much of Central and South America, Africa and southern Asia, poses severe limitations on population distribution and agricultural

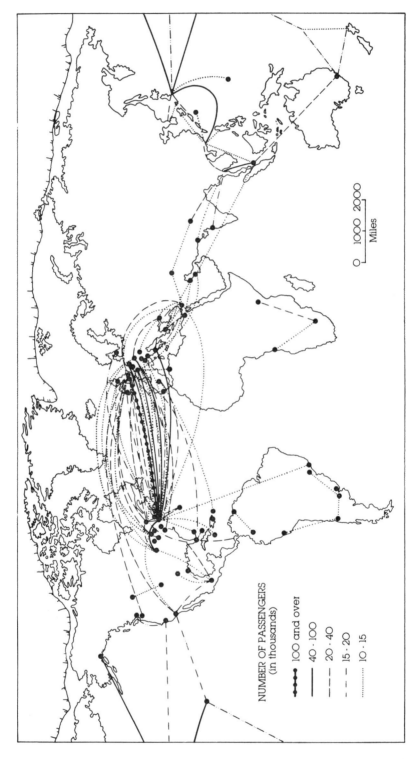

Figure 1 International air passenger flows. Source: R.A. Harper, "Metropolitan Areas as Transactional Centers," in C.M. Christian and R.A. Harper, eds., *Modern Metropolitan Systems*. Columbus, Ohio: Charles Merrill, 1982, p. 104. Reprinted with permission.

NUMBER OF PASSENGERS
(in thousands)

100 and over
40 - 100
20 - 40
15 - 20
10 - 15

0   1000   2000

Miles

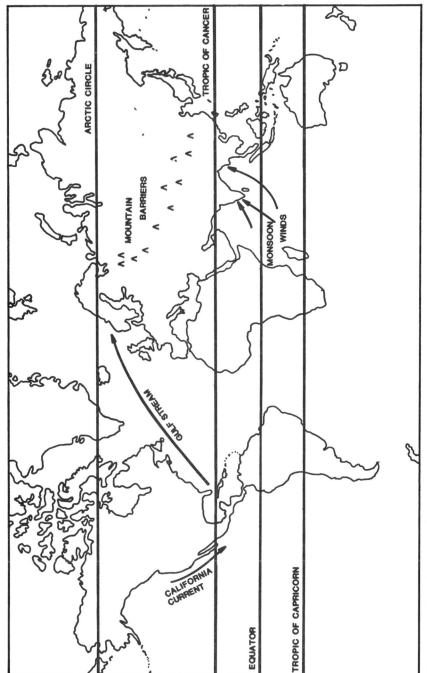

Figure 2 Climatic regions based on latitude, with moderating influences.

145

activity. Much of the population is clustered where precipitation levels are not extreme. Most people involved in agricultural production live at the subsistence level. They grow a relatively small set of tropical crops like bananas, rubber and rice. In world markets, places within the Tropical Zone typically compete with one another to sell this limited set of products. In turn, they must import other critical products, such as wheat, which they cannot produce efficiently or abundantly.

The Temperate Zone, or "middle latitude" region, stretches from 23 degrees north and south of the Equator to about 67 degrees north and south. Thus it extends from the Tropic of Cancer to the Arctic Circle in the north and from the Tropic of Capricorn to the Antarctic Circle in the south.

Because of the curvature of the Earth, solar radiation diminishes as distance from the Equator increases. Climatically this results in a distinct seasonality in temperature and tremendous variation in precipitation within the Temperate Zone. The climatic variety of this region means that a variety of crops can be produced within it. The continental areas that lie within the region, such as North America, Europe, southern Australia, southern Africa and southern Latin America, are the "breadbaskets" of the world. These regions can sell their surplus products to tropical regions in exchange for the tropical goods they cannot produce.

Finally, the Arctic/Antarctic Zone, or "high latitude" region, extends respectively from the Arctic and Antarctic Circles to the North and South Poles. Here temperature conditions are so extreme that there is, at best, a very limited summer growing season. Human settlement tends to be very sparse.

Students should learn that although these formal physical regions tell us something about the different areas and even about how they interact, world climates are more dynamic and more complex than this simple and static classification suggests. For example, Europe lies in the northern part of the Temperate Zone, but it is much warmer than would be expected from its absolute location within the zone. Europe's moderate climate results from the warm Gulf Stream, which flows northeast from the Gulf of Mexico. The waters of the Gulf Stream warm the continent in winter and cool it in summer. Throughout the year it promotes high levels of moisture. As a result, Europe has been much more heavily settled historically and produces a greater variety of agricultural crops than might have been expected in a region so far north of the Equator.

A high school world geography course should also introduce students to formal physical regions based on landform characteristics or on characteristics of soil or vegetation. The aim is not, however, to have students memorize the myriad of regions that can be defined on the basis of variations in these physical features. Rather, the aim is to help students learn to distinguish areas based on different physical characteristics and to begin thinking about the impact that physical characteristics might have on the human population. How do landform regions, for example, vary in terms of where people live or how they make a living? How can and do people modify different landform regions to make them more livable? Here students would see the impact of mountains, plains, and river valleys on human settlement. They would also see that even mountainous areas can be modified through terracing so that they are more productive agriculturally.

FORMAL HUMAN REGIONS. The second type of region based on areal content is the formal human region. The course should introduce students to formal human regions based on variations in population and culture. If time permits, it might also look at regions based on types of economic and political systems.

In examining population regions, students should see four major geographic concentrations. The first is located in East Asia in the eastern third of China. The second is in South Asia along the Indo-Gangetic Plain. Both of these are remnants and outgrowths of "culture hearth regions." In other words, they are areas where early civilizations formed several thousand years ago. Two other concentrations of population are the results of "modern" history. These include Western Europe and the east-central part of North America. Each of these has served as the focal point for the world economy at some time during the past three centuries. Students should also see that much of the rest of the world's population, the other half, is unevenly distributed along coastal regions or within interior plains regions.

The general pattern of population concentrations, combined with discussions of population totals by continental region, should give rise to questions about regional adequacy of food supplies. It should also suggest reasons for international migration to offset population pressure.

The course should also consider formal human regions based on culture. "Culture" refers to the way of life of a particular group of people in a particular part of the world. Culture regions are characterized by similar cultural traits such as religion, language, beliefs, or values.

Using culture as the basis for defining regions has great value, precisely because culture represents such an important characteristic of the human population of any place. Culture affects where individuals live, their response to outsiders, and their attitudes toward change. It even affects the way a population uses its natural resource base.

A discussion of world culture regions should begin with the "Western" culture region, which includes North America, Europe, and Australia. People in these areas speak languages that are derived from a common base. They adhere primarily to some form of Christianity. They value personal advancement, technological improvements, youthfulness, and material goods.

A second culture region, characterized by the Islamic religion, is centered in North Africa and the Middle East. This Islamic culture region extends into parts of West Africa, Western Asia, and even into parts of Southeast Asia. Within this culture region, the religion of Islam pervades daily life, influencing people's ethical, political, economic, and social behavior. Indeed, within this culture region, Islam provides a source of identity, which people use to distinguish themselves from the rest of the world. Students might ask how the differences between the Islamic and Western culture regions affect day-to-day life within the two areas. They might also look at how cultural differences have influenced interactions between the two regions, historically and in the present.

By the end of the course, students should be able to associate the different continental areas of the world with particular culture regions. Looking at the world in terms of its diverse culture regions, students should realize how similar people in Europe and Australia are to themselves. Combined with information on population regions, it should also show students how important it is to understand the languages, values, and beliefs characteristic of other culture regions.

In the process of looking at culture regions, it is critical to introduce the concept of cultural diffusion. This is the process whereby elements of culture spread from one culture region to another. By looking at the process of cultural diffusion, students will come to see culture regions as dynamic areas. Culture regions change over time, expanding geographically (as Islam did after the seventh century) or even contracting or disappearing (as the Amerindian culture region did in North America). Students should also understand that cultural diffusion can produce conflict—as in Iran, where elements of Western secular culture were adopted more quickly by the political elite under the Shah than by the population as a whole.

Although population concentration and culture may be the most important characteristics upon which to base formal human regions, students should understand that other aspects of human development also show geographic variations. For example, the contemporary world could be subdivided on the basis of different political systems. Some parts of the world, such as North America and Western Europe, have democratic systems in which more than one political party normally competes to get candidates elected to public office. Other parts of the world have one-party regimes, where a centralized leadership can make sweeping decisions with little or no organized opposition. In still other countries, the military holds power. Geographic variation in the type of political system could be discussed in terms of its impact on people's activities, their resource use, and even relations among political regions.

FUNCTIONAL REGIONS. The third type of region based on areal content is the functional region. The course should introduce students to functional regions based on variations in international trade, international migration, and international organization memberships. By looking at these three types of functional regions, students can effectively be shown the integrated nature of the contemporary world.

When shown on a map, or even in tabular form, data on international trade produce three general patterns of which students should be aware. First, within North America and Europe, countries tend to have the highest level of trade with other countries in the same continental area. Canada and the United States, for example, trade more with each other than with any other country. Second, the industrial countries of North America, Europe, and Japan account for the majority of international trade worldwide. Third, the continental regions of South and Central America, Africa, and Asia have generally low levels of internal trade. Countries within these regions tend to have a few strong linkages with one or two of the big trading regions identified above.

Students might consider why these general patterns in international trade exist. They should consider to what extent these trading patterns might be expected on the basis of the physical and human variations they have already studied in the course. For example, detailed analysis of Central American trade would show a few agricultural and mineral products leaving these regions and a larger, more diversified set of manufactured and agricultural products returning. How might the climatic region to which Central America belongs account for this pattern?

International migration provides a second important example of a functional region. Today the United States, Canada, and Australia are the major recipients of the world's permanent international migration. The flows originate primarily in Latin America and Asia. Students might explore whether this pattern of migration would be expected on the basis of what they know about existing resources and population patterns and trends. Do global maps of variations in physical or human geography help us explain this pattern?

Another important question related to international migration flows involves the impact that immigrant groups are having on the host countries. Consider Figure 3. It shows the dramatic impact that Latin Americans and Asians are having on population patterns within the United States. What are the implications of the changing ethnic makeup of our country?

The pattern of memberships in international organizations represents

Figure 3 Dominant sources of recent immigrants to the United States, by state.

a third important example of a functional region. International organizations come about as governments, individuals, and groups recognize the need for international cooperation to achieve particular goals. Thus they are important indicators of political cooperation and interaction at the global scale.

International organizations may link governments, individuals, or groups within or across continental areas. The European Economic Community (EEC) and the Latin American Integration Association (LAIA) link neighboring countries that are interested in promoting trade within the functional region. The North Atlantic Treaty Organization (NATO), on the other hand, links governments of North American and European countries for the purpose of mutual defense against threats coming from outside the functional region. Functional regions of these types should be discussed in terms of why these particular linkages were formed and what impact they could have on future global interaction.

UNEVEN DEVELOPMENT

Overall, the economic and demographic distinctions among continental areas that were seen in the previous sections of the course produce a global pattern of uneven development. Some regions of the world are resource-rich, sparsely settled, advanced technologically, and growing slowly in terms of population. Other regions are resource-poor, densely settled, technologically backward, and growing almost uncontrollably in population terms. Identifying and analyzing geographic distinctions such as this is a major focus of contemporary research in geography.

In the second half of the course, students should focus on generalizations about uneven development and apply them to an analysis of the major continental regions. The themes of location, place, internal variations, and linkages will all come together in this analysis.

Measuring the level of development

Social scientists have been interested in studying development since the 1950s, when large numbers of former colonies in Asia and Africa began achieving political independence. They have discovered that the process of development involves complicated economic and demographic changes over time. Moreover, it involves changing geographic distributions of population and economic activity. This is the dimension of the development process on which a world geography course should focus.

It is impossible to classify regions strictly as either "developed" or "underdeveloped." There is no magical, neat cutoff point at which regions can be dichotomized in this way. Regardless of the point chosen, wide variations will exist within each category. It may be more useful to think of the level of development in terms of placement on a continuum that has a "more developed" and a "less developed" part. While North America, Europe, and the U.S.S.R. all fall within the "more developed" part of the continuum, they certainly manifest quite different levels of development. Similarly Asia, Africa, and Latin America, which fall within the "less developed" part of the continuum, differ considerably from each other.

It is important to note that placement on a continuum of development need not imply that less developed regions are "following" more developed regions. Nor does it imply that they will ultimately "catch up" and become like the more developed regions. Instead, it provides a relational context to study or analyze regions at one point in time. For example, a thousand years ago China would have been the "most developed" region in the world. A century ago both Japan and the U.S.S.R. would have been classified as "less developed."

ECONOMIC MEASURES OF DEVELOPMENT. Exactly where one places a particular region on the development continuum depends on how one measures development. Various economic measures have been used to indicate the level of development of a country. Among the most popular have been per capita Gross National Product, per capita consumption of energy produced from inanimate sources, and the distribution of employment among primary, secondary, and tertiary sectors of the economy.

Based on these economic measures of development, one can distinguish a set of countries with high per capita GNP (over $5000 per person per year), high labor force participation in the tertiary or service sector (over 60 percent), and high energy consumption (the equivalent of 2000 or more barrels of oil per person per year). Although there are variations among these countries, collectively they may be classified as "more developed." They include the countries in North America, most of Europe, Japan, Australia, and the U.S.S.R.

Other countries, including most countries in Central and South America, Africa, and Asia, manifest low levels of per capita GNP (under $1000 per per person per year), a labor force concentrated in the primary sector (over 60 percent of the labor force in agriculture and mining), and low levels of per capita energy consumption (the equivalent of under 500 barrels of oil per person per year). These regions would be placed on the "less developed" part of the development continuum.

Various problems can arise from careless use of these measures of development. Per capita GNP, for example, does not measure the distribution of income in the population, nor does it measure economic activity outside the money economy. Thus it can significantly overstate the economic resources available to the average person in countries where most of the wealth is in the hands of a small elite. Likewise, it can understate economic well-being in countries where most people obtain their food, clothing, and other basic needs outside the money economy.

DEMOGRAPHIC MEASURES OF DEVELOPMENT. Measures of different characteristics of the population also provide a basis for distinguishing between more developed and less developed regions.

More developed regions have low birth and death rates. As a result, these regions are growing naturally at less than 1 percent per year. Many of these regions rely on immigration as a major source of population growth. They also have low infant mortality rates (the proportion of infants who die in the first year of life) and high life expectancy (seventy years or more). The combination of low birth and death rates also results in a relatively even or slightly top-heavy population age structure. No more than 25 percent of their population is under twenty-five years of age.

Less developed regions, on the other hand, tend to have birth rates that are higher than their death rates. Most are growing naturally at 2–3 percent per year. For countries with large total populations such as Mexico, India, and China, those rates produce large increases to the population each year. It is estimated, for example, that China adds the combined populations of Ohio and Indiana to its total every year. Less developed countries tend to have high infant mortality rates (10–20 percent) and lower life expectancy (less than sixty years). As much as 40–50 percent of the total population may be under the age of twenty-five and thus economically "dependent."

Demographic measures of development can also misrepresent a country's level of development, if accepted uncritically. For example, the measure of "dependent" population may misrepresent the economic hardships faced by people in those parts of the world where young people enter the work force at a very early age. Moreover, these measures do not give information on other aspects of development that may be important, such as the provision of health care, nutritional levels, or the role of women in the labor force.

DEVELOPMENT REGIONS. Despite their limits, these demographic and economic measures of development allow us to characterize different parts of the world at a particular point in time, so we can regionalize by grouping similar countries together. In effect, the groupings of "more developed" and "less developed" countries represent formal human regions based on level of development.

Once this pattern is established, the question of "why" should be addressed. What forces have brought it about? This entails a discussion of different theories of development.

Theories of development

Two main theories are used to explain variations in development around the world. One is modernization theory, which holds that variations simply reflect the fact that different regions happen to be at different stages of economic development. The second is dependency theory, which argues that the level of development observed in the less developed region reflects distortions caused by the exploitative policies of countries in the more developed region.

MODERNIZATION THEORY. According to this theory, all regions began the development process historically at a "subsistence stage." At this stage, the population survives on a day-to-day basis in small-scale, non-commercial agricultural activities. Population groups may shift from location to location, following water supplies or in response to depleted soil resources. There is little regional interaction. Birth rates and death rates are high as the population struggles against disease and starvation. The rate of natural increase is low.

As population groups settle in more productive or economically prosperous areas, and as technological advancements in agriculture appear, a surplus of food is created. When this happens, a part of the population becomes free to carry out other endeavors, in small-scale craft industries or service activities. Surplus food and crafts lead to trade with other regions. A regular food supply, possibly in conjunction with improved sanitation or health care, help lower death rates. The birth rate, however, remains high because the societies are still primarily agricultural, and large families are still an economic asset. Thus the total population grows rapidly.

As the population grows and agricultural productivity improves, a market for manufactured goods is created. In regions where there is an adequate supply of industrial minerals, a manufacturing base may be added to the commercial agricultural economy. Now the region interacts even more strongly with other regions as it searches for raw materials or markets for its manufactured products.

Typically, industries locate in existing urban centers to take advantage of their pool of labor, capital, and consumers. Rural populations migrate to urban areas in search of job opportunities. In urban societies birth rates are low, because large families become an economic liability. Overall, the population growth rate slows, but there is also a geographic redistribution of the population to large urban areas. This redistribution is reflected in the geographical pattern of the economy. Increasingly it is the urban rather than the rural areas that produce the society's wealth.

Finally, the growing prosperity associated with advanced commercial agriculture and specialized manufacturing creates a high demand for the provision of goods and services. The vast majority of the population now lives in urban areas, many of which are extremely large and may even be characterized by suburban growth. Birth rates and death rates are low, and the population grows very slowly. Economic prosperity exists throughout the region.

This scenario roughly describes the historical experiences of North America and Europe and also has relevance for Japan and Australia. The advocates of modernization theory argue that this pattern is also relevant to other regions. They believe that Central and South America, Africa, and the rest of Asia are progressing through this same sequence on their path to development.

DEPENDENCY THEORY. The second theory of development suggests that the countries of the less developed region will not have the same experience as the more developed region has had. According to dependency theory, when regions such as North America and Europe reached the stage of advanced commercial agriculture and early industrial development, they sought raw materials and outlets for their products in other, more primitive parts of the world. These less developed regions were colonized and became politically subject to European countries. The imperialist rulers then implemented economic policies that distorted the economy of the colony in order to benefit the colonial power. Mercantilism, for example, legally dictated that raw materials would leave the colony in exchange for manufactured goods from the mother country. While the few colonial cities that funneled the trade became relatively prosperous, for the most part the colonies languished. All the wealth flowed to the more developed countries.

In many cases this pattern of economic activity has lasted for more than a century. Even after they gained independence, the less developed countries continued to export their raw materials to the developed countries and to import manufactured goods. In addition, advocates of dependency theory point out that even if manufacturing is added to the economy of a less developed country, the manufacturing firms are typically based in North America, Japan, or Europe. Therefore less developed countries remain dependent on the more developed regions.

Dependency theorists argue there is little evidence to suggest that the less developed regions will move beyond their current stage of development. The question then becomes, "What is necessary to break this dependency?" Often, the answer is radical social and political change. This has become the basis for much of the political and economic turmoil within less developed countries today.

Both theories of development have relevance in explaining the geographic pattern of development on the Earth today. It is important, in the context of a world geography approach, that students be introduced to both theories. Dependency theory represents a powerful force within many developing countries in Africa and South and Southeast Asia. At the same time, the foreign policies of most of the countries within the more developed region, and some countries within East Asia and Latin America as well, are based on modernization theory. Thus students need to understand both perspectives to understand the pattern of events today.

The spatial analysis of development

Whether one accepts modernization theory or dependency theory, a spatial analysis can reveal much about the process of development. More developed and less developed regions exhibit quite different spatial patterns in terms of the distribution of population and economic activity. A world geography course should give particular attention to this type of analysis.

When manufacturing is added to the economy of a country, it tends to be concentrated in large urban centers. Within more developed regions, this results in the creation of a dynamic functional region, or "core area." The core area is relatively small geographically, but it contains the majority of the population. Population density—the number of people per unit of land—is also high here. The core will contain many large urban centers, most of which will be oriented toward manufacturing and will be functionally specialized. In other words, they will produce only a small set of products. These cities become tightly integrated by transportation and communication linkages as products and people move among them.

Outside the core is the periphery, which is larger geographically and more sparsely settled. It usually remains focused on the primary sector of the economy: agriculture and mining. Just as cities in the core area specialize in what they can produce best, different areas of the periphery will specialize in agriculture, forestry, fishing, or mining, depending on local resources. The periphery contains fewer large urban centers, and those that do exist are less tied to each other than those found in the core. As a result, they need to be more self-reliant and more functionally diversified. The core and the periphery have a reciprocal relationship, with raw materials moving from periphery to the core and specialized manufactured goods moving the other way.

The core–periphery pattern within the more developed region of the world is mapped symbolically as Regions A and B in Figure 4. Region C within Figure 4 indicates the quite different core–periphery pattern that characterizes most less developed regions.

In many parts of the less developed world, little or no manufacturing has been added to the economy. As a result, the spatial pattern remains what it was when the area was part of a formal colonial empire. The economies of these countries remain oriented toward the primary sector and tend to be export-based. A core–periphery pattern exists but is very different from that seen in the more developed region.

Countries within the less developed region are usually characterized geographically by single-city core areas. The city that constitutes the core area is typically located at the site of primary production (e.g., a mining city) or, more often, at a coastal location that facilitates the export of raw materials and the import of manufactured goods.

These core cities tap the resources from a periphery around them, but the relationship is not reciprocal as in more developed regions. It is parasitic. The core city, or primate city, contains a very large share of the total urban population and most of the wealth and prosperity of the entire country. These cities are "pockets" or "islands" of development in the otherwise less

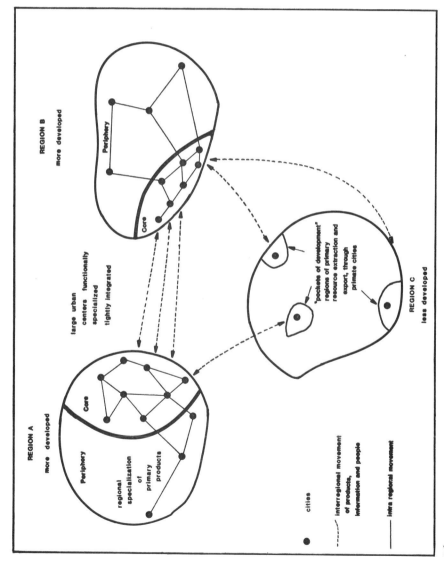

Figure 4 Core–periphery patterns of development.

developed country. The primate city is typically more strongly linked to cities in the core areas of the more developed region than to other cities in its own country.

Outside the core area, the population lives at a subsistence level. The contrast between the lifestyle and living standards of the middle class within the core city and those of the average rural person in less developed countries has been described as a "dual society." The economic contrast between the core and the periphery also prompts migration from the rural areas to the core city. As a result, primate cities in the less developed world are growing at staggering rates and are reaching enormous sizes. The degree of geographic concentration of population and economic activity in this relatively small set of core cities has gone well beyond the concentration that occurred in the more developed region.

These generalizations about measures, theories, and spatial structures associated with the development process need to be "applied" to the continental regions. To what extent are they relevant to our understanding of the geography of the contemporary world? Do they help explain why people and activities are located where they are in different continental regions? Do they help explain how and why continental regions are linked together as they are?

The global pattern of development

A high school world geography course should conclude with an analysis of major continental regions that fall within the more developed and less developed worlds, respectively. This will allow students to apply the geographic concepts and skills they have learned in the course. Areas within the more developed region that could be surveyed include Anglo-America, Western Europe, Japan, Australia, and the U.S.S.R. Areas representing the less developed region might include Latin America, South and East Asia, and Africa.

In this section an overview of two regions, Anglo-America and Latin America, is provided in order to show how a particular region might be analyzed in this context. These examples establish a format that is appropriate for analyzing any region.

A MORE DEVELOPED REGION: ANGLO-AMERICA. By most economic and demographic measures, Anglo-America is the most developed region on Earth. Canada and the United States have among the highest per capita GNPs in the world ($14,000). They are highly urbanized (75 percent) and have service-oriented economies (60 percent tertiary sector). They are growing in population at less than 1 percent per year. Life expectancy in these countries averages seventy-five years, and both countries have a relatively small dependent population (25 percent).

Historically, North America's growth has been tied to European development. Western Europeans settled North America for economic purposes; primary products that could be produced in abundance in North America, such as fish, furs, and forest and farm products, were in high demand in Europe. Trade between Europe and North America was funneled through a small set of east coast cities such as Boston, New York, and Charleston. During this phase of mercantile capitalism, which lasted until approximately 1840, the population remained small and heavily concentrated along the east coast, at locations where the materials could be collected and easily distributed to Europe.

As the population grew, primarily as a result of immigration from Western Europe, the domestic demand for manufactured goods also grew in North America. That situation, plus the vast natural resources that were discovered as the population diffused westward, prompted the beginning of a phase of industrial capitalism that lasted for about a century after 1840.

During this phase, manufacturing centers developed near resource sites, principally near the coal fields of Appalachia and the iron ore mines of the upper Great Lakes. They also developed at places that were particularly accessible because of their location along waterways or rail lines (e.g., Cleveland, Chicago, St. Louis). An urban industrial core region, extending from Boston to Chicago to St. Louis to Washington, developed. By 1920 it contained the majority of the region's largest cities, most of them oriented toward manufacturing. These cities were tightly integrated by rail and road networks. They were also highly specialized functionally. For example, Pittsburgh's economy was based on steel production and Cincinnati's on food processing. The American South and West were peripheral to the core area. With their wide range of climates, their economies were oriented to a variety of agricultural specialties, including wheat, tobacco, citrus fruit, and cotton production.

Today, the Anglo-American region is in a phase of late industrial capitalism, and its human geography is changing as a result. Manufacturing is less important to the economy than it was. New and existing industries are locating more heavily in the periphery to take advantage of cheaper labor or natural amenities. For the first time in their histories, the old industrial states of the northeast and north-central regions are declining in population as people and economic activities move to the Sunbelt. These geographic changes are producing problems. Sunbelt states must cope with strains on their ability to provide services to a growing population, and the northern states are struggling to maintain services despite lower tax bases.

Nor has North America remained self-sufficient in major resources or retained its position as the dominant world supplier of certain products. Heavy demand for energy resources has made the region more dependent upon the Middle East and Latin America for supplies. Japan and Western Europe have become major competitors in the distribution of manufactured goods to world markets.

Nonetheless, continued prosperity has made this region a magnet for international migrants. The United States and Canada are the major recipients of immigrants from Latin America and Asia. As a result, the ethnic makeup of the region is changing, not only in terms of country of origin but also in terms of the location of immigrant groups.

A LESS DEVELOPED REGION: LATIN AMERICA. In demographic, economic, and geographic terms, Latin America represents a less developed region. It has a relatively low per capita GNP and high birth rates. It is also characterized by a primate city pattern of development. Outside a relatively few prosperous urban areas, the population remains involved in primary production. With its mostly tropical climate and diversity of landform areas, Latin America remains a major world supplier of tropical crops (coffee, bananas, sugar cane) and industrial minerals (copper, tin, bauxite). There is a very uneven pattern of development within the region; a few countries, such as Venezuela, Brazil, and Argentina, produce a variety of export products and are economically more advanced than smaller neighbors like Nicaragua and Uruguay.

Latin America has a rich cultural history. It was heavily populated by indigenous Indian tribes who had a well-developed cultural and economic system for centuries before the arrival of Europeans. These groups were located inland in the mountainous areas of South and Central America. They lived in urban centers surrounded by prosperous agricultural regions. Around A.D. 1500 this pre-colonial phase came to a sudden halt. Europeans from Spain and Portugal conquered the Indian tribes and colonized the region for the next three centuries.

Culturally, the region changed dramatically during the colonial period. The Europeans forced the indigenous people to speak Spanish or Portuguese and to convert to Christianity. Economically, the region developed a mercantilist pattern, in which economic activity focused on providing precious minerals and tropical foodstuffs for European consumers. The Indians worked as laborers in this system. They were supplemented with black slaves imported to work in mines and on plantations. Ultimately the mixing of these three groups would result in a society of distinct social/racial groups: creoles, mestizos, and mulattos.

The region also changed spatially during the colonial period; it was reorganized around coastal cities and interior resource locations. The urban centers became the focal points for European investment and related economic activities. They were also the places in which Latin Americans sought economic prosperity. Outside these primate cities the population generally made a subsistence living in agriculture.

Political and economic independence did not coincide in Latin America. After political independence the pattern of the economy was maintained by those who came to power. Prosperity continued to be concentrated in a few large cities and in the hands of the owners of mines and plantations. The primate cities that arose during the colonial period, such as Caracas, Buenos Aires, Lima, and Mexico City, remained the places in which economic activity was centered.

Today, the geography of this region is beginning to change in selected areas. While an urban-industrial core area has not yet developed, manufacturing based on the processing of raw materials or the substitution of imported goods has begun to appear in the larger cities. Still, the area does not yet produce a range of manufactured goods for international markets. Likewise, the manufacturing base has been financed by foreign investments so that economic dependence on external areas remains strong.

Nonetheless, the growing economic diversity of these cities has made them magnets for the rural population. Latin American cities are among the largest and fastest growing in the world. By the year 2000, cities such as Rio de Janeiro, Sao Paulo, and Mexico City are expected to house populations of 20–30 million, making them larger than the majority of countries in the world today. Migrants from rural areas cluster around the edges of these cities, hoping that they can improve their economic welfare in the long run.

A growing disparity between core and periphery and the continued rapid growth of the population are producing considerable social unrest. Many of these countries have adopted socialist political regimes, with the aim of redistributing wealth. Policies have also been developed to redirect population and economic activities to regions outside the primate city area in order to create greater geographic equity. The governments of Latin American countries have also joined together in a variety of supranational organizations to help reorganize and develop their economies, independent of outside forces.

The geography of development

As the discussion of Anglo-America and Latin America indicates, the geography of more developed and less developed regions differs in very significant ways. In a high school course students should study such geographic differences. What are they? Why do they exist? What impact are these differences likely to have on the future development of these regions and their relationship with other regions, including our own?

Clearly the issues raised provide a basis for mapping, analyzing, and discussing the history and politics of development within these regions. More important, they provide a comparative framework for discussing other places. To what extent do Western Europe and the U.S.S.R. follow or depart from the patterns and trends found in Anglo-America? How is Africa different from Latin America?

What should also be apparent is the uniquely geographic nature of the approach. A world geography approach continually asks where people and economic activities are located. It asks how the location of these characteristics has changed over time. Finally, it asks why the characteristics are located where they are. These basic questions can be applied to analyzing the development of any continental region. In this sense history and international relations take on a distinctly geographic air. It is this geographic perspective that constitutes the essence of the approach and its principal contribution to helping students understand their world.

4. Annotated bibliography

GENERAL READINGS ON THE NATURE OF GEOGRAPHY

Hart, J.F. "The Highest Form of the Geographer's Art." *Annals, Association of American Geographers*, March, 1982, pp. 1–29. An articulate statement on the importance of the study of regional geography by a recent president of the Association of American Geographers.

Taafe, E.J. "The Spatial View in Perspective." *Annals, Association of American Geographers*, March, 1974, pp. 1–16. An important overview of three main traditions in modern geography: man–land relationships, area studies, and the spatial view. All have relevance to the preparation of a course on world geography.

MATERIALS FOR CURRICULUM DEVELOPMENT

Joint Committee on Geographic Education of the National Council for Geographic Education and the Association of American Geographers. *Guidelines for Geographic Education: Elementary and Secondary Schools.* Washington, D.C.: Association of American Geographers, 1984. A detailed breakdown of learning skills and knowledge outcomes for grades K-12. The publication stresses five main themes in geographic education: place, location, relationships within places, relationships among places, and the region. A valuable guide for curriculum developers and teachers.

Natoli, S.J., and Bond, A.R. *Geography in Internationalizing the Undergraduate Curriculum.* Washington, D.C.: Association of American Geographers, 1985. Although developed for university level courses, this collection of brief papers is useful in outlining some basic themes and methods for modern geography courses. There are chapters on environment and society, maps and cartography, realms and regions, spatial interaction, and culture and nationality.

OVERVIEW STATEMENTS FOR PHYSICAL AND HUMAN GEOGRAPHY

Marsh, W.M., and Dozier, J. *Landscape: An Introduction to Physical Geography.* Reading, Mass.: Addison-Wesley, 1981. An excellent introduction to the elements of physical geography. Patterns and processes associated with climate, soil vegetation, and landform on the Earth's surface are outlined. The book is well illustrated with photographs, diagrams, and maps. There is a 27-page glossary.

Getis, A., Getis, J., and Fellman, J. *Human Geography: Culture and Environment.* New York: Macmillan, 1985. A well-written, neatly presented overview of aspects of human geography. Of particular interest are five chapters on population/cultural geography. There are discussions of culture hearth regions, current culture realms, and the impact of humans on the environment.

GLOBAL VARIATIONS IN DEVELOPMENT

Cole, J.P. *Geography of World Affairs*, 6th ed. Boston: Butterworths, 1983. A thematic overview of the geography of the contemporary world. Chapters on natural resources and international trade precede a rather cursory and somewhat traditional set of regional discussions.

Dickenson, J., et al. *A Geography of the Third World.* London: Methuen, 1983. An excellent book on the historical background and current structure of the economy and demography of Third World nations. It contains a good overview of measures of development, theories of development, and selected themes such as urbanization and trading linkages. It may represent the best starting point for teachers who want to present the geography of Asia, Africa, or Latin America.

Jackson, R., and Hudman, L. *World Regional Geography: Issues for Today,* 2nd ed. New York: Wiley, 1986. A textbook, produced for introductory college courses, but could be used for high school classes. The framework for the book is level of development. Measures and theories of development are presented clearly. Graphs, tables, and maps are used effectively throughout the discussion. All continental regions are discussed in development terms. The basic physical and human geography of each region is handled well. It does not deteriorate into a country-by-country discussion but stresses general geographic distributions.

ADDITIONAL CLASSROOM AIDS

Resource Publications in Geography. A set of publications from the Association of American Geographers, based in Washington D.C. Recent topics include computer mapping, revitalizing cities, agricultural land in an urban society, and political restructuring. Each is less than 100 pages in length and designed for use in classroom settings.

World Population Data Sheet and Bulletins. The Data Sheet is a one-page table of approximately twenty measures of development for every nation on the Earth's surface. Published by the Population Reference Bureau, Inc., Washington, D.C., it is updated every year and is a valuable classroom aid. Copies for classroom use may be purchased.

The Bureau also publishes three or four bulletins every year. Each deals with an important population issue such as international migration, the aging of the American population, or population policies in China.

ATLASES

Several excellent atlases are available for student use. All provide absolute location information for physical and political features and also have maps showing global distributions of a variety of physical and human features, such as landform and climatic regions, population distribution, energy supplies,and economic regions. Especially good are the three paperback atlases listed below.

Crow, B., and Thomas, A. *Third World Atlas.* Philadelphia: Open University Press, 1984.
Goode's World Atlas, 17th ed. Chicago: Rand McNally, 1986.
Kidron, M., and Segal, R. *The New State of the World Atlas.* New York: Simon and Schuster, 1984.

5. Content outline for a world geography course

UNIT I: THINKING GEOGRAPHICALLY—INTRODUCING LOCATION AND PLACE

1. Geographic variations on the local scale
   1.1 Urban land use forms a pattern
       Commercial land use in the city center
       Socioeconomic and ethnic determinants of residential land use
       Suburbanization of office, industrial, and commercial activities
   1.2 Urban areas have linkages among and within land use types
       Daily activity patterns
       Location of shopping malls, public facilities, and freeway systems
   1.3 Maps of the local area show interrelated environments
       Interpreting air photo and topographic maps
       Relating the physical and human environments
2. Geographic variations on the national scale
   2.1 The U.S. can be regionalized climatically
       Dynamic forces (cold polar air, warm Gulf air)
       Impact on where people live
       Agricultural crop production
   2.2 The U.S. can be regionalized by landform area
       Dynamic forces (plate tectonics)
       Influence on where people live
       Location of mineral deposits
   2.3 The U.S. can be regionalized by human characteristics
       The distribution of population
       Cultural variations in religion, race, and ethnicity
       Economic variations (agricultural/industrial)

UNIT II: PATTERNS AND PROCESSES ON THE GLOBAL SCALE— AREAL DIFFERENTIATION AND SPATIAL INTERACTION

1. Regionalization
   1.1 Regions may be defined by location
       Absolute location (latitude and longitude)
       Relative location based on relational characteristics

    1.2 Regions may be defined by contents of area

        Similar physical or human characteristics (Corn Belt, Tropical Zone, Middle East)

        Points and linkages of functional regions (airline networks, trading organizations)

2. Formal regions on the Earth's surface: physical geography

    2.1 Climate varies regionally

        Broad regionalization (Tropic, Temperate, and Arctic Zones)

        Dynamics associated with climate regions

        Impact on where people live and what they can grow

        Impact of humans on climate

    2.2 Landforms vary regionally

        Major landform features (plains, plateaus, mountains)

        Dynamics associated with landform areas

        Where people live

        Where industrial minerals and fossil fuels are found

        Impact of humans on landforms

3. Formal regions on the Earth's surface: human geography

    3.1 There are general patterns of population distribution

        Uneven distribution

        Four major concentrations of population

        Overpopulated versus underpopulated continents

    3.2 Cultural regions can be formed on the basis of history, race, and religion

        Historical beginnings and cultural hearth areas

        Racial distinctions (Caucasoid, Negroid, Mongoloid)

        Religious distinctions (Hinduism, Islam, Christianity, Judaism, Animism)

    3.3 Culture can diffuse from one area to another

        Dynamics of cultural diffusion

        Western culture to Iran or Japan

    3.4 Cultural conflict exists on the Earth's surface

        Cultural dualism in Japan, Iran, or Canada

        Cultural pluralism in the U.S.S.R. or U.S.

    3.5 The world has a variety of economic and political systems

        The economic systems: capitalism and socialism

        The instability of economic and political systems

4. Functional regions on the Earth's surface

    4.1 International trade makes all parts of the Earth dependent upon one another

        Supply/demand relationships and trade

        Volume of trade dominated by a few highly developed countries

        Transport linkages

        Volume and nature of commodities shipped

    4.2 Political and economic relationships affect the pattern of trade

        Formal trade relationships

        Historical dimensions to current trends

        Political conflict and trading patterns

        Investment and trade

    4.3 International migration ties most countries of the world together

        Permanent international migration

        Temporary migration

Migration and labor shortage problems
Migration and internal tensions
4.4 International organizations reflect cooperation among countries
Economic, political, and security organizations
Positive impacts (EEC and work conditions)
Negative impacts (internal fighting over membership)

UNIT III: UNEVEN DEVELOPMENT

1. The development continuum
   1.1 Uneven development can mean many different things
   Developed versus undeveloped
   Technologically advanced versus technologically backward
   First World, Second World, Third World
   1.2 Development can be compared along a continuum
   Difficulties in classifying world regions
   Changing placement on the development continuum
   Variations in development among and within regions
2. Measures of development
   2.1 Economic measures reveal global variations in the level of development
   Per capita Gross National Product
   Per capita consumption of inanimate energy
   Sectoral employment trends—primary, secondary, tertiary
   Level of urbanization
   2.2 Demographic measures also show how development varies among countries
   Crude birth and death rates
   Rates of natural increase
   Life expectancy
   Dependency ratios
3. Theories of development
   3.1 Economic theories explain variations in development
   Development stage models—Rostow
   Dependency theory
   Dual economies
   3.2 Demographic theories explain variations in development
   Demographic transition theory
   Linking demographic and economic models
4. Spatial dimensions to development
   4.1 More developed regions have certain characteristics
   Core areas
   Periphery
   4.2 Less developed regions have other characteristics
   No urban industrial core
   Focus of economy on islands or pockets of development related to primary
   exports

UNIT IV: THE GLOBAL PATTERN OF DEVELOPMENT

1. The more developed regions
   1.1 Anglo-America represents the most highly developed region in economic and demographic terms

      Rich resource base

      Diversity of trade products

      Strong ties to Western Europe

      Functional specialization of the core area

      Changing relationships between core area and periphery

      Dependence on external sources of resources

   1.2 Europe has considerable internal variation in levels of development

      Resource base limited

      Dependence on external sources of food and minerals

      Functional specialization of the core area

      Periphery heavily oriented toward the primary sector

      Efforts at regional integration

   1.3 Japan is undergoing rapid change in economic development

      Weak natural resource base and trade dependence

      Strong cultural development and industrial organization

      Functional specialization of the core area

      More weakly developed periphery

   1.4 Australia's diverse physical geography promotes agricultural and mineral exports

      The impact of Australia's distance from other more developed countries

      Strong ties to Western Europe

      Less functional specialization of the core area than other developed regions

      Periphery poorly settled but resource-rich

   1.5 The U.S.S.R. is the least developed of the more developed regions

      Vast resource base

      Two main phases of development (from little urban-industrial growth to economic turnaround)

      Population heavily concentrated in the west

      Resources concentrated in the eastern two-thirds

      Functional specialization of the core area

      Periphery sparsely settled and not fully integrated

      Current problems with internal cohesion, economic diversification, and international influence

2. The less developed regions
   2.1 Latin America is the most developed of the less developed regions

      Rich natural resource base

      Distinctive historical development

      Uneven distribution of population

      Recent movement toward industrialization

      Recent efforts toward supranationalism

   2.2 South and East Asia contain most of the world's population

      Majority of natural resources exported to more developed regions

      Long cultural history and strong colonial impact

      Lack of core–periphery structure

Mostly subsistence agriculture

Some emerging industrial development and population control

Conditions of social unrest and political instability

2.3 Africa is the least developed region on the Earth's surface

Rich natural resource base

Long cultural history (colonization and late independence)

Lack of core–periphery structure

Mostly subsistence agriculture

Uneven development

Problems with inadequate food supply, desertification, rapid population growth, and racial tensions

Chapter **6**
An International Relations Approach

Patrick McGowan
Robert B. Woyach

1. **Rationale**

INTRODUCTION

Within the last generation, the idea that all Americans should be educated for "responsible citizen participation in world affairs" has been transformed from an idealistic goal of a few internationalists to a vital national need. In today's interdependent world, average Americans routinely make decisions about complicated international issues. Should we care if our corporations, universities, and pension funds retain investments in South Africa? Should we "buy American" or keep faith in the free trade system? Should we support our government's military involvement in Nicaragua, Lebanon, or the Persian Gulf?

In short, the world has become a complicated place for Americans. As a result, our need for a globally educated citizenry has grown. That need is likely to increase as today's students reach positions of leadership in the next century.

The high school world studies course can make a major contribution to preparing students for citizenship in today's world. To do so, the course must help students develop the knowledge and skills necessary to understand, interpret, and make reasoned judgments about key world issues and problems. This requires far more than traditional teaching about civics and current events. It requires basic instruction about how the world around us works and why. It requires efforts to help students understand their role in the world as individuals and as American citizens. It also requires instruction designed to teach basic critical thinking and decisionmaking skills.

AN INTERNATIONAL RELATIONS APPROACH

This chapter describes an international relations approach to the high school world studies course. This approach is highly suited to achieving the goals of citizenship education, precisely because it deals directly with the issues and problems facing the world today. What, then, is international relations? What is distinctive about an international relations approach?

The subject matter of international relations

International relations is the study of the interactions and relationships that link the various people, groups, organizations, and states inhabiting our world. These regularized interactions and relationships constitute an "international system." A key task of international relations scholars is to explore, describe, and explain the present international system, its past development, and its possible futures. While the international system has cultural and social aspects to it, international relations scholars tend to be most concerned with its political and economic dimensions.

International relations also attempts to understand the forces that affect the everyday international behavior of governments, business firms, private organizations, and other "actors" as they try to achieve their goals within the world arena. How do domestic politics affect the foreign policies of states? Under what conditions are states more or less likely to resort to violence to achieve foreign policy goals? Why do business firms enter the global marketplace?

Relative to some other approaches to world studies, the focus of international relations is relatively narrow. It is primarily concerned with the relationships among actors, not with a detailed understanding of the actors themselves. At the same time, the perspective of international relations is relatively broad. International relations scholars consciously apply the evidence, insights, and concepts of several disciplines—particularly political science, economics, history, geography, and psychology. For example, to explain the relationship between the United States and the Soviet Union, scholars might look at the personal attitudes of key decisionmakers, the military and social histories of the two states, the influence of geographic location, or the dilemma of providing security in an age of nuclear weapons.

An international relations course

The fundamental goal of an international relations course should be to give students a basic framework of knowledge and a core set of skills for interpreting and making judgments about international events.

Course content in an international relations course would focus on the contemporary world. Students would learn about international actors and about the patterns of interaction, conflict, and cooperation that make up the world system. The course would show students how the concerns and motivations of actors shape international events. More important, it would show how the international environment influences the behavior of actors. A key goal of the course would be to show how international actors create and use such things as international organizations to resolve problems and to manage conflict and change.

In addition, a high school international relations course should help students to understand the historical origins and foundations of the contemporary international system. How did the nation-state come to dominate the world system politically? How did the nations of Europe, North America, and Japan come to enjoy such high levels of economic well-being relative to the rest of the world? How did the split between the United States and the Soviet Union develop? This historical content would not be presented in the same way it would within a history course. Nonetheless, a course on international relations should give students an historical perspective on the world in which they live.

Finally, a high school international relations course should focus explicitly on fundamental and enduring issues within the international system. Students should see the way in which the world system deals with critical sources of conflict. However, the approach would not merely look at current events or the headline issues of the day. It would not even focus primarily on enduring but rather specific issues of international politics, such as the arms race between the Soviet Union and the United States. Rather, the course should focus on issues reflecting perennial concerns of all actors, such as the need for security. It should focus on issues that describe basic cleavages within the world system, such as the gap between the more and less developed nations. The issues, in short, should reflect fundamental tensions that arise from the very structure of the world system.

ADVANTAGES OF THE APPROACH

There are several advantages to approaching the high school world studies course from the perspective of international relations.

First, although the field of international relations encompasses a large body of knowledge, in comparison with some other approaches the field is reasonably well focused. International relations is not concerned with conveying detailed knowledge about the many cultures of the world or the multitude of civilizations that have existed throughout history. An international relations course would give students an understanding of the world system, a sense of how this system evolved, an awareness of the key challenges currently facing the system, and some skills necessary to participate effectively as citizens in shaping the future of the system.

Second, a frequent complaint about current high school world studies courses is that they have become compendia of facts, with no attention given to concepts. It is essential for a high school course to teach facts. Students must know something about the world in order to make reasoned judgments or to understand more abstract concepts, but facts that remain isolated from larger patterns of meaning are irrelevant. Learning isolated facts cannot contribute to the development of higher thinking skills. In an international relations approach, individual facts are selected for the explicit purpose of teaching broader concepts.

Third, international relations may well be the approach that can most easily contribute to the development of basic citizenship skills. Because it deals explicitly and directly with fundamental issues facing the contemporary world, students have maximum opportunity to analyze and make judgments. They also develop their critical thinking skills in ways integrally related to the content of the course, not as an artificial add-on.

Fourth, because the international relations approach focuses on the contemporary world, the course's knowledge base is consistently being played out in current political and economic events. This provides teachers with ample opportunities to reinforce core course content by discussing events and trends in which the students may be highly interested. As a result, the normally rigid distinction between what is done in the classroom and what happens in the real world becomes less clearly drawn.

Finally, an international relations approach has an obvious motivational appeal. The course does not become bogged down in apparently irrelevant knowledge about the past. Especially if approached through key world issues, the relevance of the material should be immediate and obvious to students, teachers, and parents alike.

DISADVANTAGES OF THE APPROACH

Many of the advantages of the approach suggest corresponding disadvantages as well.

First, while it is well suited to citizenship education, an international relations approach is less well suited to achieving some other traditional social studies goals. If curriculum planners believe the world studies course should help students understand themselves as members of a social system or understand what it means to be human, international relations may not be the most appropriate approach. If a school district is primarily interested in teaching students about other countries or cultures, an international relations approach would be far less relevant than a cultural or geographic approach.

Second, while an international relations course should help students develop a historical perspective, it cannot be expected to convey an overall image of history. Historical material is used selectively, not in a way that provides students with a chronological view of the human story. If the development of a chronological framework is a primary goal of the course, then a historical approach is clearly best suited to achieve that objective.

A final disadvantage of an international relations approach is related to teacher preparation. Very few high school world studies teachers have had extensive college-level course work in international relations. This means that school districts and teachers who opt for an international relations approach must be willing to invest in staff development as well as curriculum change.

2. Goals for students

GLOBAL AWARENESS AND CITIZENSHIP

An international relations approach to the high school world studies course should have as its fundamental goal the education of globally aware young women and men. Global awareness can mean many things, but after taking an international relations course high school students should have begun to develop three critical competencies that lie at the heart of global awareness. First, they should be able to see their place as individuals within the world system. Second, they should appreciate the multiple and often contradictory roles played by the American people and the American state in international affairs. Finally, having come to understand better the interrelationships among all people on Earth, they should be able to intelligently address issues affecting the survival and welfare of humanity. In short, they should have learned to speak for themselves, for their own people, and for the species as a whole.

MAJOR KNOWLEDGE GOALS

A high school world studies course taking an international relations approach should help students gain an understanding of the complexity and diversity of international affairs today. Specifically, the main knowledge goals of the course should be to help students:

1. Understand what it means to call the world a system and understand the major characteristics of the international system, such as interdependence, complexity, order, conflict, and change
2. Understand the nature and variety of international actors and appreciate that the spectrum of opinions, beliefs, and values held by international actors ranges far wider than the spectrum of political opinions held by Americans
3. Know in general terms how population, resources, wealth, and military power are distributed globally and how the world is divided by different political and economic systems

4. Understand how the distribution of these characteristics affects the patterns of conflict and cooperation in the world
5. Appreciate the positive and negative aspects of the global system so that they understand the need for both order and change in the world
6. Realize how scientific and technological change affects international life and generates new international issues
7. Understand how geography, culture, history, social organization, and psychological processes affect international behavior
8. Know how the local community is affected by and has an impact on actors throughout the world
9. Comprehend the critical importance of citizen participation in local, national, and international affairs
10. Understand how the structure of the international system affects national security and the different ways in which states try to make themselves secure
11. Understand the historical origins of the gap between the more and less developed countries and appreciate how the international system may contribute to and impede economic development within the Third World
12. Understand why questions about natural resources and economic growth have become important in the contemporary world and know how and why states and other actors have brought those issues into the international arena

MAJOR SKILL GOALS

An interntional relations course should also be directed toward helping students acquire the analytical, communication, and decisionmaking skills essential for informed, participatory citizenship in our American democracy. Specifically, the course should help students:

1. Develop critical thinking and problem-solving competence by identifying, describing, and analyzing problems, exploring alternative solutions, anticipating the impact of various solutions, and selecting from among different alternatives, both individually and in groups
2. Become adept at identifying the viewpoints, belief systems, and ideologies of others and thus learn to examine their own opinions and beliefs with respect to world affairs
3. Develop their capacity to accept, practice, and defend democratic beliefs and procedures, both in interpersonal relations and in government
4. Learn to gather reliable information about current international issues from a variety of printed and electronic media
5. Learn to use maps, statistical data, and other types of information to describe characteristics of the world system and to analyze how these characteristics might affect relations among international actors
6. Develop a willingness and an ability to engage in persuasive communication, both written and oral, with respect to international issues

3. Organization of subject matter

Subject matter within the field of international relations can be organized in a variety of ways. It is possible, for example, to take a foreign policy approach, looking primarily at the various domestic and international influences upon the foreign policy decisions of key states like the United States. One can also take a power politics approach, looking primarily at the forces that influence the competition among national governments for power and prestige within the international system.

The approach recommended here is a modified international systems approach. It looks primarily at patterns of political and economic interaction among various actors within the international arena. The approach is organized primarily in terms of concepts describing key characteristics of the world system, general propositions about the behavior of international actors, and issues that have arisen from the very structure of the world system.

CRITERIA FOR ORGANIZING AND SELECTING SUBJECT MATTER

Two fundamental assumptions guide our organization of the subject matter and should underlie criteria for selecting the particular facts and ideas to emphasize in the course. First, because students are likely to have limited backgrounds and undeveloped conceptual skills, the course should focus on the most basic facts and ideas describing the world system. Second, the salience of the material and students' interest in the course can be enhanced by organizing the majority of the course around key international issues.

FOCUSING ON THE BASICS. Any high school world studies course must assume that students have relatively little knowledge about the world and even less about relationships that make up the international system. One implication of this is that the course should begin by reinforcing and extending the students' basic geographic knowledge about the world. This will lay a factual foundation for understanding some of the patterns of interaction among international actors.

A second implication of students' limited understanding of world affairs is that throughout the course, explicit attention should be given to the basic concepts that describe world affairs. Such concepts as the nation-state, the international system, interdependence, deterrence, development, and dependence provide a vocabulary and a framework for discussing and analyzing world affairs.

Attention to these concepts need not make the course overly abstract. The basic concepts of international relations describe concrete relationships. They can and should be taught by describing concrete situations and events. The challenge may well be to ensure that the concepts are not lost within the factual detail but are consistently and explicitly emphasized.

Likewise, although these basic concepts make up a technical language within international relations, they do not represent a needless jargon. Many of the most basic concepts have come from or have found their way into everyday discourse. Most describe properties of the world that are central to understanding world affairs. Thus it is critically important that students be exposed to these ideas in a systematic way.

The focus on basic concepts also raises an important question with respect to historical material. An important goal of the course is to give students an historical perspective on the contemporary world system. However, the course cannot provide a detailed understanding of historical periods or a complete history of the contemporary world. For example, an international relations course should include material on past attempts to preserve the peace, such as the nineteenth-century Great Power conferences and the League of Nations. These historical experiences set a context for understanding collective security as an alternative to the current security system. The course should not, however, try to give students a detailed understanding of the political, economic, and social environment of the nineteenth and early twentieth centuries. The purpose of introducing these historical examples of peacekeeping efforts is to deepen students' understanding of the dynamics and pitfalls of collective security, not to teach them about these historical experiences *per se*.

USING INTERNATIONAL ISSUES. Issues that are of fundamental and enduring importance to actors in the international system probably provide the most attractive basis for organizing a high school international relations course. Students are likely to be attracted to questions about security or economic development that have clear and immediate relevance to their own concerns or to events happening in the world around them. These types of issues also provide a substantive focus that can bring concepts to life. Finally, material on issues can be used to reinforce basic international relations concepts, helping students develop a more in-depth understanding of the world system.

Four criteria should guide the selection of issues for detailed examination in the course.

- First, the issues should be global in scope. They should, in other words, be of fundamental concern to all international actors, not simply Americans.
- Second, the issues should reflect problems that cannot be solved by any single international actor, not even one as powerful as the United States. Only issues that require action by more than one actor will lead teachers and students to explore the bases of international conflict and cooperation.
- Third, the issues chosen should provide an opportunity for giving students a historical perspective on the international system. It should be possible to teach

each as a story, with an origin located in the past, a present dilemma, and a future that has implications for the students' own lives.

• Finally, the issues selected should represent or reflect fundamental features of the international system.

Given these criteria, three international issues seem particularly appropriate:

1. The search for security among international actors, particularly among states and their populations, and the impact of nuclear weapons on the search for security

2. The challenge of international development and the conflicts engendered by the gap between the more and less industrialized countries

3. The set of ecological concerns, such as population growth, environmental decay, and resource depletion, which have arisen as a result of growing human demands on our biological and physical environment

Each of these three broad issues highlights different properties of the international system. Each is of global concern and requires international cooperation to manage or resolve. Finally, each contributes significantly to the story of how the present international system evolved and where it may be heading in the future.

The use of issues to teach about the world system inevitably raises a final question. If students are to understand the issues being dealt with in the course, material describing the nature and evolution of the issues must be introduced into the course. As with historic content, however, analyses of the issues should be subordinated to the goal of describing and analyzing basic properties and dynamics of the international system. In an examination of an ecological issue such as population growth, for example, relatively little emphasis should be placed on understanding how and why populations grow. Primary emphasis should be given to describing why population growth has become an international issue and how the world community has tried to define and respond to the issue.

LAYING THE FOUNDATION: THE INTERNATIONAL SYSTEM

What are the fundamental concepts and information that underlie a high school international relations course? This section outlines some basic concepts and information about the world that should provide a conceptual and factual core around which a course can be built.

Political and economic maps of the world

Our cognitive maps or mental images of the world provide the foundation for thinking about and understanding what happens in the international system. The more relevant and accurate those maps are, the more comprehensible the world will be and the better will be our judgments and decisions with respect to world issues. Most students are likely to have limited cognitive maps of the world. Nonetheless, the basic geographic and political knowledge they do have represents the foundation upon which the course can and should be built.

Students undoubtedly perceive the world, albeit with little detail, in terms of the standard political map. That map highlights the various continents and countries (states) and provides a useful starting point. At the beginning of the course students should be introduced to additional maps of the world that highlight other divisions: maps that show the distribution of population, wealth, key industrial resources, military power, and different political and economic systems.

These maps of the world provide a cognitive and visual foundation for helping students understand the patterns of conflict and cooperation within the international system. Which parts of the world are most likely to have similar or complementary interests? Which are most likely to have conflicting or at least different interests and perspectives?

Throughout the course an effort should be made to enrich students' cognitive maps. By the end of the year, students should be able to visualize the world map in terms of the distribution of nuclear weapons, industrialization, urbanization, trade dependence, pollution, and well-being measured in various ways.

The evolution of the international system

An international relations approach should not try to teach a detailed history of the evolution of the present international system. On the other hand, it is critical that students understand that substantially different world systems have existed in the past and that the present world system itself has evolved through time. This understanding is important if students are to comprehend that the present international system is constantly undergoing change. It is also essential if they are to consider alternatives to the current world order.

Thus the course should help students understand some of the key developments in the evolution of the modern world. Two dimensions of this historical experience are most relevant. The first is the development of the modern "state" or "nation-state." The second is the progressively increasing scope of the international system.

The modern nation-state can be defined as a political community occupying a particular territory and ruled by a government that claims the right to make and enforce laws without approval from a higher authority. Such "sovereign" states dominate the international system. More precisely, some states, such as the United States, Japan, and the Soviet Union, dominate the system. Other states, such as Lesotho in southern Africa or the Maldive Islands in the Indian Ocean, probably have less routine impact on the system than many multinational corporations. However, the very term we use to designate the world arena, "international system," indicates the primacy of nation-states as actors in the world, both historically and today.

Yet nation-states have existed in their modern form for only a few hundred years. They have become the dominant form of political organization in the world only during the last century. Students should understand that the nation-state is a relatively recent historical phenomenon. They should understand how nationalism and the ideologies that arose through the democratic revolution and the articulation of socialism have enabled nation-states to mobilize their human resources so effectively.

The present international system is historically unique, in that it is both global—affecting the lives of most people everywhere in the world—and intensive—its effects often reach deeply and dramatically into individual societies. Today, economic decisions made in New York, Tokyo, and Brussels affect virtually the entire world. At the same time the security of New York and Tokyo is deeply affected by military decisions made in Moscow.

The evolution of the international system into an intensive, global system was only achieved toward the end of the nineteenth century. After 1850 new medical, military, and transportation technologies enabled the European nations to dominate the interior of Africa and bring it, for better or worse, fully into the international system. New communication technologies have made it possible for information about events in Asia to reach North Americans and Europeans in days and then hours. New transportation technologies made it possible to ship products from Japan to San Francisco as quickly as it once took to ship them from Chicago. These technologies have combined to alter the attitudes and behaviors of people in virtually every part of the world. Students should understand the importance of economics and European imperialism as forces for uniting and expanding the world system. They should also see the critical role played by advances in technology.

What it means to call the world a "system"

One of the most critical concepts in international relations is the idea that the world is a "system." Even as the historical background of the international system is discussed, it is important to begin introducing students to this concept.

In the field of international relations, the idea of the international system has taken several forms. Some scholars talk about fairly abstract conceptualizations of "the world system." Others discuss specific "international systems" such as the coffee trading system, the international communications system, or the international financial system.

All these systems are made up of three components. First are the "actors," or decisionmakers, including the governments of nation-states, profit-making organizations like banks and manufacturing firms, and international organizations like the United Nations and the World Council of Churches. The actors in the international system also include individuals, as consumers or producers, as rebels against injustice, or as the recipients of foreign aid. The second component of the international system includes those things that make up the "environment" of the actors, such as natural resources and the biosphere. Finally, the third component of the international system is the "relationships" among actors. It includes the patterns of past conflict and cooperation that influence current decisions and policies.

If dealt with on a relatively concrete level, the idea that the world is an international system is well within the grasp of tenth graders. Indeed, the concept of a system (or a pattern of actors and their interactions and relationships) gives order to what can otherwise be a chaotic collection of entities (governments, leaders, corporations, terrorist movements) and events.

International systems can and should be seen in the institutions and items that surround students in their daily lives. Students can, for example, see evidence of the international system in the products they consume and in the people they know from other countries. They can see the international system in their favorite music and in their family traditions. In short, the students' own families and communities provide a concrete resource for investigating different dimensions of the international system.

Interdependence and dependence

The systems concept is critical for understanding world affairs, primarily because of its implications. The systemic nature of the world results in patterns of interdependence and dependence among the members of the system. These two concepts are among the most important for students to grasp and to use in analyzing world events and making judgments about international issues.

"Dependence" and "interdependence" refer to the character of the relationships among actors within the international system. Because actors are linked together, the decisions or actions of one can have an impact on the ability of others to achieve their goals. If an actor cannot attain its goals without the cooperation of others, that actor is dependent on the others. If the different actors each have an impact on one another (that is, if the dependence is mutual), then the relationships are said to be interdependent.

Most Latin American and Western European and many East Asian states are economically dependent on North America. Economic decisions by the government of the United States or by American multinational corporations and consumers can undermine economic development plans and create recessions. Alternatively, access to the American market can stimulate local or national economies. Economic policies by Japanese or Western European governments typically have a similar if not equal impact on North Americans. Thus the relationship among these industrial states is one of interdependence. On the other hand, actions by Latin American governments, consumers, and business firms generally have little or no impact on the United States government or on American consumers and corporations. The pattern of dependence between Latin America and North America is not reciprocal or mutual. Latin America is said to be dependent upon the north, particularly upon the United States.

THE FIRST ISSUE: SECURITY AND NUCLEAR ARMS

No concern is more basic to the analysis and understanding of the international system than the issue of security. Teaching about the problem of national security reinforces basic concepts about the international system, such as its lack of central authority and the sovereignty of nation-states. The security issue also shows the impact of changing technology. Finally, the issue of security provides an opportunity to build students' understanding of world affairs by showing the impact of domestic and international forces on the decisions and policies of international actors.

Providing security in a world of sovereign states

Security concerns preoccupy states because there is no central authority to enforce laws or to safeguard the members of the international system. The system is, in other words, an example of political anarchy. But what is security? How do states try to provide for their security?

Most students will probably think first of security in terms of a military defense in the face of a military attack. However, security involves the protection of any basic value from any type of threat. It is meaningful to talk about food security or economic security, or even to see the protection of civil and human rights in terms of security.

The protection of these basic values often requires the possession of military force and sometimes its use, but states have a variety of other tools at their disposal as well. In some instances diplomacy (the negotiation of international agreements) may provide greater security than force and violence. In other situations, the use of economic rewards or threats, as in cutting off or increasing trade, can better protect basic interests and values.

The tools used to achieve security will depend on the nature of the threat, the resources or tools available to the actor, the values and goals of decision-makers, and the domestic and international constraints on the use of certain tools.

The external military threats that states face vary considerably. For example, over the centuries the Russian people have experienced several devastating invasions by hostile peoples and states. As a result, the Soviet Union today uses its resources to create a massive military establishment. They have also attempted to create a ring of docile buffer states near their frontiers, serving to protect the Soviets from future invasions.

The United States, on the other hand, has not faced a military threat along its frontiers since British troops burned Washington, D.C. in the War of 1812. Yet the United States has far-flung political and economic interests. Protecting these interests requires our government to project its military and economic power to distant corners of the globe. As a result, the United States has built an extensive system of alliances and mutual security arrangements with other states.

States with fewer resources than the Soviet Union and the United States may be forced to pursue their security interests primarily by non-military means. For example, states like India, Switzerland, and Sweden have attempted to protect their security in part through policies of neutrality. By attempting to insulate themselves from the international conflicts of more powerful states, they have tried to reduce their risks of being directly threatened by states with greater military resources. States with security problems like Cuba and Japan have taken the opposite course. Having a hostile United States only ninety miles away, the Cubans have chosen to ally themselves very closely with the Soviet Union. The Japanese, close to the Soviet Union, have done the opposite.

In seeking to achieve military security states generally practice one of three different strategies. Some states, such as Israel, South Africa, and China, are garrison states that practice an extreme form of self-help. They maintain strong, independent military forces to guarantee their freedom from foreign conquest. Other states use military alliances to enhance their security by adding the power of their allies to their own military power. States as varied as the United States, the Soviet Union, Japan, and Cuba do this. Finally, some states maintain whatever military forces they can afford but try to avoid involvement in global or even regional conflicts by practicing foreign policies of neutrality (Sweden) or non-alignment (India).

Why states choose the security policies they do will help students understand the complex way in which geography, national traditions, power, and international threats shape the international behavior of the nation-state.

Nuclear arms and security

Nuclear weapons and the ballistic missiles capable of carrying them from one continent to another (ICBMs) have radically transformed the nature of national security in our time. If students are to understand contemporary international relations, they need to comprehend the security dilemma posed by the nuclear age.

Prior to the nuclear age, military planners thought primarily in terms of the defense of their borders. Before World War II the French built the Maginot Line. The United States has long rested secure behind the shelter of the Atlantic and Pacific Oceans.

The development of long-range bombers and ballistic missiles capable of delivering nuclear weapons to targets deep inside another country changed the meaning of "security." It was no longer possible "to meet the enemy at the gate" and to think that a state's military forces could provide an impenetrable shell of defense around the state's territory. National security in the nuclear age was no longer guaranteed by geography. It was now necessary to think primarily in terms of deterring or discouraging a hostile power from even considering an attack; once launched, enough bombers and warheads would reach their targets to cause unthinkable loss of life and physical destruction.

At least within the United States, the dilemma posed by these new weapons led to the development of a new style of deterrence, based on "mutual assured destruction" (MAD). The idea of deterrence is to prevent an enemy's attack. With the new technologies of destruction, this could only be done by threatening to punish an enemy with equal or greater destruction. Mutual assured destruction is the logical outcome of a deterrence policy in a world in which both opponents have the new technology. As punishment a would-be aggressor faces the total destruction of its own society in a retaliatory or "second strike" attack. As long as all nuclear enemies fear that a surprise first strike would lead to their own subsequent destruction, the relationship between enemies is a reasonably stable, if frightening, standoff. Nuclear war would be suicidal and therefore irrational.

Just as scientific and technological changes created the nuclear era, technological change also constantly threatens to upset or "destabilize" the delicate "balance of terror." When one state develops more accurate land-based ICBMs, as both superpowers have done, it becomes possible for them to attack and destroy at least the land-based nuclear missiles of the other. Similarly, an effective antimissile defense shield, as originally proposed in the Strategic Defense Initiative (SDI), would make it possible to destroy Soviet nuclear weapons before they reach their targets. Both changes in technology create new situations in which it might become thinkable to use nuclear weapons in a crisis situation.

The United States and the Soviet Union have used arms control (negotiations aimed at setting limits on the number and nature of nuclear weapons and their delivery systems) to stabilize the balance between them. Arms control has been an attempt to use diplomacy to increase security. However, it has not aimed at eliminating nuclear weapons; rather, it has been seen as a way to increase security by increasing the stability of deterrence.

The threat to security posed by nuclear weapons may not be limited to the threat of nuclear war between the superpowers. China, France, and the United Kingdom all have significant arsenals of nuclear weapons and a number of other states, such as Israel, Pakistan, and South Africa, may now have or may soon have the ability to produce nuclear weapons. The proliferation of nuclear weapons raises significant questions about the distribution of military power in the international system and about the security of all nations. Will these new nations be more likely to use nuclear weapons than the superpowers have been? Will the spread of nuclear weapons increase the risk of accidental war? Might the spread of weapons actually increase security in the world by making regional and local wars less likely?

Alternative paths to achieving security

Is it possible to devise a realistic alternative to a security system based on self-help and military self-reliance? International relations scholars have looked at various alternatives. Exposing students to these alternatives provides a valuable opportunity for exercising analytical and decision-making skills. It also provides an opportunity to understand the implications of the ways states attempt to achieve security in the contemporary world.

One alternative to the present system is the development of a collective security system within an international organization like the League of Nations or the United Nations. "Collective security" basically refers to an agreement whereby states within the international system agree to join together to prevent aggression and to protect each other. The collective security system of the League of Nations was based on the principal of consensus. All League members needed to agree to take collective action to punish aggressors. Otherwise, no action could be taken by the League. The United Nations attempted to use a different type of collective security. It rested not on universal consensus but rather on a consensus among the most powerful states. If the five permanent members of the Security Council (China, France, the Soviet Union, the United Kingdom, and the United States) agree to take action in the name of collective security, then the organization can deter or punish would-be aggressors. If they cannot agree, as has been the case more often than not, collective action cannot be effective.

A second alternative security strategy can be described as "disarmament and national resistance." Are massive military forces necessary to attain security, or do they simply encourage war and thus lead to insecurity? Can a society defend its interests through a combination of passive and active resistance to external threats? Students should be exposed to the logical implications and political arguments for and against such a security system.

Finally, the increasing connectedness of the international system may itself lead to greater international security. If states and peoples become increasingly dependent on each other, might the likelihood of violence be decreased? In general, close contacts and high levels of interaction among states actually increase conflict among them. The more two societies are in contact, the greater the opportunity for disagreement. On the other hand, interdependence may lead to decreased use of violence to resolve conflicts. Of critical importance is the creation of new international institutions that can make authoritative decisions to resolve the conflicts that do arise.

THE SECOND ISSUE: THE CHALLENGE OF DEVELOPMENT

One of the most important characteristics of the international system today is an extreme level of inequality among nation-states. To understand how much this division affects the world's political agenda and relationships among nations, one need only look at the voting blocs within the United Nations, the array of non-governmental groups involved in development assistance, and the periodic debates over reforming the world economic system.

The implications of global inequality for the international system should be a central component of an international relations course. By learning about this issue, students will be introduced to a critical feature of the world community. They may even begin to empathize with their peers in less developed countries. They will also see how the international economy has developed over the past 150 years. Also, by discussing and debating alternative responses to the challenge of development, students can develop skills in critical thinking and communication.

Underdevelopment in the Third World

Since the 1950s it has become common to classify the more than 160 states of our world into three categories. The first group, or "First World," includes about twenty-five of the richest and most industrialized countries in the world. All have industrial market economies and were among the first to industrialize. The key First World countries are the United States, Japan, Australia, and the countries of Western Europe. A second group of countries, with industrial non-market economies, make up the "Second World." These are the nine Communist-governed states of Eastern Europe, including Yugoslavia, Albania, and the Soviet Union. In general these are middle-income countries by world standards. The remaining 140-plus states of Latin America, Africa, and Asia have grouped themselves politically into a "Third World." Some of these states have rapidly industrializing economies (such as Taiwan and South Korea); some are very rich (such as Kuwait); most are very poor (such as Haiti). Some have socialist systems (such as Cuba); others have capitalist systems (such as Singapore). Despite their diversity, these Third World states try to present a common front, on international economic issues in particular.

Taken as a whole, most Third World countries share many characteristics, which makes the term "Third World" meaningful. Among these common characteristics are (1) low standards of living, (2) low levels of economic productivity, (3) high rates of population growth, (4) high and growing levels of unemployment and underemployment, (5) economic dependence on agricultural production and the export of primary products, (6) political instability and a tendency toward authoritarian government, and (7) economic, political, and military weakness in international relations. Because these characteristics tend to appear together, they form a syndrome called "underdevelopment." With the exceptions of a few oil-exporting states such as Saudi Arabia or newly industrialized countries such as Singapore, most countries of the Third World are underdeveloped, despite their often rich cultural heritages.

One important characteristic of underdevelopment is the unequal distribution of wealth and power within most Third World societies. In Central and South America, for example, the typical country in the 1970s was controlled by an oligarchy of families who accounted for about 1 percent of the population but enjoyed as much as 30 percent of total national income. A politically informed middle class of professionals, bureaucrats, merchants, intellectuals, and skilled laborers often formed 30 percent of the population and obtained as much as 50 percent of the national wealth. At the bottom of this unequal sociopolitical pyramid were the unskilled workers, unemployed urban slum dwellers, and rural peasants. While they constituted about 60 percent of the population, this underclass subsisted on only 20 percent of the national wealth. Given such internal inequality, it is not surprising that political democracy is rare and that authoritarian regimes of both the right and the left flourish in many Third World countries.

International inequality

Even though the United States still contains pockets of economic backwardness and social deprivation, it is one of the richest and most economically developed states in the world. It is therefore very hard for most Americans, particularly high school students, to appreciate the gap between the First and the Third World, let alone understand the implications of underdevelopment.

Over two-thirds of the world's people, some 3.4 billion, live in the Third World. Although local elites in these countries often have very high material living standards, the vast majority do not. The degree of inequality is especially striking when comparing the richest fifth of the world's population, including most Americans, to the world's poorest fifth, who live in 36 least-developed countries such as Bangladesh, Ethiopia, Sierra Leone, and Haiti. In 1980 adult literacy among the world's richest was 97 percent, versus 42 percent for the world's poorest. Per capita educational expenditures were $497 per year in the richest countries, versus $6 in the poorest. Government health expenditures per capita were $432 per year in the rich countries, compared to $2 in the poorest. The percentages of the population with access to safe water were 96 percent and 39 percent, respectively.

Origins of underdevelopment

The gap between the countries of the First and Third Worlds has historic roots that reach back almost 500 years to the emergence of modern Europe.

Yet underdevelopment only began to emerge in the nineteenth century, as Europe and North America underwent an industrial revolution while the Third World remained largely agricultural.

Industrialization and the new medical and military technologies of the nineteenth century allowed the nations of Europe and North America to create vast formal and informal political empires in the Third World. Meanwhile, railroads, steamships, and new communications technologies made trade and other economic activities between different parts of the world easier. In the process, most parts of the Third World, especially those under colonial rule, came to specialize in the export of agricultural and mineral raw materials. They also came to depend on the industrial states of the First World for manufactured goods like textiles and tools.

This division of labor between the First and Third Worlds had both economic and political origins. Minerals and energy resources are where one finds them, and some Third World countries are richly endowed. Agricultural products such as coffee, tea, cocoa, and rubber, which are native to the tropics, are impossible or too costly to grow in Europe and most of North America. As the countries of the First World industrialized, their increasing wealth and growing populations created a strong demand for these products. Third World producers and foreign investors responded to that demand. At the same time, machines made it possible for First World manufacturers to make many traditional products more cheaply than they could be produced by Third World craftsmen. Increasingly, traditional crafts were replaced with imports. Thereafter, the division of labor grew progressively more entrenched, since most new technologies and innovative products tended to be developed within the industrial world.

The division of labor between the First and Third Worlds was also shaped by colonialism. Up to World War II many parts of the Third World were under the direct political control of First World nations. Others, such as Thailand and much of South and Central America, were subject to irresistible diplomatic pressure and massive foreign investment. Together these forces often led to indirect control. During the nineteenth and twentieth centuries it was rarely in the interest of First World producers, consumers, or workers to allow industrialization within the Third World.

By the mid-twentieth century today's highly integrated world economy had already emerged. This world economy is in many respects still characterized by the patterns of the nineteenth century. In the early 1980s, for example, the exports of Third World nations were still largely made up of food and raw materials (79 percent). The bulk of their imports still consisted of manufactured products (66 percent). Most Third World trade was with countries in the First World, often the former imperial country. On the other hand, most First World trade was with other First World countries (70 percent). Third World countries depended on the First World for markets, foreign investment, new technology, and even loans to pay their foreign debts.

The political and economic relationship between the Third World and First has been described as one of "dependence" or even "neo-colonialism." Third World countries, while highly dependent on First World countries economically, may not be similarly important to the First World. The country of Honduras, for example, depends on exports of agricultural products for over 70 percent of its national income. Well over 50 percent of these exports have gone to the United States. Thus American import policies or even economic cycles affect Hondurans tremendously, but Honduran policies have little or no impact on Americans. Further, since many of the plantations and larger economic enterprises in a country such as Honduras may be owned by North Americans or may depend on North American banks or foreign aid, basic economic decisions affecting Hondurans may be made by North Americans despite Honduras' formal political independence.

Third World specialization in agricultural goods and mineral raw materials has other unfortunate consequences. The prices of primary products on the world market rise and fall frequently. Thus the export earnings of a country, and the money available for investment in the local economy, can change radically from year to year. Likewise, primary products have historically accounted for a smaller and smaller proportion of the price of manufactured goods. As a consequence, Third World countries have suffered from "declining terms of trade" that also hurt their economic development efforts. Year after year they must produce more and more primary products just to buy the same amount of manufactured goods.

Responding to underdevelopment

From the point of view of international relations, the key issue in the debate over global inequality and underdevelopment is whether and how to restructure political and economic relationships between the First and the Third World. Three types of responses have been championed by various people.

The very idea of a "Third World" has its origins in one type of response to underdevelopment. Mahatma Gandhi first used the term, saying that the newly independent countries of Asia and Africa should not be forced to choose between the politico-economic cultures of the First and Second Worlds. Rather, they should find their own path to development—a third way. In part Gandhi was reacting to the dependence of Third World nations on the First World. He and some other Third World leaders held that Third World development would be possible only if relationships between the First and the Third World were radically restructured.

The most radical approach to restructuring relations between the First and Third World can be called "collective self-reliance." Advocates of collective self-reliance see development as a complex set of changes that result in (1) greater cultural, political, and economic independence, (2) a more equitable distribution of wealth and power within the society, and (3) greater assurance that all people's basic needs are met.

Collective self-reliance focuses on what Third World states and peoples can do themselves to promote this type of development. In general, advocates believe that the best policy is one of virtual autarchy. All ties with the First World, they argue, should be severed. To the extent that international trade is needed to meet the basic needs of the society, reliance should be placed on other Third World countries.

A second approach to development stresses restructuring First and Third World relationships by changing the rules of the game within the international economy. Many scholars and political leaders within the Third World argue that underdevelopment is reinforced by the division of labor between First and Third World countries. They believe that Third World reliance on primary products and on markets and economic institutions in the First World perpetuates this division of labor. Therefore, development can only occur if the international economic system is changed so that more of the benefits flow to Third World countries.

Advocates of this type of reform created the United Nations Commission on Trade and Development (UNCTAD) in 1964. UNCTAD was meant to give Third World countries greater control over international development aid. In the 1970s reformers called for a New International Economic Order (NIEO). Their plan was to establish new rules governing international trade, foreign investment, and the international transfer of technology.

The approach to development that has guided most development efforts since World War II, and is still most popular within the First World, is called the "modernization approach." Advocates of this approach argue that Third World countries can use the international economy as an engine for growth. In their view, many Third World problems, such as underemployment, result in a "comparative advantage" in international markets. In short, underemployment results in low wages, which means cheaper products. Cheaper production costs attract foreign and domestic investors. Their activities spur economic growth and development. Initially the benefits of this growth will accrue to an economic and political elite, but as development finally gets started, its benefits "trickle down" to meet the needs of the poor. The principal obstacles to development, in the eyes of these advocates, are internal to the Third World countries. They include illiteracy, inadequate communication networks, and traditional cultural values and social institutions that inhibit entrepreneurship and social change.

Variations on this basic modernization approach have provided the basis for most foreign aid policies within the First World, such as the U.S. Caribbean Basin Initiative and the Lome Convention linking the European Economic Community with many countries in Africa, the Caribbean, and the Pacific. The modernization approach has also guided development policies of key international organizations, such as the World Bank and the International Monetary Fund. Today this approach to development places great emphasis on letting market forces operate freely and on removing governmental involvement in Third World economies.

THE THIRD ISSUE: THE ECOLOGICAL AGENDA

Of all the topics on which an international relations course might focus, the issues that make up the ecological agenda may be the most powerful. In essence, the ecological agenda involves issues that arise from our dependence upon the Earth. Broadly speaking the ecological issues include population growth, food security, resource security, and environmental decay. Some specific issues that can be examined under this broad agenda include acid rain, the loss of farmland, deforestation, depletion of the ozone layer, alternative energy sources, and family planning.

The ecological issues provide a unique perspective on the international system. Each of these issues manifests both local and global dimensions simultaneously. They touch on the daily lives of students and link daily activities with problems of global import.

Ecological issues also present a unique organizational challenge. Most treatments of the ecological issues focus on the nature and dynamics of each particular issue, such as population, food, or energy. Since each issue is unique, this makes a great deal of sense. At the same time, this organization of content can quickly degenerate into an exercise in which much information is communicated but students gain little contextual understanding. Structuring content according to the particular issues can also become quickly overwhelming. Not every issue related to the ecological agenda can be taught in the time available.

The approach suggested here does not proceed with the ecological agenda issue by issue; it tries to lay a basic conceptual and historical foundation for all the issues. It also uses the concrete issues to illustrate key points about the ways in which the ecological agenda has been handled by the international system.

Sensitizing students to the ecological agenda

The ability of the planet to sustain human economic activity, and indeed human life, depends on its ability to provide the resources we need. Our dependence on these ecological resources can be seen in the food we eat and in every product we use.

In general terms we consume two types of resources: renewable and nonrenewable. Students should be familiar with both. Renewable resources include all biologically based resources (food, cotton, wood, natural rubber, coffee, and the like). These resources are renewable because they come from living organisms that grow and reproduce themselves.

With respect to renewable resources, human life and activity is sustainable indefinitely, as long as we do not exceed the "carrying capacity" of the planet. As long as we do not use up biologically based resources faster than they can be replaced, there is no problem. If we do exceed the carrying capacity, we not only face shortages but may also destroy the biological system itself, as seen in species extinction and desertification.

Non-renewable resources include all mineral-based resources, such as metals and ceramics. In the case of non-renewable resources, the planet has a finite endowment. We may discover new gold deposits, but there is presumably a fixed amount of gold on the planet. When it has been found, mined, and used, there will be no more. Thus there is no carrying capacity for non-renewable resources. Available resources can be stretched out through conservation and recycling, and we can respond to shortages by finding substitutes, but the inevitable trend is toward depletion of non-renewable resources.

Fossil-based fuels such as oil and coal are considered non-renewable. Although they are continuously being created, fossil fuels take much longer to make than to use. Thus their amount is also fixed for all practical purposes.

The ecological agenda has arisen because of the perception that modern industrial society is reaching the Earth's limits. Production of some critical non-renewable resources, such as oil, may have peaked. More important, we may be exceeding the planet's carrying capacity because of rising populations and wealth.

Ecological issues have not arisen overnight, although they have changed in the last century. Pre-industrial societies often exceeded the carrying capacities of their local areas. Famine was endemic in the pre-industrial world. The Mayan and Mesopotamian civilizations may both have declined in part because population growth and resource use depleted agricultural lands.

However, the contemporary world is experiencing ecological stress under unique circumstances. The threat to the environment is no longer local, but global. The scientific and industrial revolutions gave human societies the power to produce, consume, and pollute as never before. Medical advances have allowed human populations to swell. The emergence of a world economy means that local resource shortages now have an international impact. As a result of these changes, greater absolute stress is being placed on the environment. What were once local problems have become global issues.

The global nature of ecological issues takes on a unique dimension when juxtaposed with their equally local nature. Ecological issues are always manifest first within local communities. Pollution, whether it be air pollution, water pollution, or the pollution of toxic wastes, is produced through the everyday activities of ordinary people. Pollution is also first felt within a local area. The same is true of hunger and population growth. If a population does not grow enough food to feed itself and cannot obtain food on the market, it experiences hunger. When populations grow, the local community experiences overcrowding, diminished access to facilities and services, and rising costs for basic necessities.

Local ecological problems inevitably spill over and become national, regional, and international problems. Rapid population growth eventually leads to emigration. That is how North America was populated in the nineteenth century. Immigration continues today in part because rapid population growth continues in many parts of the world. Likewise, when a local area overruns its agricultural potential, the impact is felt in rising prices on the world market. If the population is exceptionally poor, as in the Sahelian region of Africa, the impact may be different but it is equally visible. When local power plants in the Ohio Valley use high-sulphur coal, trees and fish in Canada and New England die. If Europeans insist on using fluorocarbons and damaging the Earth's ozone layer, skin cancer rates will rise all over the globe.

Students should realize that the solution of ecological problems requires both global agreements and the cooperation of people in local communities.

Contrasting perspectives on the ecological agenda

The issues that make up the ecological agenda arise from genuine concerns about the sustainability of modern society. Students should be aware both of these concerns and of the worldview that underlies them. They should also be exposed to the "other side." In this case the other side actually consists of a set of assumptions about the world that students are likely to share.

The most widely held perspective on ecological issues can be called the "modernist perspective." Despite their obviously great differences, capitalists, socialists, and most people who participate in the world system share this perspective. In essence, the modernist perspective grew out of the scientific and industrial revolutions. Its hallmark is an image of a future world in which abundance can be had by all if only we work hard enough. All modernists believe in economic growth, though they may disagree about how the economic system should be organized. They also believe that people should strive to satisfy all their material wants and needs.

The second perspective can be called the "ecological perspective." The keystone of this perspective is the belief that modern industrial society, both capitalist and socialist, is designed to exceed the carrying capacity of the planet. Thus ecologists believe that we need a new set of values that emphasize sustainable lifestyles. We need to accept lower material standards of living so that we will extend the life of our non-renewable resources and preserve the biological systems that give us our renewable resources.

The differences between modernists and ecologists are many, but the critical differences revolve around two questions. First, can technology save us from the natural limits to growth? Second, is economic and population growth good or bad?

Modernists can point to centuries of scientific and technological accomplishments as proof that modern industrial society can overcome any obstacle. If oil runs short, technology will find alternative sources. If food production falls behind population growth, bio-engineering will save the day. If pollution becomes life-threatening, we will create the technologies needed.

Modernists relaize that in order to invent these technologies, we need economic growth. Some argue we need population growth as well. Without economic growth, the money needed to invest in technological research and development will not be there. We will not be able both to sustain high living standards and to spend what is needed to produce new and more expensive technologies.

Ecologists doubt both the efficacy of technology and the wisdom of depending on economic growth. Economic and population growth merely push us closer to the planet's limits by increasing our use of natural resources. Also, do we really want to increase our dependence on technology? Can we increase food production fast enough to feed a world of 10 billion people, twice as large as today's? Might the danger of such technologies as fusion energy and bio-engineering be greater than their benefits? As problems multiply, can we produce the technology to solve all of our problems simultaneously?

For students the debate between modernists and ecologists can reveal why there is controversy about something so obviously wrong as hunger and "overpopulation." The two worldviews also help students to link assumptions about the world to practical policies and to link policies to their long-run implications (i.e., images of the future). This ability is critical to skillful decisionmaking.

The politics of the ecological agenda

Ecological issues have not been a traditional part of the agenda of world politics. Yet the ways in which the international system handles these issues is the central concern for international relations.

Unlike security or even development issues, the tendency for ecological issues to spill over national boundaries has led to an emphasis on multilateral rather than bilateral efforts to deal with them. On these issues, diplomacy between states, two at a time, gives way to simultaneous diplomacy among many states. Students can see the importance of multilateral diplomacy in the range of international conferences sponsored by the United Nations over the past two decades.

The World Population Conferences of 1974 and 1984 provide an excellent look at multilateral diplomacy. They also demonstrate how changeable perspectives on ecological issues can be and how difficult it can be to build a consensus on them. Although the 1974 conference did agree on a World Plan of Action, it did not create a consensus on the population problem. Indeed, by 1984 major actors, including the United States, had dramatically shifted their positions on the population issue, but consensus remained as elusive as ever.

In general, national governments have emphasized national solutions to the ecological issues despite their global nature, as was clearly evident at the World Population Conferences. This has also been the case with respect to the energy issue. The continuous dissension within OPEC, the quadrupling of oil prices in the 1970s, the failure of oil-consuming nations to work together, and the preference for nationalistic responses like Project Independence all demonstrate the dominance of national interest and national solutions. Students might use the energy issue to look at the pattern of interests among different actors. They might then be asked to construct and assess some set of rules or agreements for managing petroleum resources. The exercise would demonstrate how difficult it can be to achieve accommodations, even when cooperation would benefit everyone involved in the long run.

Finally, an important aspect of the politics of the global ecological agenda has been the critical role of non-governmental groups. Despite their wide diversity, virtually all national governments have pursued ecological policies based on modernist assumptions about the world. In this sense they have rarely tackled what ecologists regard as the significant long-run issues. Even in the case of energy, it was only short-run needs that encouraged a search for sustainable energy sources like solar power. When the crisis passed, interest in sustainable but less efficient energy sources evaporated.

The modernist perspective of national governments can also be clearly demonstrated in the area of environmental decay. Here the role of non-governmental groups comes to the fore as well. Third World governments have consistently denied the relevance of environmental problems. Despite horrendous pollution in major Third World cities, environmental quality has a far lower priority than economic and industrial development. Even in the First World, where environmental groups have been quite successful in getting national laws enacted, interest in the enforcement of anti-pollution laws typically waxes and wanes with the fortunes of the economy.

Thus non-governmental groups have taken the lead in placing environmental issues on the world's agenda. Students should be encouraged to find out about some of these groups, such as the Sierra Club, the Cousteau Society, the Nature Conservancy, Zero Population Growth, and the Club of Rome. They might explore how these groups raised the ecological agenda in the United States during the 1960s and early 1970s. They should be familiar with the Green Party in Germany as an offshoot of this multinational movement.

THE FUTURE OF THE INTERNATIONAL SYSTEM

Organizing an international relations course around key issues has one important drawback. It lacks a conclusion. Unlike historical approaches, in which the course naturally ends when you get to the present, a course organized around concepts or issues needs some device for tying the threads together. One such device could be an examination of current trends that foreshadow significant changes in the international system.

Of course, "significant changes" is far too broad an agenda to be left unstructured. Students' attention should be directed toward a specific change in question. For example, scholars have speculated about the future of the nation-state as the basis for organizing the world politically. Will it become more powerful and relevant, or less? Alternatively, scholars continue to explore whether the world is becoming a more or a less violent place. The degree of violent conflict has important implications for human survival in a nuclear age. Finally, students might ask whether current trends are leading to a world of poverty and misery or a world of wealth and prosperity. All three questions are related, and all three also rest on an understanding of where we have been historically, what the international system is like today, and what forces may present irresistible opportunities for change.

What trends, then, are important? International relations scholars have no better crystal ball than historians, geographers, or anthropologists. While the efforts of futurists provide useful grist for the mill, they too must be taken with a grain of salt. There are three trends, however, that may prove highly important to the future of the international system: (1) the further globalization of economic life, (2) changing technology, and (3) the increasing scope of international regimes.

Trend 1: The globalization of economic life

As students will have seen earlier in the course, the international system is characterized by a genuine world economy. However, globalization of economic life is a continuing process, not a completed one. In the United States there is a new awareness of the world economy and the impact it is likely to have on us. The shift to a service economy is in part an adjustment to the world economy. The decline and restructuring of manufacturing is also a response, as is the shift toward robotics. In businesses of all kinds, there is a new awareness of the importance of the international market. The impact goes beyond business. Churches have become more aware of global issues. Interest groups and individuals are finding or creating new international organizations as they discover problems that defy local or national solutions.

At the same time, a backlash has appeared. Protectionist sentiment has grown strong, not only in the United States but elsewhere in the world. Nostalgia for a simpler life has increased the appeal of patriotic sentiment. Even the resurgence of fundamentalist religions in the United States and elsewhere in part reflects the need for a unique national identity and a simpler life.

Students might explore these contrasting trends. They could see evidence of them in their own communities and schools. They could explore the implications of these trends in terms of the future of the nation-state and the stability of the world economy. Is the nation-state still a viable political unit within a global economy? Can the search for national identity and economic security be reconciled with the increasing scale of economic organization? Should we try to maintain the global economy?

Trend 2: Technological change

Technological change has become a way of life in the contemporary world. Many new technologies will have the potential for radically changing the shape of the international system, our perception of global issues, and our everyday lives.

Areas in which foreseeable technological breakthroughs could revolutionize aspects of our lives include biotechnology, superconductors, fusion energy, solar technologies, and supercomputers. Students might explore how these technologies would affect life within the international system. Will new communications and transportation technologies tie the world's nations even more closely together? Will biotechnology hold the promise of greatly expanded food production? Superconductors and changes in energy technology will create new industries and add extensive new energy resources, but will they also widen the gap between rich and poor?

The impact of new technologies on the distribution of power and resources within the international system is a key issue. Technological change has already increased the gap between the skilled and the unskilled in the United States. Will it create a permanent underclass of people who lack the education and skills to participate in the economy? In the world community, will new technologies only increase the development gap? Will they create additional conflict and additional momentum toward fundamental changes in the international economy? How can the benefits of new technologies be quickly distributed throughout the international system?

Trend 3: The increasing scope of international regimes

One of the chief implications of the growing world economy and increasing interdependence has been the increase in the number and scope of international regimes.

"International regimes" can be defined as the rules, expectations, and institutions that coordinate relations among actors in the international system. While states have studiously maintained their formal sovereignty in the modern world, they have also recognized the need to create mechanisms for making international activity more predictable. As a result, national governments have created a variety of regimes to manage and coordinate their actions: to permit mail to flow between nations, to coordinate international airline traffic, to coordinate the use of radio and television frequencies, to prevent the spread of nuclear weapons, and to manage our use of ocean resources.

Nation-states create regimes only when it is in their interest to do so. However, the growing number of regimes inevitably constrains national sovereignty. Precisely because it is in the interest of nation-states to abide by the regimes, these abrogations of sovereignty are not easily reversed.

Students might be exposed to some of the more important international regimes that have been created. They should understand the cumulative nature of this trend and explore its implications for radical change in the international system. Should we create more and more regimes to coordinate international activity? What is the impact of these regimes on the ability of states to govern themselves? In the long run, might regimes so constrain national power that some new form of international authority will be needed to coordinate the disparate regimes? Do regimes create the conditions for peace and in that way make us more secure?

The world in 2020

With these trends in mind, students should speculate on the shape of the world in the year 2020 or beyond. Will the world be facing the same problems, or will some of these problems have changed? Will changes in technology, the integration of the world economy, and the growth of international regimes have led to some new international system? How will the world be different? Are the differences desirable or not?

This final topic of the course should be seen as an opportunity for students to construct a realistic image of a future on the basis of what they have learned. Projecting these images of the future, perhaps in terms of scenarios of a future world order, can provide a critical exercise in citizenship and leadership. The exercise could not only help students summarize course learning; it could also give them an opportunity to set their own agendas for the future.

4. Annotated bibliography

Ambrose, Stephen E. *Rise to Globalism: American Foreign Policy Since 1939;* 4th revised ed. New York: Penguin Books, 1985. Unquestionably the most balanced and comprehensive history of U.S. foreign policy since World War II. Essential reading. Much of the book can be read by tenth-grade students.

Barraclough, Geoffrey. *An Introduction to Contemporary History.* Baltimore, Md.: Penguin Books, 1967. Defines the essential elements of the contemporary period in history (roughly 1890 to the present). An easy-to-read and reliable guide to twentieth-century international relations.

Brown, Lester R., et al. *State of the World 1986.* Washington, D.C.: Worldwatch Institute, 1986. An annual assessment of the political, military, and ecological state of the world. Written from a liberal viewpoint. It contains a great deal of useful and up-to-date information, as well as informative essays on contemporary issues.

Chirot, Daniel. *Social Change in the Twentieth Century.* New York: Harcourt Brace Jovanovich, 1977. An introductory college-level textbook on social change from a world systems point of view. Emphasizes how international political and economic forces shape developments within states and nations. Also looks at the role of the Second World in international relations.

Dyer, Gwynn. *War*. Homewood, Ill.: Dorsey Press, 1985. Traces the development of warfare from its ancient beginnings to our present nuclear stalemate. This book has useful accompanying materials, including a telecourse made up of eight one-hour programs, available from Films Incorporated Education, 1213 Wilmette Avenue, Wilmette, Ill. 60091.

George, Susan. *Feeding the Few: Corporate Control of Food*. Washington, D.C.: Institute for Policy Studies, 1979. A penetrating book that explores how international markets and the investment decisions of transnational agribusinesses shape world agricultural activity.

Haley, P. Edward, Keithly, David M., and Merritt, Jack, eds. *Nuclear Strategy, Arms Control, and the Future*. Boulder, Colo., and London: Westview Press, 1985. A useful collection of essays and documents by American and Soviet policymakers and policy implementors. A good source for contrasting Soviet and American perceptions and doctrines regarding security. Includes a glossary and chapter bibliographies. Many readings are short and could be assigned to students.

Harf, James E., and Trout, Thomas B. *The Politics of Global Resources: Energy, Environment, Population, and Food*. Durham, N.C.: Duke University Press, 1986. Examines the ecological issue areas from an international relations perspective. Part of a series of books published by Duke University Press. Four other books are devoted to individual ecological issues.

Kidron, Michael, and Segal, Ronald. *The State of the World Atlas*. New York: Simon & Schuster, 1981. An atlas of 65 world maps, beautifully produced, which describe the "state of the world." An excellent source of maps for introducing an international perspective. Available, along with a Teaching Guide, from the Center for Teaching International Relations, University of Denver.

Polanyi, Karl. *The Great Transformation: The Political and Economic Origins of Our Time*. Boston: Beacon Press, 1957. A great and long-ignored classic. Polanyi presents a challenging interpretation of the origins of the modern international system and its breakdown in World War II. The themes addressed are central to an understanding of the present world system.

Russett, Bruce, and Chernoff, Fred, eds. *Arms Control and the Arms Race*. New York: W.H. Freeman, 1985. A collection of articles from the journal *Scientific American*, focusing on SALT and START, arms control negotiations, and European security. For educators who wish to dig deeply into this most troublesome subject, this is the place to start.

Russett, Bruce, and Starr, Harvey. *World Politics: The Menu for Choice*, 2nd ed. New York and Oxford: W.H. Freeman, 1985. The best introductory college-level international relations textbook currently available. Widely used throughout the U.S. and other English-speaking countries.

Seligson, Mitchell A., ed. *The Gap Between Rich and Poor: Contending Perspectives on the Political Economy of Development*. Boulder, Colo.: Westview Press, 1984. Presents evidence on both sides of the debate on whether the gap between rich and poor is growing. The book critically examines the contending theories and policies that attempt to explain the origins of the gap and remedy it.

Sewall, John W., Feinberg, Richard E., and Kallab, Valeriana, eds. *U.S. Foreign Policy and the Third World: Agenda 1985–86*. New Brunswick, N.J. and Oxford, U.K.: Transaction Books, 1985. An annual publication of the Washington-based Overseas

Development Council. The book presents a series of articles on current problems of world development and the role of the United States from a liberal perspective. Each volume contains a glossary and an appendix that provide extensive data on the foreign assistance efforts of developed countries.

Southwick, Charles H., ed. *Global Ecology*. Sunderland, Mass.: Sinauer Associates, 1985. A comprehensive and balanced collection of recent evidence regarding the current state of the environment and long-term trends. Defines basic ecological terms and looks at divergent views on ecological policy.

Stavrianos, L.S. *Global Rift: The Third World Comes of Age*. New York: Norton, 1981. An historical account of the sources of the economic and political backwardness of less developed countries from a liberal-radical point of view. Particularly good at relating today's Third World protest and revolution to their historical origins.

Todaro, Michael P. *Economic Development in the Third World*, 2nd ed. New York and London: Longman, 1981. The best undergraduate college text on development economics. A place to start for those unfamiliar with this issue. Full of data and notable for its sympathy and understanding of the problems and points of view of less developed countries.

Wein, Barbara J., ed. *Peace and World Order Studies: A Curriculum Guide*, 4th ed. New York: World Policy Institute, 1984. A well-edited collection of more than one hundred college-level course syllabi in the areas of international relations, international political economy, global ecology, militarism and the arms race, and alternative futures. Also includes descriptions of global studies courses and programs at some 30 colleges and universities.

Weston, Burns H., ed. *Toward Nuclear Disarmament and Global Security: A Search for Alternatives*. Boulder, Colo.: Westview Press, 1984. An excellent and comprehensive collection of readings covering the nature of nuclear weapons, arms race processes, the nature of security and deterrence, disarmament and arms control as approaches to security, and the possibilities of global transformation. Includes extensive bibliographies and a useful glossary of key terms.

Zars, Belle, Wilson, Beth, and Phillips, Ariel. eds. *Education and the Threat of Nuclear War*. Cambridge, Mass.: Harvard Educational Review, 1985. A special issue of the *Harvard Educational Review* that clearly and non-ideologically discusses the dilemmas of teaching and learning in the nuclear age. Presents recent research on children's attitudes and fears. Also reviews teaching practice at all levels and critiques major published curricula. Very helpful for those concerned about the psychological impact of teaching children about war and nuclear weapons.

5. Content outline for an international relations course

UNIT I: THE WORLD TODAY

1. Differences within the world
   1.1 The countries of the world differ from each other culturally and racially
   Population distributions across countries and regions
   Differences in language, ethnicity, and race
   Differences in religion

    1.2 There are important economic and political differences as well
       Democratic and authoritarian governments
       Capitalist, socialist, and mixed economies
       Industrial and non-industrial economies
       Resource-rich and resource-poor
2. Relations among countries
    2.1 Differences across countries produce international relations
       Trade and investment
       Travel and communication
       War and diplomacy
       Interaction is international relations
    2.2 Differences across countries also affect international relationships
       Culture and communication problems
       Ideology, politico-economic systems, and conflict
       Resources, division of labor and national interests
    2.3 Two key political conflicts dividing the world reflect and reinforce these differences
       The East-West conflict
       The North-South conflict

UNIT II: THE INTERNATIONAL SYSTEM

1. The world as a system
    1.1 Thinking of the world as a system highlights the regularity of interactions among countries and their impact on each other
       The concept of a system
       Political interactions routinely distribute power and security among countries even without a world government
       Economic interactions distribute wealth and resources within the world system
       Cultural and social dimensions of the world system
       Interdependence and dependence within the world system
    1.2 The present global system emerged after 1850, although its origins are much older
       The state and capitalism in early modern Europe
       The nineteenth-century transportation revolution in railroads and steamships
       European imperialism after 1880 created a global economic and political system
       Improvements in communication and transportation have increased interaction
    1.3 The United States helped fashion some key parts of the international system after World War II, but not others
       American hegemony in the world
       American interest in an open economic system
       The United Nations system
       Decolonization
2. The variety of actors in the international system
    2.1 "Countries" are really "states"
       The essential characteristics of states
       National government and state power

The anti-apartheid movement
Support for the IRA
Human rights in the Soviet Union
Amnesty International

UNIT III: SECURITY AMONG STATES AND PEOPLES

1. The international context of security policy
   1.1 Security means protection against threats to basic national values by other international actors
       Basic values—physical safety, welfare, form of government
       Types of threats—subversion, terrorism, boycotts, war
   1.2 Governments and states exist to provide security for their citizens
       Cities and empires in the ancient world
       Conflict in Europe and the rise of nation-states
       The American Constitution and national security
   1.3 States must practice self-help because of the nature of the international system
       International anarchy and the doctrine of self-help
       Self-help and the threat of war
2. Differing approaches to achieving security
   2.1 Different states have different security needs
       Geography and security
       Local and regional conflicts
       The superpower conflict
       The balance between perceived threats and defense capabilities
   2.2 Virtually all states maintain some military forces
       Global military spending
       Japan and Switzerland
       Trends in military spending
   2.3 Garrison states practice extreme self-help
       Isolated states: Israel and South Africa
       Israeli self-sufficiency versus dependence on the outside world
   2.4 Alliances can be used to augment a state's military power
       Nineteenth-century alliances
       Why the United States and the Soviet Union have created alliances
       Why the Europeans joined NATO and the Warsaw Pact
   2.5 Some states try to insulate themselves from global or regional conflicts through neutrality or non-alignment
       The Swiss tradition of neutrality
       Indian neutrality in the East-West conflict
       The movement of non-aligned states
       Can neutralism and non-alignment work?
3. Nuclear weapons and security
   3.1 Nuclear weapons have changed the meaning and logic of national security policy
       Destructiveness of nuclear weapons

Delivery of nuclear weapons
Fighting a nuclear war
3.2 The United States and the Soviet Union compete in a nuclear and conventional arms race, driven by the doctrine of mutual deterrence
Arms races
Current stockpiles
Strategy of mutual deterrence
3.3 Technological and scientific change often make deterrence unstable
Stable and unstable deterrence
The impact of MIRVs
"Star Wars" and the future of deterrence
3.4 Arms control tries to create stable deterrence
Arms control versus disarmament
SALT and START
Can the Russians be trusted?
3.5 Many more states may acquire nuclear weapons in the future
Which states can do it or have done it?
Why might a state want nuclear weapons?
The effects of proliferation
The Nuclear Non-Proliferation Treaty
4. The social base and impact of national security policy
4.1 Many domestic groups try to influence security policy
Advocates of arms control, disarmament, and "freezes"
Advocates of nuclear war winning and peace through strength
4.2 Social and political norms affect the security policies of states
Nuclear war and "life, liberty, and the pursuit of happiness"
Soviet doctrines of nuclear war and deterrence
4.3 Security policy affects a nation's economy and society
The military-industrial complex
The garrison state
The Soviet standard of living
5. Alternative paths to security
5.1 International organizations have tried to provide collective security
The concert of Europe and efforts to create a security regime in the nineteenth century
Collective security and the League of Nations
The United Nations and its Security Council
5.2 Do greater contact and interaction lead to greater security?
Cultural and educational exchange
A world of peoples?
5.3 Can disarmament or national resistance provide the basis for national security?
Past disarmament efforts
Prospects for nuclear and conventional disarmament
Gandhi's alternative

UNIT IV: THE CHALLENGE OF DEVELOPMENT

1. World inequality
1.1 The world is a very unequal place and is growing more unequal

UNIT V: THE ECOLOGICAL AGENDA

Chapter 7
Measuring the Effectiveness of World Studies Courses

Judith Torney-Purta

1. Program evaluation

Offerings of world studies courses have expanded rapidly in secondary schools within the United States during the last decade. Despite their often enthusiastic reception, however, there has been little attempt to measure the extent to which these courses actually help students to understand the world better. Only minimal information exists about the extent to which given program goals are being implemented or about the effectiveness of different types of approaches. Yet such information should be of great interest to administrators, supervisors, staff developers, evaluators, and school board members.

This chapter deals with ways of assessing the effectiveness of world studies courses. This type of assessment has been called "program evaluation." Program evaluation, and this chapter, do not deal with testing aimed primarily at giving grades to individual students or at evaluating teachers.

THE LACK OF ASSESSMENT EFFORTS

There are several reasons why there have been relatively few assessments of the effectiveness of world studies programs. Evaluation systems exist in many districts, but they are often best adapted to measuring the implementation and outcomes of long-established courses such as biology and American history. These systems are rarely designed to measure the effectiveness of world history courses, let alone the more novel approaches to world studies described in this handbook. Likewise, existing evaluation methods often do not assess skills (such as critical thinking or the ability to see a problem from another culture's perspective) or attitudes (such as support for international cooperation) that may be important objectives of world studies courses. In fact, the general absence of valid and readily available instruments for testing those knowledge, skill, and attitudinal objectives that might be appropriate to a world studies course is one of the major reasons so little measurement of course effectiveness has taken place. Many project directors have had to choose between using an instrument that was poorly adapted to their program's objectives or creating new questions without sufficient time, expertise, or resources to validate them.

ASSESSMENT AS PART OF CURRICULUM DESIGN

Ideally, program evaluation should be built into a course development effort from its inception. This is in part so that baseline information about teachers and students can be collected before the program is implemented. Early attention to evaluation also ensures that the evaluator understands why the goals and objectives have been defined as they have been and why given content areas or methodologies have been selected. It can also ensure that those designing and implementing the curriculum have some input to the evaluation process.

If the individual responsible for evaluation cannot be present from early in the program planning, it is essential that there be briefings about the goals and objectives that have been selected once he or she does arrive. Many potential problems in evaluations can be minimized by good communication among evaluators, curriculum specialists, and teachers. Indeed, all participants should see themselves as evaluators.

Similarly, it is important that resources for evaluation be allocated from a project's inception. Evaluation is rarely successful if resources must be pieced together from funds remaining after the program has been developed.

Thinking about program evaluation from the very start can usefully orient the entire process of program design. What are the goals of the course? Would a single approach serve those goals, or should a blend of approaches be adopted? What are the relative merits of different approaches? By focusing on evaluation, individuals with different opinions and responsibilities can explicitly discuss which goals are most appropriate for their district. In some districts the major focus will be on ensuring that students have knowledge of the major forces and events in world history. In other districts motivating students to obtain a variety of points of view on global issues and to examine them critically will be seen as of greatest value. Nearly all evaluation approaches that use goals and objectives as their starting point can be part of a coherent program development effort from its inception.

One technique for integrating evaluation into program design is to ask planners (teachers, supervisors, or members of the community) to project themselves into the future by two or three years. How would they judge the success of the world studies program they are planning? Would higher student scores on a knowledge test of place-name geography or important dates in world history be sufficient evidence of success? Would they also want students to understand the influence of climatic conditions on economic productivity or the differences in Western and non-Western approaches to issues? What importance would they attach to enhancing students' motivation to read international news in the newspaper, or to raising teachers' confidence about their ability to lead discussions on global issues, or to increasing students' tolerance of the views of others?

In summary, curriculum goals and objectives can often be clarified by beginning to look at how their success will be evaluated. At the same time, concrete suggestions about how to measure course effectiveness will be generated. If teachers as well as school district personnel are involved in this process, they are more likely to participate willingly in evaluation and to use the resulting information to improve their program.

The integration of program evaluation throughout curriculum planning is related to the process of "formative evaluation." That term has usually meant that there is feedback from an evaluation process at one or more points during the implementation of the project, not merely at the end (summative evaluation). What is proposed here is evaluation or assessment that is interwoven with program design at all phases, including the earliest phase, when program goals and objectives are being set.

2. Principles for assessment planning

Recent educational research, including research on program evaluation efforts, suggests at least four key principles that should guide the planning and implementation of assessment efforts.

PRINCIPLE 1: THERE IS NO SINGLE METHOD OF ASSESSING CURRICULUM IMPLEMENTATION OR MEASURING COURSE OUTCOMES THAT WILL BE UNIVERSALLY APPROPRIATE. There are many models of program assessment. Most of these evaluation designs include assessments of (1) the context of the program, (2) the input, (3) the process, and (4) the expected product. However, the perspective from which these elements are assessed varies greatly from one model to another. Past efforts to assess world studies programs have generally faced twin problems. On the one hand, they have attempted to find simple answers about program effectiveness using instruments not well matched to a given program's content. On the other hand, they have sometimes produced exaggerated generalizations based on insufficient data. In general, the most useful and satisfying evaluations are those in which the measures of outcomes or products are carefully tailored to the objectives and content of the program being evaluated.

A number of instruments and procedures for measuring the effectiveness of world studies programs have been created over the years. If combined with thoughtful reflection about specific program goals, these instruments and procedures may have great utility for program evaluators. Thus educators responsible for program evaluation can benefit from networking with other evaluators and sharing information on instruments, data, and interpretations.

PRINCIPLE 2: PLANNING FOR THE ASSESSMENT SHOULD BEGIN EARLY IN THE PROJECT AND SHOULD TAKE PLACE IN PHASES. The interweaving of evaluation and program planning should, if possible, take place throughout the project. Guides to evaluation usually break down the process into four phases.

First, one must focus the evaluation by deciding what its purpose is and what critical questions are to be answered. What are the objectives of the program to which the evaluation design must be tailored?

Second, one must design the evaluation. This involves making basic decisions about overall strategies and scope. Often individuals from local colleges or universities—both faculty and advanced undergraduates or graduate students—can be usefully involved in this process. It also involves making decisions about the collection of information. What groups will be assessed, and how will a sample be chosen? How often and when will groups be assessed? For example, will assessments take place at the beginning and end of a semester, or only at the end? What methods will be used—observation, questionnaires, interviews? Do the available methods closely match the purposes of the program and the evaluation? Are the measures objective, reliable, and valid? What methods will have to be newly developed? Which methods can be adapted from existing techniques? There are three key criteria for judging the adequacy of the resulting design. First, is it relevant to answering the basic questions posed? Second, is it flexible enough to accommodate unexpected problems? Third, is it feasible?

Third, one must decide how the data are to be analyzed. This includes plans for coding and computer analysis as well as the interpretation of the data collected.

Finally, one must write and disseminate the evaluation report. Sometimes several reports must be prepared, each tailored to the needs of specific audiences.

PRINCIPLE 3: WHENEVER FEASIBLE, SEVERAL METHODS SHOULD BE USED FOR GATHERING INFORMATION ABOUT BOTH THE IMPLEMENTATION OF A CURRICULUM AND ITS OUTCOMES IN TERMS OF STUDENT LEARNING. The use of multiple methods has been likened to "taking out insurance on usefulness." It is sometimes referred to as "triangulation"— meaning the use of at least three measures, such as student surveys, teacher interviews, and classroom observation.

Multiple methods are useful in part because there are built-in sources of error in any method of data collection. Observational methods can lack objectivity or specificity. Interview questions may be worded in a misleading way. Written instruments may suffer from students' limitations in reading ability. Thus using only one type of question or one individual's rating of a program's success may result in distorted findings or in a list of new questions that cannot be answered with the available data.

PRINCIPLE 4: TEACHERS WHO ARE IMPLEMENTING THE CURRICULUM SHOULD ALSO BE INVOLVED IN THE PROCESS OF EVALUATING IT. The building of trust between program evaluators and the teachers or administrators carrying out the program is essential in making evaluation integral to course design and implementation. In addition to being involved in formulating goals, objectives, and criteria, teachers can and should be encouraged to undertake research or evaluation projects in their own classrooms as part of the evaluation process. These research projects may be conducted individually or in teams.

The information teachers collect can be the starting point for reflection on the strengths and weaknesses of the curriculum. It can also provide data to be examined by someone who plays the more traditional role of evaluator. For example, material such as answers to open-ended questions, which teachers originally collected as class assignments to assess the students individually, can be used later as a measure of group outcomes.

3. Types of measures for evaluating world studies programs

As the bibliography for this chapter indicates, there are many sources of information on general evaluation design and on assessing the organizational context of schools. There are very few sources of information on how to collect data on world studies programs. This section will deal with how to measure curriculum implementation and outcomes that are likely to be important for several of the specific approaches to world studies described in this volume. It cannot be stressed too much, however, that program evaluation methods must be tailored to the particular construction of a course or curriculum. These are examples of possible approaches, not sets of questions ready for use by program evaluators.

MEASURES OF CURRICULUM IMPLEMENTATION

There has been little published research about the implementation of various world studies approaches in actual classroom settings. Yet implementation is obviously a key concern. Simply saying that world geography or world history is the title of the course is no guarantee of learning opportunities for students.

Whether or not the learning objectives of a world studies course are met will in part depend on whether the program is actually implemented. Students obviously cannot be expected to learn in school what is not taught there. Unless assessment of implementation is included in the evaluation, it is impossible to judge the success or failure of the program. Thus a key question in any evaluation is whether the program is being taught in a way that closely resembles how it was designed to be taught.

At least three questions should be addressed when assessing program implementation. First, were the student materials used? Second, to what degree were materials used as intended? If they were not used as intended, why not? For example, were they too hard for the students? Was there not enough time? Did teachers lack confidence in their appropriateness? Third, to what degree were the suggested pedagogical techniques actually followed?

Even if a full study of program implementation is beyond the resources of a district, some information from teachers about their perceptions of the program is always better than no information at all.

Assessing students' opportunity to learn

There are several standard methods that can provide useful information about program implementation.

Observational techniques are clearly useful in assessing what is actually taking place in the classroom. The reliability of observational data can be increased by using several individuals with different points of view as observers. Some districts may also have the resources to hire individuals outside the system to conduct classroom observations. If there are trusting relationships between teachers, they may be able to observe each other in the classroom. Whenever an observational method is undertaken, a form for recording observations should be used. The form should focus on objectives that the observed teacher has accepted. The information should also be kept confidential.

In the absence of funds to hire outside observers, or as a supplementary source of information, teachers can also be asked to generate data on how often they use the course outline or associated materials. This information can be collected in a checklist that asks how often each type of material was used, and if it was not used, why not. Interviews either in person or by phone are also an appropriate way to collect this type of information. Teachers can be asked a series of open-ended questions about their implementation of the program. Questions such as the following are sometimes appropriate: "If an observer had visited your class before you adopted the new approach and again this year, what would he or she see that would be different?"

In conjunction with the preparation of criterion-referenced tests (described in the next section), one can also collect ratings from teachers, or a subset of students, about whether particular topics or objectives were actually taught in class. In other words, to what degree did students have the opportunity to learn the information or skill being tested? Teachers can be instructed as follows:

> Please look over this test but do not answer the questions. (Correct answers are indicated.) Indicate by circling one number next to each question the degree to which the average student in your world studies class this year had the opportunity to learn the information or skill necessary to answer the question correctly.

Each item can then be presented with the correct answer indicated and with the following scale: (4) students had a lot of opportunity to learn this; (3) students had some opportunity to learn this; (2) students had a little opportunity to learn this; (1) students had no opportunity to learn this. Teachers may also be instructed in how to interpret the scale. For example, "a lot" of opportunity to learn may mean that the topic was taught and reviewed several times. "Some" opportunity may mean that the topic was taught, but not with consistent review. "A little" opportunity may mean that the topic was mentioned but not specifically taught.

Assessing implementation using teachers' logs

For many teachers, world studies will be a new course in an area with which they have little familiarity or training. They may be very certain of their knowledge and associated pedagogy in some areas, and very uncertain in others. They may believe that some concepts contained in the course outline are too difficult for their students. Because of this, it is very useful to ask teachers to keep logs of their experience with the world studies course and to share their information at several points during the school year.

The guidelines below have been adapted from instructions that are routinely given to teachers involved in the California International Studies Project.

> It is our belief that you are the best source of information about how you respond to materials, people, and staff development activities. Therefore, in a notebook, we would like you to keep a dated, running log of professional and classroom activities that are related to the world studies approach you are using.
>
> Suggestions for log entries include: (1) records of your in-class use of lessons, units, or other instructional materials—especially non-textbook materials—that have been suggested; (2) adaptations in these lessons, materials, or approaches that you feel would make the lesson more suitable for your class or for meeting specific objectives in your situation; (3) students' reactions to different instructional strategies (e.g., role playing, small group discussions, divergent thinking activities) or the use of visual or cultural resources (e.g., maps, slides, artifacts, international visitors), noting in particular the proportion of the class that was involved and any problems that students encountered in achieving the objectives of the activity;

(4) anecdotes or quotations describing noteworthy student responses, learning, or insights.

Most entries should be divided into two parts. The first should be a straightforward description of what took place. The second should be your assessment, comment, or interpretation.

Logs such as these, especially if discussed by groups of teachers, can be outstanding sources of information about which parts of the world studies approach are being implemented successfully (from the teacher's point of view) and about those parts that seem to require further teacher education.

Assessing teachers' workshops

The degree of program implementation will vary in part with teachers' confidence in their understanding of the subject matter and associated instructional techniques. If workshops are given, it is useful to know how teachers judge their knowledge both before and after the workshop.

A technique such as the following can be used to assess the impact of teachers' workshops.

On a scale from 1 to 9, with 9 representing a very high level of knowledge or confidence, please rate the following by circling one number in each line:

How much knowledge do you presently have about the agricultural revolution and its impact on world history?

1 2 3 4 5 6 7 8 9

The specific topics addressed would depend on the particular world studies approach to be used. It is best if the topic is stated as a relatively specific concept that received attention during the workshop.

A similar scale can be used to let teachers assess their confidence in performing various types of classroom activities:

How confident are you of your ability to correct stereotypes or misconceptions that students have about other countries?

1 2 3 4 5 6 7 8 9

This type of rating technique can also be used to assess teachers' confidence with respect to the use of unfamiliar methodology. (How confident are you of your ability to use a role-playing situation to meet a content objective with your class?) It can even measure their confidence in teaching certain skill objectives. (How confident are you of your ability to teach students to use atlases or to read and interpret maps?)

Ratings such as these are easy to collect. About forty scales can be completed in ten minutes. One could administer an instrument using these scales before the first in-service workshop, after the conclusion of major in-service workshops, and again after there has been an opportunity to work with the curriculum in the classroom.

Because many of the concepts dealt with in the world studies approaches described in this volume will be new to teachers, it is important to communicate that they are not expected to have all the necessary knowledge and confidence in advance and that the assessment is not aimed at them individually. It is also important to assess the levels of knowledge and skill the teachers believe that they have at several points during the implementation of the curriculum. A successful workshop experience may sensitize teachers to what they do not know or to the complexity of the subject. This can lead to artificial drops in post-test ratings.

Assessing classroom climate

Most approaches to world studies require a classroom atmosphere in which students are free to discuss ideas and to question the opinions presented by the teacher, other students, or the textbook. Therefore some measures of the classroom climate for discussion will also be important.

The IEA Civic Education study (Torney, Oppenheim, and Farnen, 1975) used items such as the following to measure how much independent expression of opinion was encouraged in the classroom.

- Teachers try to get students to speak freely and openly in class.
- Students can feel free to disagree openly with their teachers.
- Students are encouraged to make up their own minds.
- Knowing the reason for events is more important than memorizing facts and definitions.

These types of statements can be used as the basis for observational methods or in written surveys in which teachers or students are asked to agree or disagree with a given statement.

MEASURES OF STUDENTS' KNOWLEDGE AND SKILLS

Enhancing students' knowledge of the world, its history, its geography, and the way it is governed are major knowledge objectives of world studies courses. Major skill objectives include such things as developing students' ability to explain historical events, recognize biases, interpret information on maps, and systematically compare and contrast cultures. How is attainment of these knowledge and skill objectives to be measured? This section will discuss the use of criterion-referenced tests, multiple-choice items, and open-ended techniques to assess knowledge and skill outcomes of world studies courses.

Criterion-referenced tests of knowledge

Much of the current concern about the poor preparation of young people with respect to world studies has been generated by findings that many students do not have basic factual knowledge of the world, nor are they able to comprehend basic concepts used in the discussion of world issues.

Criterion-referenced testing can be an especially useful technique for assessing this dimension of the effectiveness of world studies courses.

A "criterion-referenced test" is constructed to assess performance levels in relation to a set of well-defined objectives or competencies, identified prior to instruction. Criterion-referenced tests are often distinguished from "norm-referenced tests" (usually published standardized tests) in which student performance is compared with that of a large normative group. It is important to note, however, that students can be compared with each other on a criterion-referenced test as well as on norm-referenced tests.

Criterion-referenced tests can often take advantage of available standardized tests. However, only those parts of the standardized tests that closely match classroom or district objectives will be useful. Thus it is almost inevitable that some parts of a criterion-referenced test will have to be developed within the school district.

The preparation of items for criterion-referenced tests can be undertaken by evaluation specialists or by teachers themselves, with some guidance in the technical aspects of item and test construction. In criterion-referenced testing the domain, objective, or major idea is defined as unambiguously as possible. After the definition has been clearly stated, questions can be generated.

Multiple-choice questions dealing with basic factual information are relatively easy to construct. The process is to construct a test item with one clearly correct expression of the major idea and, if possible, with wrong answers representing major misconceptions a student might have. For example, one of the major ideas or content objectives of a recently developed state syllabus is that "the student should appreciate the quality of technological and cultural development of pre-Columbian societies." An item to measure students' achievement of that objective might be the following:

> Farming in Latin America at the time of the Spanish colonialization: (1) included advanced methods developed in that region for farming in swampy and mountainous areas; (2) improved markedly after the importation of cows and horses from Europe; (3) depended on methods of terracing originally developed in North America; (4) was less important than fishing.

The correct answer is (1). Choices (2) and (3) present statements reflecting a potential misconception, that advanced farming methods would have either a European or North American basis. This item is factual, but given the state's curriculum objectives, it measures a more important idea than an idea that merely asked students whether cows and horses were imported from Europe.

The development of items measuring concept attainment is somewhat more difficult. It requires an ability to unequivocally define the attributes of the concept. Only then can students be tested as to their ability to recognize those attributes or distinguish concepts on the basis of differing attributes.

The following example demonstrates a two-stage format for defining the objective and domain and generating appropriate test questions for the concept of irrigation.

> The pupil will demonstrate that he or she holds the concept irrigation, defined as having two attributes: first, the application of water to crops; and second, used at times when the natural water supply is insufficient for crops' requirements.
>
> How will acceptable performance be recognized? The pupil will correctly discriminate between positive and negative examples of the concept irrigation in a multiple-choice or true/false test in which approximately equal numbers of positive and negative instances are included. [Modified from Black and Dockrell, 1984, p. 55.]

This format was developed in response to problems Black and Dockrell encountered in instructing teachers to write criterion-referenced items. In one instance, for example, an objective was that students understand the concept of the Third World. The following item was written:

> Mexico is a poor country, but its people have a higher standard of living than many other poor nations. What is the best explanation for this? (1) it is near the USA; (2) most of its people speak Spanish; (3) it sells oil to other countries; (4) it has a large area; (5) it has many beautiful mountains.

While this may be an adequate question for testing basic factual material covered in a world studies course, it does not assess whether the student understands the concept of the Third World. Black and Dockrell concluded that more appropriate items would be written if domain definitions clearly set out the criteria for defining the concept. Positive and negative instances of the concept could then be generated.

Ideally, as part of curriculum planning in the school district, a group (including teachers and curriculum specialists) would generate a set of knowledge items related to each major area covered in the world studies course. In parts of the course where the textbook was closely related to the outline, items from the teachers' guide could be considered for use in a criterion-referenced test. A pool of two to three times as many items as one wished to have in the final test should be generated. Each item or set of items would be referenced to a specific domain or objective. All items would then be reviewed for appropriate content.

All multiple-choice items should also be reviewed in terms of criteria of good item construction. For example, the stem of the item should in most cases include the subject and verb so that the answer alternatives can be shorter. Negatively stated items should be avoided or stated as: "All of the following are true EXCEPT." There should be one and only one answer that is clearly the best answer. It should be an answer on which both sources and experts agree. Finally, all incorrect alternatives should be plausible—if possible, representing a common misperception.

As a final step in test development, all items should be administered to a small group of students. Items that are either too easy (95 percent or more of the students answer them correctly) or apparently confusing should be eliminated or rephrased.

Even with limited resources, key parts of this process can be implemented. Then a reasonable if not elaborate criterion-referenced measure of knowledge will be available for assessing course effectiveness. Perhaps equally important, those who have participated in the test construction will have gained a much clearer understanding of the course content.

Multiple-choice items measuring critical thinking skills

For several decades the development of critical thinking has been included on lists of objectives in the social studies. Some of the current interest in these skills coincides with advances by cognitive psychologists in understanding how individuals encode information and arrive at solutions to problems. It is only within the last few years that reasonably valid and reliable paper-and-pencil measures of critical thinking skills have been developed. Norris (1986) has reviewed tests for evaluating students' success in the process of critical thinking. Some of these tests may be useful to districts wishing to assess students' abilities to do such things as draw suitable inferences, recognize assumptions, and evaluate arguments.

The California State Department of Education has recently developed an eighth grade test in history and social sciences that also includes a substantial section for assessing critical thinking skills. Seventy school districts participated in field testing the California state test. Three general categories of critical thinking skills are identified. The first category is "Defining and Clarifying the Problem":

> ... identifying the central issue or problem, for example, in a political argument or the point of a political cartoon; comparing similarities and differences between people, ideas or events; determining which information is relevant in a given situation; formulating appropriate questions which will lead to a deeper and clearer understanding of an issue or situation; expressing problems clearly and concisely.

Multiple-choice items have been developed for all except the last skill. One of the illustrative items to assess formulating appropriate questions presents a map of Central Europe in 1935 and in 1949. The question is as follows:

> Which of the following questions might lead to a better understanding of the relationship between these two maps? (1) Who is the present political leader of Poland?; (2) What are the main differences between the governments of Hungary and Rumania?; (3) Is Czechoslovakia a major world power?; *(4) What happened in Central Europe between 1935 and 1949?

A second category of critical thinking skills on the California state test is called "Judging Information Related to the Problem":

... distinguishing among fact, opinion, and reasoned judgement; checking consistency, for example, between statements; identifying unstated assumptions; recognizing stereotypes and cliches; recognizing bias, emotional factors, propaganda, and semantic slanting; recognizing value orientations and ideologies, their similarities and differences.

Sample questions released by the California State Department of Education deal with domestic rather than international issues. Nonetheless, they could serve as models for further question development. For example, one could ask:

> Which of the following statements about Japan is a fact rather than an opinion? *(1) The Japanese consistently export more goods to the U.S. than they import from the U.S.; (2) The Japanese engage in many unfair trading practices; (3) U.S. companies should take Japanese business practices as a model; (4) 1, 2, and 3 are all facts.

Some test development specialists prefer not to use an "all of the above" option, like option (4) above. Others, like myself, find that when they are plausible, such options successfully distinguish students with well-developed understandings from those who have some major misunderstandings as well as from those who stop reading when they come to the first plausible alternative.

A final category of critical thinking skills in the California state test is "Solving Problems/Drawing Conclusions":

> ... recognizing the adequacy of data from graphs, identifying reasonable alternatives, testing conclusions or hypotheses, and predicting probable consequences.

Multiple-choice techniques are used to measure all except the last skill.

Although not traditionally included in tests of critical thinking, the ability to take the perspective of someone else in looking at a situation or problem is a cognitive skill of special importance in world studies. Some attempts have been made to measure this skill. For example, items might ascertain whether students realize that people in another country are likely to prefer their own customs.

Open-ended techniques assessing knowledge and skills

Multiple-choice questions are limited in their ability to assess certain types of skills and certain levels of knowledge. In many of these instances open-ended techniques can fill the gap. In some cases it may even be possible to generate multiple-choice items by examining students' responses to open-ended questions.

One key contribution that open-ended techniques can make is suggested by current research on the distinction between novice and expert "thinking patterns." What is it that distinguishes the answers of individuals with a high level of training in a field when compared with individuals who do not have such training? In research conducted by Voss, Tyler, and Yengo (1983), undergraduates taking a course on domestic Soviet policy and faculty members specializing in the Soviet Union were asked to solve this problem:

> Assume you are the head of the Soviet Ministry of Agriculture, and crop productivity has been low over the past several years. You have the responsibility of increasing crop production. How would you go about this?

Respondents were to think aloud while solving the problem. What they said was recorded.

The experts spent a large proportion of their time developing a representation of the problem and identifying constraints on solutions. These included such things as Soviet ideology and the negative outcomes of solutions attempted in the past. By the time this problem representation was complete, the expert had usually delineated the problem carefully enough to identify a cause. Solutions could then be derived, taking various constraints into account.

By contrast, the novices were more likely to suggest specific solutions in a more or less random way. They had little concern for an overall representation of the problem or for constraints on their suggested solutions.

Although world studies courses are not trying to turn students into experts, Voss' findings are instructive. They suggest that it is important to assess the representation of the world to which students assimilate individual facts and concepts. An important and potentially measurable criterion for the success of a world studies course is the extent to which students can reason out problems in an organized way and visualize constraints on solutions.

One evaluation system that attempts to get at such complex levels of understanding is the Structure of Observed Learning Outcome or SOLO Taxonomy (Biggs and Collis, 1982). In this system, responses to open-ended written questions are classified on a scale that ranges from Prestructural to Extended Abstract. Each level is defined by students' use of data and arguments to support a position and by their ability to generalize. Specific examples from this work are given below in the sections on the Western civilization and world geography approaches.

MEASURES OF STUDENTS' INTERESTS AND ATTITUDES

Attitudes and motivation are sometimes seen as the soft side of social studies evaluation. There is a feeling in many school districts that change in attitudes about world issues is not an appropriate objective of world studies courses. Further, there is a continuing debate in the psychological literature concerning the relationship of attitudes, as measured in pencil-and-paper tests, to behavior.

Nonetheless, all the approaches to world studies described in this handbook share certain attitudinal goals. For example, they all seek to encourage students to become more interested in learning about their own nation's behavior in the context of other nations. This goal can be seen in objectives like the following: The course will enhance students' interest in taking further world studies either in high school or college; will increase students' interest in reading the newspaper or watching television programs dealing with international issues; will make students more likely to participate in discussions of these issues with family and friends; or will make students more likely to seek out and critically evaluate the ideas and perspectives of individuals from other countries, either interpersonally or in their reading.

While homework assignments, tests, and grades serve as extrinsic motivation for students to learn about the world during their school years, the long-range aim of education is to foster intrinsic motivation to learn outside the classroom. There are few extrinsic rewards for informed citizenship. Enhancing intrinsic motivation, interest, and curiosity about the world is thus a major aim of world studies courses and has often been linked with greater interest in domestic politics as well. Ideally a world studies course will arouse students' interest so that they go on to complete the partial mental picture or representation of the world they have begun to build during the course.

Apart from motivation and interest in world studies, attitudes toward international cooperation and the problems of developing countries may also be influenced by world studies courses. One key attitude is sometimes phrased in a negative form as "ethnocentrism" or "national chauvinism." In a positive form it may be called "the ability to appreciate cultural diversity" or "enlightened patriotism." The history of attempts to measure this constellation of attitudes goes back at least forty years to the F-scale, a measure of authoritarianism and ethnocentrism that has been both extensively used and criticized. Studies of attitudes toward people in other nations have also developed a variety of stereotyping scales, but there have been serious problems with many of them as well.

Measures of international interest

There are many questionnaires in the research literature that are designed to assess attitudes toward school subjects. A questionnaire specific to world studies is preferable to more general instruments that assess whether students like social studies more than some other subject.

In all attitude measures based on self-report, it is important for students to be informed that these questions do not have right or wrong answers and that their responses will be anonymous. There will always be a tendency for some students to present their attitudes in a favorable light, but research with high school as well as with college students suggests that most of the responses on these scales are relatively accurate self-reports. In the Study of Stanford and the Schools, for example, some students responding to an open-ended question about interest in world affairs said that they did not see much reason for them to be concerned with such things. Their responses were consistent with findings on a ten-item scale measuring interest and concern about international issues.

There are two approaches to measuring interest or intrinsic motivation. One could give students a brief questionnaire early in the school year and repeat the questionnaire near the end of the year, looking for changes in interest and motivation. Alternatively, one could question students only at the end of the year about how much they believe their interest has changed. The pre- and post-test design is somewhat stronger, but may not always be feasible. Assuming a pre- and post-test, one might include the following types of questions on both surveys:

> How likely are you to take further elective world studies courses? (4) almost certain, (3) very likely, (2) somewhat likely, (1) not likely.

It might also be of interest to ask whether students would be likely to take world studies courses on different topics. For example, are you likely to take courses dealing with developing countries, courses dealing with Asia, courses dealing with international current events, or courses dealing with world geography? Some programs have the dual aim of interesting students both in courses in the content of world studies and in foreign languages. Students could be asked at the beginning and end of the year how many years of foreign language they expect to take.

Attention to media reports on international affairs is another important dimension of international interest. How often a student reads the newspaper or how much attention a student pays to international news has generally shown a positive relationship to knowledge about international issues. A variety of items can be used to measure media interest. For example:

> How often do you read the newspaper? (4) every day; (3) 4 to 5 days a week; (2) 1 to 3 days a week; (1) very seldom.
>
> How much attention do you pay to international news when you read the newspaper? (4) I read it and pay the most attention to it; (3) I read it but pay equal attention to other sections; (2) I read it but don't pay as much attention to it as to other sections; (1) I don't read international news.

Similar questions can be asked about watching television news.

The IEA Civic Education project (Torney, Oppenheim, and Farnen, 1975) used a slightly more direct measure of interest in international topics, asking students to rate how likely they were to watch a television program on a specific topic, national or international. For example, students might be asked to rate a program about hunger and poverty in other countries and also a program about hunger and poverty in the United States. They might also be asked about their interest in watching programs about the cultural heritage of India. In questions using television program titles such as this, however, it is often a good idea to include some topics that are not politically relevant, such as programs dealing with human interest. One should avoid listing topics in which boys and girls tend to have different levels of interest, such as sports.

An approach similar to these self-report rating scales can also be used to measure interest in participating in discussions about international issues. For example,

> How often do you talk about world issues with your parents? (1) almost never; (2) once a month; (3) once every two weeks; (4) once each week; (5) several times each week.
>
> How often do you talk about world issues with your friends (outside of the classroom)? (Same scale.)

The same pair of questions can be asked about how often national political issues are discussed. Then a comparison can be made between types of issues. In this and other dimensions of interest, one would expect higher scores at the end of the year if a course stimulated intrinsic interest on the part of students.

A final dimension of intrinsic interest that program evaluators may want to measure can be called "global concern." The following seven items, selected and adapted from items originally used by the Educational Testing Service (Barrows, 1981), could be used with the following response format: (1) True about me, (2) Not sure, (3) False about me.

> 1) The fact that a flood can kill 25,000 people in India is very depressing to me (True indicating global concern); 2) I am most comfortable with people from my own culture (False indicating global concern); 3) I feel that I am basically very similar to students my age in other countries (True); 4) When I hear that thousands of people are starving in another country, I feel very frustrated (True); 5) I feel it is a waste of my time to learn about other cultures (False); 6) I have almost nothing in common with people in poor countries (False); 7) I make an effort to meet people from other countries or cultures whenever I can (True).

This scale would have a range from 7 to 21. If used as a early-year/late-year measure, it has enough range to be sensitive to possible changes. In a school with large numbers of immigrant students, it would be possible to add additional items dealing with the extent to which respondents include these students in their activities.

In some cases it may not be possible to give measures of interest and motivation both at the beginning and at the end of the school year. In that case, questions such as the following can be used at the end of the year:

> I am more interested in reading international news in the newspaper than I was at the beginning of the year: (4) strongly agree; (3) agree; (2) disagree; (1) strongly disagree; I can better understand the international news in the newspaper than

I could at the beginning of the year (same responses); I am more likely to take additional courses in world studies than I was before taking this course (same responses).

Some type of assessment of motivation and interest should be part of every evaluation of world studies. If no intrinsic motivation is generated by a course, its value in the long-term education of citizens will be severely limited.

Measures of attitudes toward issues

Whether or not change in attitudes toward international issues is conceived of as a goal of a world studies course, it can be useful for program evaluators to know what impact courses are having on students' attitudes.

One key issue that emerges from all five of the approaches outlined in this volume is the value of international cooperation in solving problems. Another attitude that all these approaches address is related to the belief that citizens should be knowledgeable about foreign policy and ready to express their opinions about it. Associated with this are attitudes toward the responsiveness of the government to input from citizens. There are many examples of items measuring these types of attitudes. A sample can be found in Torney, Oppenheim, and Farnen (1975).

The measurement of attitudes and attitude change with respect to issues such as these has most often relied on agree/disagree items. The following items, for example, were used with a group of eighth to eleventh graders involved in a program called the Maryland Summer Center for International Studies:

> An international authority should be established and given direct control over the production of nuclear energy in all the countries of the world: (1) strongly agree: (2) agree: (3) don't know; (4) disagree; (5) strongly disagree.
>
> Citizens should consider the impact foreign policy decisions might have on less powerful and poorer countries before deciding whether to support those decisions. (Same scale.)

Note that the statements are relatively simple in structure. These two items were selected from a much larger group of available items because they tend to go together. In other words, students who agree with the need for an international energy authority also tend to believe that citizens should consider the impact of foreign policy on less powerful countries. To form a reliable scale, these items should be supplemented with items assessing other dimensions of the attitude in which the evaluator is interested.

This type of agree/disagree item, often called a Likert item, is difficult to write in an unambiguous fashion. (See Mueller, 1986, for a complete discussion of the process for developing a Likert scale.) Items that include negatives (for example, "Developing countries are not very important to the world economy") may be especially confusing.

A more sensitive way to measure attitudinal goals may be to use specific labels for each alternative rather than an agree/disagree format. In this format, a hypothetical situation would be posed, followed by specific questions about the situation. For example,

In an ideal situation, how important would each of the following be in making decisions about U.S. foreign policy:

1. Whether the decision would increase our power over other countries:
   (1) should be the most important thing to consider;
   (2) should be a very important thing to consider;
   (3) should be a somewhat important thing to consider;
   (4) should not be an important thing to consider.
2. Whether the decision would benefit poorer or less powerful countries: (Same scale).
3. Whether citizens in our country agreed that it was a good policy: (Same scale).

The rating given on the first item would be a way of measuring the importance given to national power. The second item would measure support for international cooperation. The third would measure the perceived importance of citizen support. Note that each response is clearly labeled and varies along a dimension from more to less important. Such questions are often less confusing than Likert items in which the student may disagree with some aspects of the statement and agree with others.

The item format just illustrated is somewhat similar to the "semantic differential" format. For example, the following types of semantic-differential items were taken from an ETS study on global understanding and used in a follow-up study with secondary students:

Hunger and inadequate health care:

This problem is very important.	1 2 3 4 5	This problem is not important.
The American government can do a lot to solve this problem.	1 2 3 4 5	The American government can do very little to solve this problem.

Similar scales were used for "This problem is solvable" to "This problem is not solvable"; "International organizations can do a lot to solve this problem" to "International organizations can do very little to solve this problem"; "This problem is of concern to people in many parts of the world" to "This problem is of concern to people in only a few parts of the world," and several other dimensions. Attitudes toward war, pollution, and other problems with potential global ramifications could be rated in this way.

It is not clear just how much one can expect a broadly targeted world studies course to influence attitudes about topics like war, international cooperation, and citizen participation in foreign policymaking. Here again the importance of tailoring the evaluation to the curriculum being taught cannot be overemphasized. For example, if the international relations approach is taught in a way that involves students in information analysis or in role-playing, it might well increase students' support for international cooperation to solve global ecological problems. It is less likely that a world history approach would have this impact. On the other hand, a world history approach with a strong cultural component might increase appreciation of cultural diversity in a way that an international relations course probably would not.

4. Measures appropriate to the specific approaches

The different approaches to world studies outlined in this book represent different conceptions of content, concepts, skills, and attitudes important for students. In other words, each of the approaches has implicit in it a structure for representing the world, which students are expected to understand and learn. The representations of the world built through the Western civilization and world history approaches have a number of similar dimensions, since an orientation to time and the past is important to both. They do not have as much in common with the world geography approach, oriented as it is around spatial rather than time dimensions. Thus to some extent each of the five approaches poses its own special challenges for program evaluation. In this section we consider measurement strategies specific to each approach.

WESTERN CIVILIZATION APPROACH

The Western civilization approach to world studies attempts to aid students in building a representation of the world, present and past, characterized by three dichotomies: Western/non-Western, capitalist/communist, and less developed/more developed. Students are introduced to relatively complex views of social organization and the dynamics of social change to understand how this world emerged. Explanations of change look to social, economic, political, and cultural factors, along with the physical environment. The uniqueness of Western culture is stressed because it represents a substantial part of the cultural legacy of the society in which American students live. Both knowledge of these cultural values and attachment to them are explicit objectives. At the same time, the approach seeks to guard against an ethnocentric attachment to Western values by representing other traditions as having vitality and integrity.

Students' representation of the history of the world as it is built in this approach also includes thinking about cause and effect in both past and present and the ability to see events organized chronologically in a time line.

Particular attention is given to benchmarks or turning points in history, such as the world in 1000 and the world in 1700. The ability to assess historical events and see the relationships between them are also central to the approach.

Measuring knowledge

There is a considerable factual base to the Western civilization approach, which can be assessed using criterion-referenced tests. There are also concepts that can be tested either through tasks, in which students are asked to discriminate between instances and non-instances, or through multiple-choice questions, in which students choose the correct definition. Among the concepts that might be assessed are definitions of the industrial revolution; distinctions between social, economic, political, and cultural factors in historical change; and distinctions between Western and non-Western. For example, a clear set of defining characteristics distinguishing the Western and non-Western experience could be developed. Test items would ask students to distinguish instances of each from non-instances, presented in the form of descriptive phrases. For example:

> Indicate whether each of the following is more characteristic of Western (W) or non-Western (NW) traditions: (1) has roots in Greece and Rome (W); (2) is related to Buddhism (NW); (3) had Charlemagne as an important leader (W).

In assessing students' grasp of the time line or comparative chronology, a series of questions could be generated as follows:

> In which of the following periods were China and the Middle East relatively advanced and stable, while the West was relatively poor and crude: (1) the world in 200 B.C.; *(2) the world in 900 A.D.; (3) the world in 1600 A.D.; (4) the world in 1900 A.D.

Similar questions could be asked concerning other periods—for example, when Britain was building colonies or the period in which a world economy was emerging. These items are built on the premise that it is more important to give students a grasp of the time dimension and major periods of world history than to have them memorize numerous specific dates.

There are also a large variety of possible multiple-choice questions relating to understanding historical change and the meaning of trends and values important in the cultural heritage of the West. For example, the students' ability to see the relevance of democracy, colonialization, or nationalism in situations other than those discussed in class could be assessed.

Measuring skills

Skills associated with using and evaluating historical sources could be assessed with multiple-choice items. Students could be asked in which of four sources a given type of information could be most reliably found. Critical thinking skills could be assessed with instruments similar to those used in the California state test. Items could be used, for example, to assess students' understanding of multiple dimensions of historical causation, their ability to distinguish facts from values, and their ability to generate questions to clarify the meaning of a historical situation. Students' abilities to recognize flaws in historical reasoning and to hypothesize and generalize about an event could also be assessed in this way.

Other skills are more difficult to measure. For example, one of the aims of the course is to help students understand that not everybody in the world wants to be like them in every way. It requires a type of perspective-taking skill to analyze Western values and recognize which ones would be unimportant to someone raised in another cultural tradition. A similar skill is involved in analyzing the experience of colonized nations and recognizing the conflicts of values that colonialism created. This type of skill could be measured using a paragraph that set out a choice faced by someone raised in another tradition or living in a recently colonized society. Students could be asked to choose the best summary of the vignette. The correct answer would recognize the different value perspective involved. The incorrect alternatives would attribute contemporary American values to individuals living at another time and/or place.

Although multiple-choice questions will probably predominate in most assessments, the understanding of historical change and the relations between political, social, economic, and cultural factors can better be assessed using written answers or essays. The SOLO Taxonomy has been applied to brief written answers to questions about history. The following example from Biggs and Collis (1983) provides an illustration.

A particular lesson designed for seven- to fifteen-year-olds dealt with Stonehenge. It presented a paragraph of factual information and a picture. The students were asked: "Do you think Stonehenge might have been a fort and not a temple, and why?" The essay answers were scored on the basis of the extent to which students were able to construct a plausible interpretation from incomplete data. Answers such as the following were labelled Prestructural because they either dealt with irrelevant information or were tautological: "It looks like a temple," or "It can't be a fort or a temple because those big stones have fallen over."

Answers such as the following were labeled Unistructural because they dealt with only one aspect of the given data before arriving at a conclusion: "It looks more like a temple because they are all in circles."

A third level was called Multistructural because several features of the given information were included in the answer, but they were treated as independent and unrelated. There was also no weighing of the pros and cons of each alternative and no attempt to deal with inconsistency: "It is more likely that Stonehenge was a temple because it looks like a kind of design all in circles, and they have gone to a lot of trouble."

A fourth, Relational, level incorporated several pieces of data on both sides, considered alternatives, and tried to balance inconsistencies: "I think it would be a temple because it has a round formation with an altar at the top end. I think it was used for worship of the sun god. There was no roof on it so that the sun shines right into the temple. There is a lot of hard work and labor in it for a god and the fact that they brought blue stones from Wales. Anyway, its unlikely they'd build a fort in the middle of a plain."

According to the research conducted by Biggs and Collis, answers at the Unistructural, Multistructural, and Relational levels account for almost all the responses of students in the ninth or tenth grade. There is still another stage, Extended Abstract, in which students introduce data beyond what is given and consider logical alternatives, not merely alternatives present in the material given. Biggs and Collis also give examples of uses of the SOLO Taxonomy in assessing students' ability (1) to draw conclusions from historical data, (2) to make value judgments about an historical event (e.g., whether William of Normandy should be called cruel for his behavior after the Battle of Hastings), (3) to reconcile divergent evidence from conflicting sources (e.g., two views of the conditions of the working class in Britain in the 1830s), (4) to define concepts such as committee, and (5) to induce the meaning of a concept from a context. These are all important skill objectives in world history and are also related to course content.

Measuring attitudes

It is especially important to assess students' attitudes toward history and their motivation to engage in further reading and study about history. The Western civilization approach helps students to begin building a representation of the world that is relatively complex. Because it is so complex, a full structure is unlikely to be fully achieved by most tenth graders, no matter how well the course is taught. A student's representation of the periods and major movements in Western civilization will remain rudimentary unless he or she is motivated to engage in further study. Since the historical perspective is not widely available in the mass media, which the average student is likely to watch or read, students must be intrinsically motivated if they are to seek out additional learning opportunities.

There are a variety of other values and attitudes that could also be important outcomes of this course. These include enlightened patriotism, as well as an understanding of and commitment to such democratic Western ideals as the rule of law, democratic decisionmaking, and free enterprise. Likert or other types of attitude scales might be developed for assessing these attitudes. Some scales developed in studies of civic education might be appropriate. (See Torney, Oppenheim, and Farnen, 1975, for a scale measuring support for equality.)

WORLD HISTORY APPROACH

The world history approach attempts to aid students in building a representation of the world, past and present, which can be organized along either chronological or topical lines. It is especially focused on giving students a sense of both the remoteness and relevance of the past and an understanding of major forces, such as religion, that have shaped history. It also emphasizes an ability to understand such concepts as borrowing, adaptation, and change as they are illustrated in different world areas and periods.

Measuring knowledge

Many of the techniques described for the Western civilization approach would be equally valuable for a world history approach. Items developed as part of widely used tests may also be useful. A number of items in the California state test deal with issues related to world history. For example:

> How did the Industrial Revolution lead to the growth of empires? (1) it slowed the development of nationalism; *(2) it created a need for raw materials that could be found in new territories; (3) it created a need for new manufacturing centers; (4) it caused leaders to think of problems within their own countries.

The ETS/Council on Learning questionnaire also included items related to world history that were relatively easy for college students and might be appropriate for younger students:

> Chinese culture has been characterized by all of the following except: *(1) a caste system; (2) patriarchal control; (3) a strong family cult; (4) ancestral concern.

Many appropriate items could be developed using the process described above for developing criterion-referenced tests. For example, students can be asked to recognize the approach to development in China as contrasted with India, or to distinguish between Confucian social structure and Roman social structure.

Because of the emphasis on linking past with present in world history, an assessment technique might present an event, such as the invention of the printing press, and query students about both its immediate historical results and its long-term effects. This would indicate whether students could distinguish between plausible and implausible outcomes of technological advances. A school district with access to news retrieval services could develop tests asking students to apply some of the concepts learned in the course to current news events. A short news story would be presented, followed by a series of questions asking students to relate historical concepts to it.

Measuring skills

A major skill objective of the world history approach is to help students better detect bias and prejudice. This skill might be assessed by presenting two sources having different biases, followed by a question asking students to identify the biases in each. The responses could be scored both for correctness in identifying the particular biases and for the level of argument and the way in which different factors were taken into account. The SOLO Taxonomy could be used as the basis for this scoring. Multiple-choice questions could also be used to assess students' ability to recognize bias or to distinguish between fact and opinion.

The world history approach also pays particular attention to students' self-consciousness about their own perspective and their skill in recognizing that those who lived in different time periods had different technologies and perspectives. In assessing the success of the course's efforts to overcome the "bias of the present," one might generate a number of situations set in other time periods to see whether students realized that certain inventions (either material or social) were not available. For example, what factors would a craftsman in China in the 1500s consider in deciding whether to take a particular job? Certainly they would not include the convenience of bus lines or health insurance benefits.

Measuring attitudes

The need for assessing students' interest in world history and intrinsic motivation to seek out further learning opportunities is as important for the world history approach as for the Western civilization approach. Further, the world history approach gives even greater attention to the question of stereotypes. There are paper-and-pencil stereotyping measures that present a series of rating scales such as the following:

> Which of the following best describes Africans: (1) all are poor; (2) most are poor; (3) some are poor, some are rich; (4) most are rich; (5) all are rich.

Answers at the extreme, (1) or (5), are scored as stereotyped. These types of ratings can be applied to any racial or national group, such as Africans or Japanese, or to groups in a particular historical period, such as medieval Europeans or Arabs during the Abbasside Caliphate.

HISTORICAL CULTURES APPROACH

World studies courses that use the historical cultures approach attempt to aid students in building a highly complex representation of the world's past and present. It emphasizes the conscious examination of cultural premises and the appreciation of the meaning of culture at several different levels. Although based on anthropology, the model's content is historical rather than ethnographic. It is organized around a listing of social principles, which are applied in telling the story of the human species from the far past, to the near past, to the present, to the future. Thus the representations built by students would have at least two dimensions, chronology and the social principles that are at the heart of human culture. Both dimensions are used to show how humans adapt to new challenges by developing culture.

Measuring knowledge

It is quite possible to develop factual questions testing students' knowledge of the content of the historical cultures approach. For example:

> In which world region has the connection between religion and political conflict led to a state of almost constant war: *(1) Middle East; (2) Russia; (3) Latin America; (4) Asia.
>
> Which statement about the changing nature of work throughout history is correct? (1) work began for subsistence, then became a source of identity, and recently became a source of status; (2) work began as a source of identity, and recently became important for subsistence and status; *(3) work began for subsistence, became a source of status, and recently became a source of identity; (4) the function of work has been subsistence, status, and identity throughout human history.

Both of these items relate directly to major factual concerns of the course. They also measure the acquisition of information that would help students understand world events. However, if the representation of the world proposed in the chapter on the historical cultures approach is accepted as the criterion for student learning, these questions are not adequate. Indeed multiple-choice items in general may not be suitable measures of knowledge attainment. The items above measure knowledge only at a factual level; the model proposed is much more complex conceptually.

For the historical cultures approach it would be necessary to measure students' understanding of concepts central to the model. In some cases, the extended definitions given in the chapter approximate the concept specifications required for criterion-reference testing. For example, definitions of social system, adaptation through culture, and civilization are all fairly well developed. Students could also be asked to distinguish between types of empires, or between situations where individuals have common cause and those where they are bound by contract, or between the Spanish and British approaches to colonization. If some kind of multiple-choice assessment is required, this is reasonable.

Measuring skills

A major aim of the historical cultures approach is to help students learn to recognize social patterns and social principles in historical material, in understanding present adaptation, and in predicting future conditions. The skill of recognizing pattern and principle could be assessed by presenting students with news stories or brief fictional vignettes and asking them to identify the social principles operating in them. Such an instrument would be labor-intensive to write but could assess this skill reasonably well. For example, one could write a vignette about someone who held political office because of close relationships to relatives but was threatened with ouster for not having performed adequately. Students could be asked questions to assess their ability to identify principles such as hierarchy, kinship, and office. The solution for this dilemma might illustrate principles such as common cause and networks.

An ability to see chains of social causes and principles extending into the past and forward into the future is another important objective of this approach. This skill could be assessed by having students label instances in vignettes or current news events that demonstrate a given chain or a particular social principle.

The course also emphasizes the ability to identify one's own premises and recognize that the premises of one's own time and place should not be confused with universal premises. The process of identifying premises is a kind of perspective-taking that could also be assessed with the analysis of vignettes. A class assignment to bring in news articles illustrating these patterns, principles, and premises might generate the subject matter upon which vignettes for use in a written test could be based. Here too, the complexity of students' thought processes could be scored using the SOLO Taxonomy.

Alternative ways of measuring students' analysis of the causes of historical events could also be developed on the basis of techniques suggested by history educators. (See Dickinson and Lee, 1978.) In this technique, students are presented with extensive material on a decision made by an historical character (for example, a battle decision made during World War I). Students are then asked a series of questions to ascertain their view of the decision-makers' intent. They are scored on a scale that goes from failure to grasp the notion of intent, through situation-based explanations, to the ability at high levels of thinking to distinguish between the historian's point of view and that of the historical actor. A similar exercise might be adapted to ascertain students' ability to grasp the premises underlying an action, which are similar in many ways to intentions.

Measuring attitudes

The types of assessments of student interest and motivation suggested in the general section on measurement can be readily applied to the historical cultures approach. Indeed, the questions might be expanded to indicate in what real-life situations students believe they could apply such techniques as back-chaining. Students could also be asked to imagine an event at a future point in time and to identify plausible or necessary antecedents of such an event in the present.

The historical cultures approach places some stress on deepened patriotism, defined as "an appreciation for what our country has done right."

Attitude scales could be developed to assess this, concentrating on democratic government and technological expertise.

In the historical cultures approach, it is also important that students see various issues as global in character. Some of the scales suggested as rating techniques for world problems could be used for this. For example, students might rate to what extent people in many parts of the world are concerned about a problem. In general, however, this approach is more focused on analytic attitudes than on the kind of attitudes usually assessed with rating scales.

WORLD GEOGRAPHY APPROACH

The world geography approach to world studies attempts to aid students in building a visually oriented representation of the earth's surface. This visual representation would include facts about the specific location of physical features, conceptions of the way in which place influences human activities, and dimensions along which the earth can be partitioned into regions. A well-developed geographical representation would include an understanding of the linkages between physical and human geography, the ways in which geography affects interactions among regions, and the particular problems of developing countries.

Measuring knowledge

Geography is unique in that it includes an almost infinite array of factual information on locational specifics and place-name geography. Teaching about and testing students' grasp of the absolute and relative location of places on the earth's surface is a basic task. However, modern geography is not merely a catalogue of names associated with a two-dimensional map. It is also a way of understanding, identifying, and solving such problems as pollution, urban crowding, poor agricultural yields, and ethnic conflict. It is the ability to think like a geographer that this approach attempts to foster, and that should be part of the focus of evaluation.

There is a tradition of multiple-choice testing in geography. A number of standardized and criterion-referenced tests are available. A recent set of competency-based tests developed by the National Council for Geographic Education (NCGE) has substantial world geography content.

Measuring skills

It is difficult to separate skills from content in world geography, because of the importance of map and graph reading in the presentation and assessment of knowledge. For example, the NCGE test contains a section called "Map Skills and Locations." In it the student is presented with an outline map of the world with thirty-eight locations numbered. Nine of the twelve questions ask students to identify the name of a nation. Questions are also asked about commonalities within a region in terms of government, economy, or religion. There is also a section on physical geography. Students are asked to refer to characteristics of the African continent, such as tropical rainforest, and to read graphs relating to climate. They are shown shaded portions of maps and asked what the shading indicates (e.g., mineral wealth, mountains) and what kind of economic activity is likely to take place there as a result.

Similar questions are included in the ETS/Council on Learning test. In that test shaded maps are presented, and students are asked whether the shading represents average annual surface temperature, elevation above sea level, or average annual precipitation. Similar techniques could be used to assess learning of various world geography concepts, especially climatic regions and natural resource distribution. the ETS/Council on Learning instrument also includes skill-based measures of students' grasp of human geography. The emphasis is on reading and applying population graphs and on answering questions on how individuals live, work, and trade in different world areas.

The pool of available items in these tests does not adequately deal with integration or differentiation across regions, the concept of cultural regions, or the problem of uneven development. In these areas, tasks involving concept definition/differentiation might be appropriate. For example, students could be asked to identify examples of uneven development, of core and periphery, or of cultural regions. Other questions could be written to assess their ability to use demographic or resource data in making appropriate generalizations or in diagnosing problems and generating plausible solutions.

Assessing critical thinking in geography is made easier by a published set of questions developed at the Ontario Institute for Studies in Education. (See Ross and Maynes, 1981.) For example, there is a question that looks at students' abilities to gain useful information through questioning:

> Someone studying a country in Africa notes considerable variation from year to year in crop yields. Which of the following questions would be most useful to ask in finding out why this was? (1) What was the crop yield in each of the last ten years? (2) What political leader was in charge during each of the last ten years? (3) What was the crop yield and amount of rainfall last year? *(4) What was the crop yield and the amount of rainfall in each of the last ten years?

This publication also gives sample items to measure students' abilities to assess the accuracy of information sources and to get information from statistical tables.

The SOLO Taxonomy has also been applied to geography. In one instance, students were asked to account for areal characteristics from a written description (Biggs and Collis, 1982). A passage describing farming in the Andes detailed the disappearance of a fertile soil cover after the tree cover was cut and burned. Students were asked "why did the deep fertile soil cover disappear and make farming impossible?"

At the Prestructural level two of the answers given were: "Because solid rock was under the soil" (focusing only on the end result), and "because the sun was too hot" (focusing on an irrelevant aspect of the situation).

At the Unistructural level one answer was: "The soil was washed away by flooding" (responding to only one dimension of the situation).

At the Multistructural level a sample response was: "because when the trees were taken away, the rain fell directly onto the soil washing it away down the hillside." This response shows an awareness of cause and effect, considering more than one aspect of a situation, and referring to a combination of events.

At the Relational level more aspects are considered and related, while at the Extended Abstract level the explanation is comprehensive and material from outside the reading is included in the student's answer. It might be possible with extensive piloting to take a short passage and written answers to such a question and generate multiple-choice options from which large groups of students could choose the best answer. Biggs and Collis (1982) also give examples of the application of the SOLO Taxonomy to the interpretation of maps and to the explanation of natural phenomena.

Perspective-taking, in the sense of understanding how a place looks from different locations or points of view, has a special role in geography. The study of geography could make students more aware of how living on a plain rather than a mountain or in a developed rather than a developing country can shape an individual's point of view. This is an important area to consider, but one in which good instruments do not yet exist.

Asking students to draw a freehand map of a certain continent or country and to fill in as many features as they can, often called an assessment of "mental maps," might also be useful. How big are countries and continents with reference to each other? What are the predominating features: cities, deserts, mountains, rainforests? Certainly maps drawn after the study of a region should have more detail than ones drawn beforehand. A further question is whether grasping these details helps students to understand human experience in those regions.

Measuring attitudes

As with other approaches, student interest in the subject of geography and in taking further courses should be assessed. Because world geography has some stereotypes to overcome as a relatively unpopular subject, these attitudinal objectives may be of particular importance. Ratings of various global problems such as pollution, hunger, and the waste of natural resources could demonstrate other attitudinal effects relevant to a world geography approach. Examples of these types of measures were suggested in the general section on attitude measurement above.

INTERNATIONAL RELATIONS APPROACH

The international relations approach attempts to aid students in building a conceptually rich representation of the world, focusing on international actors as they function in a world system. It emphasizes the present and the near future, considering the historical context primarily as it illuminates current international issues. Countries are important primarily in their roles as international actors. Factual information is closely linked to skills, especially to those required for informed citizen participation.

Measuring knowledge

A long and rich list of cognitive objectives is presented for the international relations approach. Because of its stress on problem solving and on security and the economics of development, many of the items included in the ETS/Council on Learning survey and in the Study of Stanford and the Schools would also be appropriate. Among the ETS/Council on Learning items (Barrows, 1981) is the following:

> Since the Second World War, the gap in per capita income between the world's richest and poorest countries has: *(1) widened; (2) remained about the same; (3) narrowed slightly; (4) narrowed a great deal.

About 60 percent of both college and high school students answered correctly.

The Study of Stanford and the Schools also included many items relevant to the international relations approach. Two examples are:

> Many American companies are moving their production increasingly to Southeast Asia: (1) to support the national economies in that area; (2) to promote good relations with countries in that area; *(3) because of lower labor costs; (4) because of special skills among South Asian people.
>
> A country is considered to have serious foreign debt problems when: (1) it imports less than it exports; (2) the country is low in natural resources; (3) it cannot pay its civil servants; *(4) it is unable to pay back international banking loans.

About 50 percent of the high school students involved in the study answered each of these questions correctly.

The chapter describing the international relations approach discusses a large number of concepts. In many cases these discussions could easily serve as the basis for concept/domain definitions for multiple-choice items. For example, the definitions of nation-state, Third World, interdependence, and underdevelopment could all be turned into domain specifications and criterion-referenced test items through the process described earlier. For example, "ideology" is defined as "a set of beliefs which serves to explain the past and present, and to indicate how to achieve goals posited by the ideology in the future." After studying the topic, students could be asked whether each of the following is a statement of support for an ideology:

(1) I support socialism (an ideology); (2) I support democracy (an ideology, but students may be used to thinking of ideologies as negative and may not recognize this as an exemplar); (3) I support Mr. Jones' election to Congress (not an ideology, because no set of beliefs is supported); (4) I support building more space vehicles (again not an ideology, although it is related to the future).

Another level of cognitive understanding is addressed in the international relations approach and could also be measured with multiple-choice items. That is whether the student sees links or connections between various conditions and world problems. For example, does the student connect underemployment with a nation's poverty? Do students see the connection between the production of cash crops for export and inadequate production of food crops for local consumption?

Measuring skills

A substantial list of skills is also related to the international relations approach.

Critical thinking in this approach is defined as the generation of alternative solutions to complex problems, the analysis of these alternatives, and decisionmaking based on rational analysis. One method for evaluating critical thinking skills of this sort is to observe small group discussions. The number of alternatives generated before a decision is reached would be counted. Observers would also note whether students participated in a constructive way in criticizing their own ideas and the ideas of others in the group. It should be noted that this is not an easy thing for fifteen- and sixteen-year-olds to do. They generally require instruction and support from adult leaders in the form of leading questions.

Other open-ended methods for assessing critical thinking could also be developed. A "thinking aloud" process, such as that described in the general section on skills assessment, would be a good approach to the evaluation of these critical thinking skills. Computer-assisted evaluation, in which a student is presented with a problem on a terminal and asked to enter alternative solutions, indicating in each case why the solution is preferable and what the constraints are, would be a good assessment technique in this skill area as well.

Most districts, however, will not have the resources for observations, individual interviews, or computer-assisted testing. As an alternative, a series of paper-and-pencil questions could present a problem and a solution with some major but hidden flaw in it. For example, a solution might require an illiterate population to read agricultural instruction manuals. Similarly, a solution might require individuals to violate their religious beliefs in order to adopt a development strategy. Students could be asked to identify the hidden flaw. These questions would need careful piloting.

A strategy developed for the Maryland Summer Center Project could also be useful. In that evaluation students were asked to rate on a four-point scale either how often they participated in a given type of activity or how much they had learned about a given topic during the session. For example, "I tried to think of several alternatives before deciding on a position"; and "I learned about differences between nations in negotiating style." In the Maryland Project observations of group interaction in generating and criticizing messages corroborated these self-report data. While the use of a rating scale alone would not be ideal, self-ratings may be preferable to collecting no information at all.

The perspective-taking skill related to the international relations approach has a slightly different emphasis from other approaches. The question is not whether the student can take the point of view of individuals in a single other country, but rather whether a systems perspective about the whole world can be adopted. This is one frequently used definition of the ability to take a global perspective. In spite of several attempts, however, no satisfactory measure yet exists to measure attainment of this skill.

Finally, the international relations approach pays substantial attention to the use of statistical comparisons, the reading of graphs, and the interpretation of tabular material. A variety of ways to assess these skills are included in the ETS/Council on Learning questionnaire. There are also illustrations in most books on educational evaluation and social studies methods.

Measuring attitudes

Because the international relations approach emphasizes encouraging participation and active interest in current events, the measurement of motivation and interest are particularly relevant to this approach. Positive attitudes toward oneself and one's country, in the form of enlightened patriotism, could be assessed with attitude scales developed for that purpose. Attitudes of willingness to accept, practice, and defend democratic beliefs and practices in relating to governmental decisions are also appropriate.

One of the attitudes introduced in this approach is appreciation of positive and negative aspects of international order and peaceful international change. Some measures of support for international cooperation address aspects of this. See for example, the ETS/Council on Learning cooperation scale in Barrows (1981). Most other existing scales relating to world order focus on whether the respondent believes that war is ever justified or whether war is a satisfactory way to solve international disputes. Attitudes toward war are not coincident with attitudes toward international order, however. Appropriate measures in this area still need to be developed.

5. Past research and evaluation in world studies

RESEARCH ESTABLISHING BASELINES FOR
STUDENT KNOWLEDGE AND ATTITUDES

There have been several attempts to develop reliable and valid measures of student knowledge and attitudes in world studies. Most have been part of research efforts designed to establish baseline information on international understanding among young people and to understand what factors are related to students' understanding of world problems. All these studies provide relevant models for designing evaluation instruments. Some also contain specific items that evaluators may find useful.

During the 1960s and 1970s three studies laid the foundation for most subsequent research efforts in world studies. The first, more than twenty-five years ago, was an interview study of children's attitudes toward foreign people. Lambert and Klineberg (1967) developed profiles of how children from eleven different national groups perceived other peoples, including the extent to which they saw those people as similar or different from themselves.

More recently, an analysis of data from the IEA survey of civic knowledge and attitudes indicated that adolescents in the United States were considerably more knowledgeable about domestic political institutions and processes than about international issues. The difference was especially striking when compared to students in eight other countries (Torney, 1977).

In the mid-1970s a large-scale survey of knowledge and attitudes regarding persons in other countries was conducted by the Educational Testing Services (ETS) on a national probability sample of fourth, eighth, and twelfth grade students in the United States (Pike and Barrows, 1979). Some of the knowledge questions used in this study, known as the "Other Nations Other Peoples" project, are now out of date, but others might be quite relevant to the objectives of some world studies projects. The attitudinal questions asked respondents to make paired comparisons between countries. The analysis relied on rather complex statistical techniques.

In the early 1980s, ETS and the Council on Learning followed up the Other Nations Other Peoples study with their Survey of Global Awareness among college students (Barrows et al., 1981). The instrument used for the study was constructed by a committee of scholars in disciplines such as world history, sociology, international economics, and international relations.

The survey instrument was based on a model for topic coverage which represented different historical periods and different geographic areas. As is often the case in questionnaire design, however, some items had better test characteristics than others when they were tried with a pilot sample. As a result, the historical/geographical model could not be fully implemented. Nonetheless, the final 101-item test has proven useful in generating baseline information on students' knowledge and attitudes about international matters.

The instrument includes substantial numbers of items dealing with geographical issues, relations between nations, major events in world history, problems of development, and attempts by international organizations to protect human rights. Forty-two attitude items contained in the test have been used to develop scales assessing national chauvinism, support for world government, support for human rights and concern for global problems, as well as attitudes toward international cooperation and war as a national policy instrument. There is also a set of items assessing attitudes toward foreign language and self-assessed proficiency.

About two years after the ETS Survey on Global Awareness was administered to college students, twenty-eight of the easier knowledge items and the ten-item global concern scale were also administered to approximately 1500 secondary school students in nine states (Torney-Purta, 1985). The purpose of the study was to determine whether students who had taken global education courses or participated in special global education programs had higher levels of global awareness (knowledge) or concern for global issues (attitudes) than those who had not. An analysis of the data showed that some but not all of the global education programs succeeded in enhancing the knowledge and concern of students. Particularly successful were programs designed for select groups of very able students and a program that had been in existence for a number of years and had done extensive teacher workshops on international relations. Students in global education programs that had been in existence for a short time, those that used quite traditional approaches to world history, and those that focused on a single world area were not as successful.

Both the ETS/Council on Learning survey for college students and the short form for secondary students represent important resources upon which world studies program evaluators might draw. Neither, however, is a ready-made evaluation instrument. The subgrouping of items in geography or world history, for example, would need to be augmented by additional items to make reliable subscores. Many of the objectives of world studies courses are not covered in these items at all. Likewise, many of the questions were difficult for college students and high school seniors, so they are likely to be far too challenging for younger students. Some of the knowledge items have gone out of date. Thus the survey is primarily useful as a pool from which some items may be chosen and as a model for test construction.

RESEARCH ASSESSING SPECIFIC WORLD STUDIES PROGRAMS

In recent years some very innovative efforts have been made to develop program evaluations for specific world studies programs. While all of these efforts are idiosyncratic to some degree, they also provide important models of evaluation design.

When the Study of Stanford and the Schools undertook planning to assess global awareness in a group of schools in the San Francisco Bay Area, the available assessment instruments clearly did not suit the objectives of the project. Given the specific objectives of the programs being evaluated, a new set of knowledge items dealing with international peace or conflict and another set of items dealing with international economics were needed.

New items were written, pre-tested and analyzed. Knowledge subscales on these topics were constructed. In addition, the project staff interviewed teachers and collected observational data, resulting in case studies of several classrooms. Thus the evaluation self-consciously combined qualitative and quantitative approaches. (See Torney-Purta and Landsdale, 1986, for details of the evaluation and analysis.)

Regression analysis of the data resulting from the Study of Stanford and the Schools suggests some important conclusions about what makes world studies programs effective. For example, the extent to which students felt able to express opinions in the classroom that were contrary to those of the teacher was a predictor of knowledge about peace/conflict issues and international economics. In short, this project has not only provided instruments for use in assessing course outcomes but has also suggested several important dimensions for assessing the implementation of world studies curricula.

A recent effort evaluating the Maryland Summer Center for International Studies has also combined quantitative (questionnaire) with qualitative (observational) methods (Torney-Purta, 1985). During the summers of 1985 and 1986, groups of secondary school students participated in a computer-assisted simulation. The students role-played the foreign policy makers of six different countries. Questionnaires were administered both before and after the simulation. The items included ratings of the foreign policy of each country on dimensions such as rationality and responsiveness to allies. They also included five-point agree/disagree attitude items on scales such as Support for International Cooperation, and Support for Rationality, and Moderation in Foreign Policy. In addition, students were asked specific questions about what they believed they learned during the simulation and how they expected their experience to influence future choices of courses and careers.

More than one hundred fifteen-minute observations were also conducted during meetings of the foreign policy making teams. The observations focused on students' critical thinking ability with respect to foreign policy alternatives and their ability to take the cultural or policy perspective of another nation into account.

The combination of qualitative and quantitative information provided a much richer picture of the program's impact than a paper-and-pencil instrument alone could have. In particular, it allowed assessment of students' abilities to generate and examine alternative points of view. It also provided evidence of how the simulation goals were actually carried into practice.

These efforts to assess particular world studies programs clearly demonstrate how important it is that measures of both program implementation and student outcomes be tailored to the specific world studies program. They also demonstrate the importance of using multiple methods to ensure the utility of program evaluations.

6. Annotated bibliography on evaluation methodology

Baron, J. "Evaluating Thinking Skills in the Classroom," in J. Baron and R. Sternberg, eds. *Teaching Thinking Skills.* New York: Freeman, 1987, pp. 221–248. A basic introduction to and review of the evaluation of thinking skills programs. A short list of criteria for effective evaluation is included, as well as suggestions for the involvement of teachers and administrators.

Barrows, T., ed. *College Students' Knowledge and Beliefs: A Survey of Global Understanding.* New Rochelle, N.Y.: Change Magazine Press, 1981. A report on the ETS/ Council on Learning survey of American college students. Various reports related to the project have been published by Change Magazine Press. Some provide technical information on the survey items; others focus primarily on the results of the survey, which involved 3000 college students from throughout the country. An analysis of the data, with special emphasis on its implications for teacher education, is contained in Torney-Purta, J. "The Results of the Global Awareness Survey: Implications for Teacher Education," *Theory Into Practice 21* (1982), 200–205.

Biggs, J., and Collis, K. *Evaluating the Quality of Learning.* New York: Academic Press, 1982. Presents in detail the SOLO (Structure of the Observed Learning Outcome) methodology. SOLO Taxonomy is a model for the objective and systematic analysis of essay responses. It has been applied to history and geography at both the elementary and secondary levels.

Black, H.D., and Dockrell, W.B. *Criterion Referenced Assessment in the Classroom.* Edinburgh, U.K.: Scottish Council for Research in Education, 1984. A report on a project in which teachers participated in the construction of criterion-referenced tests for use in individual diagnostic assessment in their own classrooms. The description of the way in which the tests were constructed is concrete and very useful. A number of examples of knowledge and attitude items relating to Third World countries are included

Bloom, B., Hasting, T., and Madaus, G., eds. *Handbook on Formative and Summative Evaluation of Student Learning.* New York: McGraw-Hill, 1971. One of the classics in the field of evaluation. The chapters on evaluation techniques for assessing knowledge and comprehension, application and analysis, synthesis and evaluation, and affective objectives will all be of interest. So will the chapter on evaluation of learning in secondary social studies. Many examples of specific items are included.

Brinkerhoff, R., Brethower, D., Hiuchyj, T. and Nowakowski, J. *Program Evaluation: A Practitioners' Guide for Teachers and Educators.* Boston: Kluwer-Nijhoff, 1983. A basic guide to the evaluation process. This sourcebook provides extremely detailed descriptions and checklists that would be useful in planning an evaluation or in working with an outside evaluator. Chapter titles include Focusing the Evaluation, Designing Evaluation, Collecting Information, Analyzing Information, and Reporting Information.

Case, R. *How Are We Doing? A Framework for Evaluating Development Education Programs.* New York: InterAction, 1987. A how-to-evaluate guide prepared by a Canadian and U.S. team to be used by individuals working in programs to educate the public about problems of international development. It is the most concrete and useful guide focused on material specific to world studies content, with sections on design, instrument construction, data collection, analysis, and presentation, as well as a glossary of terms.

Dickinson, A., and Lee, E. *History Teaching and Historical Understanding.* London: Heineman, 1978. Looks at techniques that history educators have suggested for assessing students' abilities to analyze the causes of historical events.

Fitz-Gibbon, C., and Morris, L. *How to Design a Program Evaluation.* Beverly Hills, Calif.: Sage, 1978. Part of a series of short booklets produced by the Center for the Study of Evaluation at UCLA. The series deals with all aspects of program evaluation in education. This volume deals with design issues (e.g., control groups, time series, before and after designs).

Gronlund, N. *Measurement and Evaluation in Teaching,* 4th ed. New York: Macmillan, 1981. One of the standard textbooks for teaching teachers how to use and construct tests that are useful across the curriculum. It includes many examples, but only a few of them deal specifically with world studies.

Henerson, M., Morris, L., and Fitz-Gibbon, C. *How to Measure Attitudes.* Beverly Hills, Calif.: Sage, 1978. Also part of the UCLA series on educational program evaluation. Especially good for its examples of measuring attitudes toward a class or toward class activities. It includes sections on measuring attitudes through attitude scales in questionnaires, interviews, and observation.

————. *How to Measure Program Implementation.* Beverly Hills, Calif.: Sage, 1978. Also part of the UCLA series. This volume discusses the use of existing records as well as observations and self-reports in measuring the extent to which a curriculum plan is being implemented.

————. *How to Measure Achievement.* Beverly Hills, Calif.: Sage, 1978. Part of the UCLA series. This volume describes both sources of published tests and methods of constructing one's own test. Some of the published tests reviewed are now out of date.

Lambert, W., and Klineberg, O. *Children's Views of Foreign Peoples.* New York: Appleton Century Crofts, 1967. A report on the early interview study of children's attitudes toward people in other countries.

Mueller, D. *Measuring Social Attitudes.* New York: Teachers College Press, 1986. Discusses the nature of attitudes, reliability/validity, and several measurement methods. The section on Likert scales is especially detailed and helpful, going step by step through the process of scale construction.

Norris, S. "Evaluating Critical Thinking Ability," *History and Social Science Teacher* 21 (1986), 135–146. A recent review of tests that have been developed to assess children's critical thinking skills.

Pike, L., and Barrows, T. *Other Nations, Other Peoples.* Washington, D.C.: U.S. Government Printing Office, 1979. The major report on one of the early international assessment studies designed to provide baseline information on the attitudes and knowledge of students with respect to foreign peoples and world affairs.

Renwick, G. *Evaluation Handbook for Crosscultural Training and Multicultural Education.* La Grange Park, Ill.: Intercultural Network. Describes in detail the context and methodology for evaluating cross-cultural training programs (e.g., workshops to train overseas volunteers or to reduce multicultural tensions). It would be especially applicable to evaluations of teacher workshops with a strong experiential component, because of its extensive coverage of intercultural/interpersonal skills. Available from Intercultural Press, P.O. 768, Yarmouth, ME 04096.

Ross, J., and Maynes, F. *Geographic Thinking Skills.* Toronto: Ontario Institute for Studies in Education, 1981. Presents a set of questions that can be adapted to assess critical thinking skills related to world geography.

Sichel, J. *Program Evaluation Guidelines: A Research Handbook for Agency Personnel.* New York: Human Sciences Press, 1982. A short introduction to program evaluation, written in a very informal style. This would be useful as an introduction for anyone who wants to know the basics of program evaluation in non-technical language.

Torney, J., Oppenheim, A.M., and Farnen, R. *Civic Education in Ten Nations: An Empirical Study.* New York: John Wiley, 1975. A report on the International Association for Evaluation of Educational Attainment's (IEA) Civic Education Survey. A shorter report on some key findings is contained in Torney, J. "The International Knowledge and Attitudes of Adolescents in Nine Countries: The IEA Civic Education Survey," *International Journal of Political Education 1* (1977), 3–20.

Torney-Purta, J. *Predictors of Global Awareness and Global Concern in Secondary School Students.* Columbus, Ohio: Mershon Center, 1985. A report of the use of a 28-item knowledge test and a 10-item attitudinal survey derived from the ETS survey with secondary school students in nine states.

————. *Maryland Summer Center for International Studies, 1985: Evaluator's Report.* College Park, Md.: University of Maryland, 1985. Provides models of several techniques for evaluating knowledge and skills, including self-rating scales and observation techniques.

Torney-Purta, J., Brown, J.E., and Cloud, J. *Evaluating Global Education: Sample Instruments for Assessing Programs, Materials and Learning.* New York: Global Perspectives in Education, 1986. A compendium of annotated instruments developed and used by global education projects across the country. It includes measures for assessing a district's curriculum, materials, teacher in-service workshops, and student outcomes. Many of these instruments could be adapted to meet the needs of districts interested in measuring course effectiveness. Available for purchase from Global Pespectives in Education, 45 Johns St., Suite 1200, New York, NY 10038.

Torney-Purta, J., and Landsdale, D. "Classroom Climate and Process in International Studies: Qualitative and Quantitative Data from the American Schools and the World Project." Paper delivered at American Educational Research Association, San Francisco, 1986. Assesses the results of data gathered as part of the Study on Stanford and the Schools.

Voss, J., Tyler, S., and Yengo, L. "Individual Differences in the Solving of Social Science Problems." In R.F. Dillon and R.R. Schench, eds. *Individual Differences in Cognition.* New York: Academic Press, 1983. Looks at differences in the ways experts and novices solve content-related problems. Suggests ways of finding out how detailed students' representations of the world are and how well they can reason about problems and visualize constraints on solutions.

Glossary

Absolute location — the specific position of a place or area on the earth's surface. Absolute location is usually specified by referring to the latitude and longitude of a place.

Actors, international — the decisionmakers or participants in international relations, including but not limited to national governments, the leaders of national governments, multinational business firms, organizations made up of national governments, and non-governmental organizations engaged in international activities.

Adaptation — the process of reconciling a society's overall culture to changes in its environment or in certain aspects of the culture itself. For example, adaptation may occur in response to changes in climate or as a result of contacts with other peoples (environmental changes). It may also occur in response to changes in technology (a change in one aspect of the culture itself).

Aerospace revolution — a fundamental change in human society initiated by the development of airplanes and rockets. These developments have increased communication and interaction among peoples around the world, made possible satellite mapping and communications, and, coupled with nuclear weapons, have transformed the logic of national security. As space technology opens up the resources of outer space, even more startling changes in human culture may occur.

Agricultural revolution — a fundamental change in the way human societies obtain their food. The term can refer to the initial development of agriculture and animal husbandry during the Neolithic revolution or to the much later change in agricultural production preceding the industrial revolution in Europe.

Alignment — self-conscious efforts by national governments to coordinate their foreign policies and international actions. Alignment is thus similar to forming a coalition. It may or may not result from a formal treaty-based alliance.

Alliances — formal groupings of two or more states, usually for a fixed duration and purpose such as defense. Alliances are usually established through written treaties among the member states. The North Atlantic Treaty Organization (NATO) is a contemporary example of an alliance.

Anarchy, international — a term used to refer to the absence of a world government capable of enforcing agreements among countries and keeping the peace internationally. Anarchy results from the sovereignty of states.

Apartheid — the system of strict racial separation and discrimination practiced in the Republic of South Africa. Apartheid laws not only require separate public facilities for people of different races but also legally restrict the political and economic rights and the economic prospects of nonwhite groups within South Africa.

Areal content — the characteristics of a place, such as its landform features, population, or dominant culture, that enable the place to be differentiated from and compared with other places.

Arms control — any measure undertaken by one state or agreed to by two or more states that limits or reduces military forces, regulates armaments, or restricts the deployment of troops or weapons. Arms control aims primarily at reducing tensions between states. It is not the equivalent of, or even necessarily a step toward, disarmament.

Arms race — a competition between two or more states in which each state attempts to create the most powerful military force. Arms races tend to get out of control because actions taken by one state result in additional efforts by the other(s). It is generally thought that arms races ultimately end in war, although they do not necessarily cause wars.

Artifact — any product of human workmanship that can be observed by human senses. Artifacts are the tangible components of human culture.

Assimilation — the absorbing of an individual or a group into the culture or social system of another society.

Audience — any set of individuals who experience the same phenomena. The mass audience is a novel characteristic of modern society, whose complex communications systems can simultaneously deliver the same message to large numbers of people.

Authoritarianism — a form of government or a political system in which power is exclusively concentrated in a leader or ruling elite not responsible to the people.

Autonomy — the status of not being under the influence or control of another. In international relations, all states seek autonomy, but few if any ever achieve it, because of the interdependence characteristic of international systems.

Back-chaining — identifying a desired future condition or goal and then working backward in time to the present to determine what conditions (links in the chain) must be met before the objective can be achieved.

Balance of power — a relationship among two or more states in which no state is militarily or politically able to dominate the others. Balance of power became a doctrine of diplomacy because it was believed that a balance among states would lessen the chance of war or limit the scope of any wars that might occur.

Ballistic missiles — rocket-propelled vehicles used to deliver a weapon, usually a nuclear weapon, to its target. Ballistic missiles may be launched from submarine (SLBMs or sea-launched ballistic missiles) or from land. Land-based missiles are distinguished in terms of the distance they can travel. Intercontinental ballistic missiles (ICBMs) are capable of traveling from one continental area to another.

Bilateral — literally, two-sided. In international relations this term refers to negotiations or other interactions carried on between two and only two actors.

Bureaucracy — administrative intermediaries between leaders and citizens/subjects. The development of bureaucracy made far-flung and heterogeneous empires possible in the ancient world. Without administrative intermediaries, kings and emperors could not have controlled the diverse functions of government across large areas. Bureaucracy encourages an increasingly centralized, impersonal, and routinized style of government, which distances government from the people under it and encourages continuity despite changes in leaders.

Caliphate — a system of government, organized according to the tenets of Islam, in which the ruler is a direct successor of the prophet Muhammad. Historically the Caliph was a symbol of the authority and unity of Islam, but the Caliph did not necessarily enjoy great power within Islamic societies.

Capitalism — a form of economic organization and practice that became predominant in Europe sometime after A.D. 1500. Capitalist economies are characterized by the concept of private property and existence of markets in which land, labor, and capital are treated like commodities. Under capitalism the aim of economic activity is seen as the rational pursuit of profits and material welfare.

Carrying capacity — the maximum number of people or other biological organisms that a particular area or a particular renewable resource system (e.g., ocean fisheries) can sustain without damaging its ability to replenish itself.

Caste system — a rigid and hierarchical set of social classes, in which people are distinguished on the basis of ethnicity, profession, or position in society. In a caste system it is virtually impossible to move from a lower to a higher level in the hierarchy.

Center or **core** — the most economically advanced and politically powerful area within an international or national economic system. In the international system Western Europe, North America, and Japan constitute the center or core area.

Chaining — the attempt to understand the past by looking at events as they fit into a pattern or "chain." Each event creates conditions that allow the next major step to occur. It is based on the assumption that events have many causes.

City-state — a sovereign political unit made up of a city and its surrounding territory.

Civilization — a highly complex culture, exhibiting such characteristics as (1) a written language and knowledge of mathematics and science, (2) an economic division of labor including specialized farmers, skilled craftsmen, and traders, (3) a specialization of social and political roles including priest, king, and soldier, and (4) the creation of explicit religious, moral, or legal norms governing behavior within the society.

Classical — that which a people regard as the origin of or the model for their culture. In world history those civilizations that developed the defining characteristics of important contemporary cultures are considered classical.

Cold war — the extreme hostility between the United States and the Soviet Union, involving arms races, heated propaganda, diplomatic conflict, and even wars by proxy, but never direct violent conflict.

Collective security — the doctrine behind both the League of Nations and the present United Nations, in which aggressor states will be punished by sanctions or war organized and directed on behalf of the member-states by an appropriate agency of an international organization. Collective security is seen as an alternative to self-help as a means of ensuring security within the international system.

Collective self-reliance — a theory of economic and social development favored by some Third World leaders, which emphasizes what the less developed countries can do to help themselves and each other to develop economically.

Colonialism — the process whereby one nation exercises direct, formal control over the political, military, and economic affairs of another people. Colonialism may involve the settlement of large numbers of people from the colonizing state in the colony.

Commercial revolution — a fundamental transition in European economies, beginning in the fifteenth century, in which the expansion of trade in everyday goods created a truly integrated international economy. An intimate part of the commercial revolution was the emergence of capitalism within Europe and the rise of such economic institutions as banking and the joint stock company.

Communism — in Marxist theory, a final stage of society in which the state has withered away and economic goods are distributed solely on the basis of need. Such states as the Soviet Union, all of Eastern Europe, China, Cuba, and Vietnam claim to have communist systems. However, classical Marxist theorists would argue that these states are still characterized by socialist systems.

Comparative advantage — the idea that for every place there exists some set of goods or services that can be produced there more efficiently (that is, more cheaply) than they can be produced in most other places. This principle provides the theoretical basis for the current international trading system. Economic welfare can theoretically be maximized if each place specializes in those industries in which it has a comparative advantage and imports those goods in which other places have a comparative advantage.

Conflict — disagreement between or among actors because of differences in perceptions or interests. Conflict can take many specific forms. In international affairs, conflict can result in threats of war, economic boycotts, sanctions, a decline in communication, or actual violence. Conflict is not the same as violence or war but can easily lead to them.

Contract — a social principle that provides one basic form of social agreement. Contracts involve agreements among two or more people to exchange services or goods in the expectation that the exchange will benefit everyone involved. Contracts are usually made by people who have no other basis of relationship.

Cooperation — the act of working together or coordinating goals, policies, or activities in order to achieve some mutually desired result. When the interests of international actors coincide, cooperation among actors may take the form of alliances, economic unions such as the European Economic Community, cartels, or coalitions. Cooperation or common cause is considered a social principle by anthropologists.

Criterion-referenced test — an evalution method constructed to access performance levels in relation to a set of well-defined objectives or competencies identified prior to instruction. Criterion-referenced testing is usually distinguished from norm-referenced testing.

Cultural diffusion — the process through which some elements of one culture, such as its technology, ideas, or tastes, spread to another culture region.

Culture — all the things and ideas that a people create in order to deal with their environment and make their interactions with each other predictable. Culture includes both the material or observable phenomena that people create (artifacts) and the equally or even more important mental phenomena we cannot see (mentifacts). Elements of culture include such things as the organization of a society (social, economic, and political institutions and principles), language, religious beliefs, and tools.

Culture crest — a fundamental cultural turning point at which small changes that have taken place over time have multiplied to such an extent that people within the society now regard the old culture (that is, the old ways) as irrelevant or even strange.

Culture hearth region — a geographic area in which a major contemporary culture originated or was elaborated.

Decisionmaker — in a political system, anyone whose decisions and choices are likely to have an impact on other people. In international affairs, the leaders of large national and international organizations, national governments, and multinational business firms are routinely considered decisionmakers. Yet average individuals and local groups can also make decisions that have an impact internationally—through boycotts, fund-raising, foreign investment, or trade.

Democracy — a form of government in which governing elites such as members of Congress and the President are accountable to the mass of the people, generally by means of periodic elections.

Democratic revolution — a fundamental transition in European political life beginning in the sixteenth century, during which institutions were created that effectively extended the rights of political participation to the mercantile middle class and later to the industrial working class. The political changes surrounding the English, American, and French Revolutions are seen as part of the democratic revolution. The rise of workers' rights, socialism, and even the expansion of the democratic ideology to the non-Western world are also aspects of it.

Demographic transition theory — an explanation of why populations in less developed countries are growing so fast and why population growth rates might be expected to decline as a result of economic development, urbanization, and industrialization. The theory actually describes the historical experience of the more developed countries.

Dependence — an unbalanced relationship between actors, in which one actor is affected by the actions or decisions of the other but not vice-versa. In international affairs, dependence between countries may result from unequal wealth, resources, or even size. The idea of dependence (as opposed to interdependence) has often been used to describe the relationship between many Latin American countries and the United States.

Dependency theory — an explanation of economic and social underdevelopment, which argues that the lack of political, social, and economic development in the less developed countries has resulted from political and economic exploitation by the more developed countries.

Deterrence — preventing another actor from taking some action by creating uncertainty or fear about the consequences. In the pre-nuclear age a strong defense could deter aggression. If a war could not accomplish its objectives, there was no reason to start it. Between nuclear powers today, deterrence has come to rest on the threat of punishment. A nuclear attack is unlikely because any attacker would also suffer unacceptable damage.

Development — most commonly used to refer to the creation of an integrated and productive national economy in which the material living standards of people generally rise as part of or as a result of the process. This is best called **economic development.** Different people emphasize different aspects of the economic develoment process, such as expanding production, raising living standards, or distributing income broadly. The term "development" is also used to refer to **political development,** which is the creation of stable political institutions capable of governing the society, and **social development,** which is the creation of modern social institutions—typically defined as Western social institutions and norms.

Dictatorship — a form of government in which an individual, a small closely knit group, or a single political party governs without being accountable to the people.

Diplomacy — the art and practice of conducting relations among sovereign states. Modern diplomacy originated in Italy during the fourteenth and fifteenth centuries A.D.

Disarmament — the severe reduction or elimination of military forces or armaments. Disarmament can occur as a result of international agreements among two or more competing states. It can also result from the decisions of one state, in which case it is called **unilateral disarmament,** (literally, one-sided disarmament).

Distorted development — a condition that occurs when an economy grows only in response to external demand or when it does not grow in ways that satisfy the needs and desires of its own people. The chief characteristic of distorted development is that the benefits of economic growth do not filter to the general population but remain concentrated within an elite group.

Division of labor — the result of economic specialization, in which different people within an economic system produce different goods or services. A division of labor is characteristic of urban society. To some extent an international division of labor has emerged in the global economy. Different countries or regions specialize in different types of production. A division of labor produces greater economic efficiency and interdependence, but overspecialization also makes people and nations overly sensitive to events and trends affecting their particular industry.

Dual society — a characteristic of underdeveloped societies, in which profound economic and even cultural differences exist between an advantaged sector of the society (usually an urban elite) and a disadvantaged sector (usually the vast majority of rural people). Dual societies have emerged historically because some people have been able to take advantage of the benefits of international trade while the vast majority have not.

Ecological agenda — controversial questions, within and among nations, regarding the use of natural systems and resources. The most commonly debated ecological issues within the international system are population growth, hunger and food security, energy security, the depletion of fossil fuels and other non-renewable resources, and environmental decay or pollution.

Ecological challenge — in anthropology, any change in the status quo that requires some corresponding change in the culture of a people. Ecological challenges thus may arise in the natural environment (e.g., climate change) or within the society itself (e.g., population decline or increase, changing attitudes toward work). The changes may occur quickly or gradually; they may be clearly recognizable as challenges at the time or only in retrospect.

Ecological perspective — a worldview that sees people and their natural environment as an interdependent system.

Economy, the international — the worldwide production and exchange of goods and services through international trade, foreign investment, and (to a lesser extent) international migration. The present international economy is organized according to capitalist principles. It emerged as a result of the economic and political expansion of the West, beginning in the fifteenth century. It became a highly integrated, global economy only in the latter part of the nineteenth century.

Elites — the small but powerful groups of people in virtually every society who control important aspects of the society.

Empire — political entities characterized by a centralized government, relatively large geographic area, and a large and usually heterogeneous population, often including several national or racial groups. A key aspect of empire is the central authority's disregard for the sovereignty of the various national groups.

Energy crest — changes in the key sources of energy or ways of harnessing energy. Historically, energy crests have preceded and led to culture crests.

Ethnocentrism — the attitude that the way of life that is characteristic of one's own time and place is superior to or more advanced than other ways of life.

Fascism — a political ideology whose most basic concepts include anti-egalitarianism and anti-democracy, collective organization, racial superiority, and the cult of the leader.

Feudalism — a highly decentralized and militarized political system based on a mutual bonding of a lord and his vassals. In return for military services to a lord, vassals received land over which they exercised virtually autonomous control. Feudalism was practiced in Japan and Sassanian Persia as well as in Western Europe. In Europe the implicit system of rights and obligations between vassal and lord laid the foundation for many civil and political rights.

First-strike capability — the ability to attack an opponent possessing nuclear weapons in such a way that it becomes impossible for that opponent to use those weapons effectively in a counterattack. Thus "striking first" is not the same as having a first-strike capability.

First World — the economically more developed and politically democratic states of Western Europe, North America, Japan, Australia, and New Zealand. Most definitions would also include the state of Israel, and some definitions would include South Africa.

Foreign aid — financial grants or loans made by a state or an international organization to a less developed country for the purpose of promoting economic development in the recipient country.

Foreign investment — using one's money (capital) to establish a new productive enterprise or to buy an existing one in another country. Foreign investment comes in two types. In **direct foreign investment** the foreign investor seeks at least some management control over the productive enterprise. In **indirect foreign investment** the foreign investor buys stocks or bonds in an existing company but does not seek management control.

Foreign policy — the course of action that international actors pursue in order to preserve or enhance their interests or to achieve their goals within the international system.

Formal regions — contiguous areas on the earth's surface that are characterized by similarities in physical makeup (landform or climate) or in some quality of their human population (language, culture, religion, race) throughout their area. In general, little concern is given to the exact boundaries of formal regions.

Formative evaluation — feedback from an evaluation process at one or more points during implementation of a project, which allows the evaluator to make adjustments in the project's objectives or plan of action.

Free trade — an economic philosophy that rejects the establishment of barriers to international trade, such as tariffs or quotas, in the belief that a free world economy will allow the most efficient division of labor globally and thus will maximize global economic welfare.

Functional regions — a way to differentiate the earth's surface in terms of points (usually cities) and the linkages between them. A functional region may be defined in terms of any type of interaction among places, such as airline traffic, telephone communication, or flows of trade and foreign investment.

Fundamentalism — a movement within any religion or political doctrine to maintain and stress the basic principles out of which the religion or political doctrine has grown. It is a refusal to deviate from the central or original foundations.

Garrison state — a heavily armed state in which military institutions and priorities dominate virtually every aspect of life. Ancient Sparta, the Soviet Union, and Israel may be considered garrison states.

Global village — the concept that humanity is becoming a single community due to the development of technologies that enable individuals all over the world to communicate and interact with one another directly. The term draws attention to the interdependence that results from economic integration and nuclear weapons. As never before, citizens of different states have become dependent on each other in the same way that people in local communities have always depended on each other.

Gross National Product — the total value of goods and services produced by the people of a given state in a single year. Commonly called GNP, the Gross National Product includes the value of a nation's international exports and imports. **Per Capita Gross National Product** is a measure of the average economic product per person for a given year. It is calculated by dividing the nation's GNP by its population.

Hegemon — a leader or an actor with predominating influence. In international relations, a state capable of establishing the norms or relationships among states. In the nineteenth century Great Britain was in many respects a hegemon. After World War II the United States exercised a similar kind of power. A hegemon exercises **hegemony** over the system.

Hellenistic — anything that is based on classical Greek models. "Hellenistic" is used to refer to Greek culture and political institutions after the time of Alexander the Great, when the Greeks no longer controlled their society politically. **Hellenic** refers to Greek culture and institutions before the time of Alexander.

Hierarchy — a differentiation between and among individuals that puts one person in a position of power over another or over others. The existence and maintenance of a hierarchy is generally dependent upon the threat of coercion, in one form or another.

Human regions — areas of the earth's surface that are distinguished on the basis of certain characteristics of the people inhabiting the place, such as population density, culture, or language. A type of formal region.

Ideology — a set of beliefs that serve to explain the past and present and to indicate how to achieve goals posited as important by the ideology in the future. Major twentieth-century political ideologies are communism, socialism, facism, and democracy.

Imperialism — the policy or practice of extending national power by exercising direct or indirect control over the economic, political, or military policies of another nation. Widely practiced by European nations and the United States in the nineteenth and twentieth centuries, imperialism is a broader concept than colonialism.

Independence — a political condition of being free from the political rule or authority of another state.

Industrialization — a kind of economic development process in which a society changes from being primarily engaged in producing agricultural or other primary products to being primarily engaged in producing manufactured products. Production of agricultural or other primary products need not disappear as a result of industrialization, but they become less important to the overall economic life of the society. The process of industrialization so transforms a society that it is usually called an **industrial revolution.**

Inequality — a distribution of valued items such as wealth, education, power, or rights, in which some members of the society have more of the valued item than others. There is an important distinction between the actual level of inequality and perceptions of whether that level of inequality is just or unjust. Virtually all societies have some level of inequality, but the perception of existing inequalities will depend on the values of the society and may change as those values change. As the international connections among societies have grown, people have also become aware of **international inequality,** or the differences in the distribution of valued items across societies.

Influence — a relationship among actors in which one actor is able to use positive or negative rewards get the other actor to behave in desired ways. The idea of influence is related to that of power but often refers to a more general and subtle relationship.

Interdependence — a characteristic of the relations among actors in the international system in which changes which affect an actor in one part of the system, or actions taken by that actor, tend to affect other actors elsewhere in the system. Interdependence results from the regularized flows of goods, money, people, and ideas that connect national societies, but it is not the same as those flows. Imperial Rome and Han China were linked by flows of trade goods, but they did not become interdependent as a result of those connections.

International organizations — formally structured groups wnose members come from at least three countries. There are two key types of international organizations: international government organizations (IGOs) have states as their members, and international non-governmental organizations (INGOs) have private individuals or groups as their members. Examples of IGOs include the United Nations, the North Atlantic Treaty Organization, the Organization of African Unity, and the Food and Agriculture Organization. Examples of INGOs include the International Red Cross, Amnesty International, and the World Council of Churches.

International relations — all intercourse between and among states and all movements of peoples, goods, capital, and information across national boundaries.

International system — all the individuals, groups, business firms, states, and international organizations that participate directly or indirectly in international relations, and the interactions among them. The international system has certain important properties, such as complexity, interdependence, insecurity, conflict, inequality, and issue-focused regimes.

Issues — general problems characterized by deep and firmly held disagreements among actors about the nature of the problem or how to resolve it. **International** or **global issues** are general problems about which international actors disagree.

Kinship — a relationship between and among people, based ultimately on a biological relationship, specifically a sharing of genes. There are two types of kinship found in human and certain animal species: vertical (that is, between parents and children) and horizontal (between siblings). Human cultures generally create a third type: affinity kinship (that is, the relationship between spouses and their families).

Latitude — the angular distance, north or south of the Equator, of a point on the Earth's surface. Since it is a measure of angular distance (that is, distance on a curved surface), latitude is measured in degrees and minutes north or south of the Equator.

Less developed countries — states that manifest at least some of the key aspects of underdevelopment. Often used synonymously with the term "Third World," but focused particularly on those states with low per capita incomes and little or no industrialization.

Liberalism — a political point of view that arose in the eighteenth and nineteenth centuries and originally favored minimum governmental interferences in people's lives. During the twentieth century, liberalism has come to represent a political point of view that favors governmental intervention aimed at helping the disadvantaged members of society.

Longitude — the angular distance of a point on the earth's surface east or west of the Prime Meridian, which is a line running north and south through Greenwich, England. Since longitude measures an angular distance (that is, distance on a curved surface), it is calculated in degrees and minutes east or west of the Prime Meridian up to 180 degrees, which is the International Dateline.

MAD — Mutual assured destruction, the reasoning or doctrine upon which American nuclear deterrence policy has rested since the 1960s. The essence of the doctrine is that no rational actor will dare begin a nuclear war as long as its opponent can retaliate and inflict "unacceptable" damage on the attacker even after suffering an initial attack.

Manorialism — a system of economic organization that characterized much of Europe during the ninth through the fifteenth centuries. Manorialism was a system of land tenure that governed relationships between landholders and the serfs or dependent tenants who worked the land. Manorialism preceded the development of feudalism and provided its economic foundation. While manorialism involved a set of legal and administrative rules and processes that were later elaborated in feudalism, the two concepts should not be equated.

Market — a system of exchange in which buyer (demand) and seller (supply) interact with each other to determine a price. The term can be applied to any context, place, or mechanism through which the sale and purchase of goods and services takes place.

Marxism-Leninism — Vladimir Lenin's adaptation of the political, economic, and social philosophy of Karl Marx. The most important assumptions of the philosophy include: (1) economic considerations and forces dominate political and social affairs, (2) the destruction of private property is necessary for equality and the end of exploitation, and (3) a truly egalitarian/communist society can only occur if the proletariat (working class) is mobilized and directed by an organized group of ideologically committed leaders. The third point represents the key contribution of Lenin and provided legitimacy for the Bolshevik/Communist Party.

Matriarchal — a form of social organization in which the mother is considered the head of the family or tribe, and familial descendance is traced through the female line. **Matriarchy** can also refer to a system of rule or domination by women.

Medieval — related to a "middle age," or a time between two ages. The medieval period in European history is the period between the classical Greco-Roman world and the modern world. It is associated with feudalism and, somewhat unfairly, with limited cultural accomplishment. The term is sometimes applied to historical periods of other societies that are contemporaneous with the European Middle Ages or exhibit similar social and cultural characteristics as feudal Europe.

Mentifact — the concepts, values, logic, premises, techniques, and other intangibles that are part of human culture.

Mercantilism — an economic philosophy and set of economic policies that characterized sixteenth- and seventeenth-century Europe. Mercantilist theory held that the wealth and power of an economy would be maximized if foreign trade were controlled so as to ensure that exports always exceeded imports. Free trade theory demonstrated that greater prosperity would result from the economic efficiencies that free trade and specialization made possible.

Migration — the movement of people across national boundaries, for the purpose of temporary or permanent residence. Migration includes both legal and illegal flows of people. Most international migration today involves the movement of people from the Third World to the First World.

MIRV — an acronym for multiple interdependently targeted reentry vehicles. A MIRV consists of between two and ten nuclear warheads placed on a ballistic missile. Each warhead can be accurately directed toward a target that is distinct and even widely separated from the others.

Modernist perspective — a worldview or set of assumptions about the world that sees the natural world as something to be used for the benefit of humans and views science and technology as the means for understanding and exploiting the natural world. Shaped by the industrial and democratic revolutions, this worldview places great importance on economic growth and efforts to raise material standards of living.

Modernization theory — one explanation of how a society can change from having a traditional, agricultural-based economy with low average incomes to a modern, industrial, and service-based economy with high average incomes. The theory sees economic development as the movement of an economy through a series of fixed and predictable stages. It emphasizes the need to accumulate and reinvest capital and assumes that international trade and foreign investment can help societies develop economically.

Monotheism — the belief that there is only one deity or god who is responsible for creation. The trend toward monotheism was a characteristic of Middle Eastern history and represents an important cultural contribution of that region.

Monsoon — a seasonal wind that sweeps from the Indian Ocean northeast across Asia between April and October and then blows southwest from the Asian land-mass between November and March. The unswerving monsoon winds not only determine seasonal changes in Asia but also affected commerce and transportation in the age of sailing vessels.

More developed countries — states or countries with extensive manufacturing or service industries that depend largely on domestic consumption for their earnings and growth. All countries of the First World are considered more developed. Second World countries are usually considered more developed as well.

Multilateral — literally, "many-sided." This term is used to describe international organizations, activities, or negotiations in which more than two states or actors are involved simultaneously. Negotiations over how to respond to global ecological issues have typically been conducted within multilateral conferences.

Multinational corporations — capitalistic business companies with operations in more than one country. Multinational corporations (MNCs) may be engaged in primary industries, manufacturing, service industries (including banking), or in a mix of industries. Some people prefer the term **transnational corporations** because most MNCs are owned and managed by citizens of their country of origin. Examples are IBM, Exxon, Sony, Volkswagen, Nestlé, and Chase Manhattan Bank.

Nation-state — a political unit characterized by a population that (1) occupies a particular territory, (2) has a relatively homogeneous culture and a sense of common identity, and (3) is ruled by a sovereign government. The majority of the states of Western Europe can be characterized as nation-states. However, states like the Soviet Union, Nigeria, and India are ethnically plural, with many subnational identities. Thus not all states can be described as nation-states.

National interests — the goals and conditions sought by the governments of states. National interests may arise from the collective self-interest of the people within states (e.g., security) or from the interest of influential segments of the population (e.g., access to the North Atlantic fisheries, the retention of an empire).

National resistance — a strategy of civilan defense that would overcome political and military domination through well-defined acts of non-compliance that make it impossible for an invader to establish and maintain political control over the society. National resistance is inherently non-violent and thus does not depend on military technology. It would, however, require careful planning and widespread support of the population.

Nationalism — the psychological and cultural identification of individuals and groups with a nation-state. Originating in Europe at the time of the French Revolution, nationalist sentiments have spread worldwide. Nationalist sentiments have a positive side, generally referred to as "patriotism," which can help states maintain order and mobilize the energies of their people. Nationalism can also have a negative side, usually referred to as "ethnocentrism" or "national chauvinism," which can become a barrier to international cooperation and understanding.

Neocolonialism — the *de facto* continuation of colonial rule through the domination of key economic institutions within a now independent country. The term is used to describe the situation of some Third World countries whose national economic policies are still dependent on multinational corporations or international economic agencies.

Neolithic — a term literally referring to the new and somewhat more sophisticated tools characteristic of New Stone Age societies. The term has come to refer to the culture of New Stone Age peoples, in particular the sedentary agriculture-based cultures that arose out of the **Neolithic revolution.** That fundamental change in human culture was brought about by the development of agriculture and animal husbandry. The neolithic revolution was the first agricultural revolution.

Network — connections among individuals within a society that allow those people to share information and competencies and to develop common perceptions and agendas about public issues and affairs. Networks provide a basic framework for integrating the social and political life of complex and dispersed societies where face-to-face contact among most people in the society is impossible.

Neutralism — the practice of treating both sides of a conflict with total impartiality. Neutralism was originally more isolationist and less positive a concept than non-alignment.

Newly industrialized countries — sometimes referred to as NICs, these are states such as Mexico, South Korea, and Singapore, which have become significantly industrialized since 1950.

NIEO — the New International Economic Order, a plan advocated by many Third World states and designed to change what they regard as their unfavorable role in the international economy.

Non-alignment — a foreign policy doctrine that became popular among some Third World leaders in the 1950s. The doctrine of non-alignment states that the countries that achieved their independence after 1945 should not align with either the First World (Western countries) or with the Second World (communist states) but should join together to preserve their freedom of action in world affairs.

Non-governmental organizations — formal associations of people that do not include governments as members and whose policies are presumably not determined by the policies of the government. Non-governmental groups are informal associations of people that do not have governments as members.

Non-renewable resource — any material that humans use in their daily lives and that cannot be replaced on a continuous basis by the growth or reproduction of biological organisms. Minerals and fossil fuels are non-renewable resources.

Norm-referenced test — usually a published, standardized test that allows student performance to be compared with the performance of a large group of students who are presumed to be similar in age, development, or learning experience.

Nuclear proliferation — the spread of nuclear weapons to states that at present do not have them. Most analysts believe that nuclear proliferation would make nuclear wars more likely.

Nuclear weapons — weapons whose destructive or killing potential is based on either atomic fission (the splitting of atoms in materials such as uranium 235) or atomic fusion (the joining together of atoms in certain isotopes of hydrogen). The process of splitting or fusing the atoms releases enormous amounts of energy, radiation, and radioactive material.

Paleolithic — literally, referring to the types of tools characteristic of people living in the Old Stone Age. The term has come to be associated with the culture of Old Stone Age people. That culture was based on hunting and gathering. It involved nomadic lifestyles and uncomplicated forms of social, political, and economic organization.

Parliamentary government — a system of government in which the executive is part of and directly responsible to the legislative branch. The chief executive is usually the elected leader of the political party that has the greatest voting strength in the parliament. Parliamentary forms of government are based on the assumptions that the executive and legislative should work efficiently together and that the executive should not exercise power independent of legislative approval.

Patriarchal — a form of social organization in which the father is considered the head of the family and familial descent is traced through the male line. **Patriarchy** also refers to a system of rule or domination by men.

Peace — a condition in which states or other actors with similar military capabilities are not fighting each other. While peace is generally considered a good thing, it is nonetheless possible for peace to coexist with injustice and oppression.

Periphery — the economically and politically weaker actors or areas within national and international political and economic systems. Peripheries are usually dominated or dependent on core areas within a system. In the international system the Third World is often referred to as the periphery.

Physical regions — areas of the Earth's surface that are distinguished on the basis of such characteristics as landforms (mountains, river valleys, plains), climate, or vegetation. A type of formal region.

Place — a particular point or contiguous area on the Earth's surface.

Pluralism — a state of society in which the members of diverse political, religious, racial, social, or ethnic groups are able to participate freely within the political system. This participation is often conducted through interest or pressure groups — that is, organizations designed to promote the narrow interests of a particular group.

Polis — a state or society, usually limited in size to a city and its surrounding territory, that is characterized by a high sense of community and face-to-face interaction.

Power — the ability to compel another state or states to act in a certain manner regardless of their perceived national interests; similarly, the ability to dissuade another state or states from a particular action regardless of their perceived national interests. International politics is often thought to involve a struggle for power.

Premises — in logic, statements that, once established, serve as the basis for an argument. In anthropological analysis, premises are the most basic truths or axioms a people use to explain and understand themselves and their world.

Primary industry — a type of economic production based on the resources of the land. Farming, mining, and forestry are the chief examples of primary production or primary industries. If primary industries are dominant within a particular national economy, that economy is said to be in the **primary stage of development** according to modernization theory.

Primate city — an urban center containing a very large share of the urban population and most of the wealth of the entire country. Primate cities are a characteristic of underdevelopment. They constitute pockets of development in an otherwise less developed country.

Progress — cultural changes interpreted as positive or beneficial by those people involved in the change. Often used by people in one society to refer to cultural changes that appear to be making another, culturally different, society more similar to their own.

Protectionism — economic policies and practices that give advantages to domestic industries and investors by limiting or preventing foreign trade and investment. The purpose of protectionism is to insulate domestic producers from foreign competition.

Ranking — a social principle that involves placing one thing over other, similar things. Ranking can be applied to any culture element, to individual people, or to social groups. It is often used to determine or limit the rights or privileges of individuals or groups.

Realpolitik — in the nineteenth century, a foreign policy based on careful calcula-
tions of national interests, self-consciously discounting sentimentality or ideology.
Currently, a perspective on international relations that sees the possession and
use of power (usually, military power) as the most important determinant of
of international relationships.

Regimes, international — sets of implicit and explicit principles, rules, expectations, and decisionmaking procedures that serve to regularize the behavior of
actors with respect to a given dimension of their international relations. Very
stable international regimes have been created to coordinate the flow of mail,
airline traffic, and similar international activities. Less stable regimes have helped
prevent the proliferation of nuclear weapons and have coordinated policies
regarding the uses of the open sea.

Regionalization — the process of locating and identifying various regions on the
Earth's surface.

Regions — areas on the Earth's surface that have distinctive characteristics.

Relative location — the position of one place on the Earth's surface in terms of
its spatial relationship to other places.

Renewable resource — any material that humans use in their everyday lives and
that can be replaced on a continuous basis by the growth or reproduction of
biological organisms. Renewable resources include wool, cotton, forest products,
fish, grain, and other foodstuffs.

Role — a social principle governing the differentiation of people based on their
specialized functions within the social group. Role has a meaning similar to **office.** Roles and offices exist independently of the individuals who occupy them
and thus allow functions to be identified and ranked without reference to particular individuals.

SALT — Strategic Arms Limitation Talks, negotiations aimed at producing arms control agreements between the United States and the Soviet Union, beginning in
1969 and ending in 1979. Two SALT agreements were reached. One component of the SALT I agreement was the Anti-Ballistic Missile Treaty, which was
signed and ratified by both parties. The SALT II Treaty was never ratified by
the United States Senate. The **START** negotiations, or the Strategic Arms Reduction Talks, were begun in 1982 and replaced the SALT process.

Scale — the principle unit of analysis for a map or geographical analysis. Local scale
maps show features of a city or other local area. Global scale maps show features
of the entire Earth or variations across the entire Earth's surface.

Scientific revolution — a process of cultural change beginning in the seventeenth
century, which brought about a fundamental reorientation in Western thinking about the world. People began looking for scientific laws, rather than religious
dogma, to explain the natural world. The scientific method, especially the willingness to question established theories, came to characterize intellectual life.

Secondary industry — types of economic production that are based on manufacturing. **Manufacturing industries** — productive enterprises that use machines
to fashion raw materials into useful products — make up the **secondary sector** of an economy. If manufacturing industries are the dominant source of income and employment within an economy, according to modernization theory
that economy is at the **secondary stage of development.**

Second-strike capability — the ability to suffer a nuclear attack and still be able
to counterattack with enough nuclear weapons to cause unacceptable damage
to the attacker. Having and maintaining a second-strike capability is the foundation of the policy of mutual assured destruction.

Second World — the middle-income, communist-ruled states of Eastern Europe
and the Soviet Union.

Security, national — the protection of basic national values such as territory, population, form of government, and economic well-being from threats or attack by other international actors. National security does not mean only defense against military or terrorist attack; it also has economic and psychological aspects.

Self-help — the assumption underlying the current international security system. It is asserted that because of international anarchy, a state must provide for its own security in whatever ways it can. Thus war is seen as a legitimate means of protecting national interests in international relations, although murder is not a legitimate means of protecting personal interests.

Socialism — an economic ideology that asserts that the means of producing goods and services should be collectively owned by all the people in a society in order to enhance economic equality. In practice, economic systems organized according to socialist principles accomplish collective ownership through state control and ownership.

Social principles — the set of basic rules that explain how people in a society behave toward each other. The key social principles anthropologists have identified include kinship, hierarchy, specialization, role, common cause, and contract. They are found in all societies, although their particular form will vary from one society to another.

Social stratification — a relatively permanent ranking of status and roles in a social system, based on differences in knowledge, wealth, power, or social respect. Stratification implies inequality among individuals and is often accompanied by implicit or explicit differences in rights, privileges, and responsibilities within a society.

Sovereignty — a condition and a right claimed by all states, in which a political unit is seen as independent and thus may legitimately make its own decisions according to its own interests without being legally accountable to any other political unit. The emergence of the doctrine of state sovereignty some 400 years ago in Europe provided the foundation for the current international system.

Spatial linkages — the relationships between two or more places that emerge as a function of their location relative to each other (e.g., paths linking the places).

Spatial variations — differences in the physical and human characteristics across different places or regions. Spatial variations of interest to geographers include differences in climate, landform, population density, wealth, dominant economic activities, and political system.

Specialization — the concentration of one's efforts on a particular economic, social, or political activity. Specialization within and across groups leads to a division of labor that allows a group or society to diversify its activities overall, attain higher levels of skill, and become more productive.

Stable deterrence — a situation in which military adversaries with nuclear weapons believe that no adversary, including themselves, possesses a first-strike capability or would in any way benefit from using nuclear weapons first in a crisis. Contrasts with **unstable deterrence,** in which one or more of the adversaries believes that one adversary, not necessarily itself, would somehow benefit from being the first to use nuclear weapons in a crisis.

State — the basic political actor in the international system, represented by a government that has or is recognized as having control over a particular territory and people.

Strategic defense — the ability to protect the home territory of a state from attack. Strategic defense was considered technically impossible with the advent of ballistic missiles carrying nuclear weapons. The 1972 ABM (Anti-Ballistic Missile) Treaty between the United States and the Soviet Union formalized the assumption that efforts to build a strategic defense system against missiles would lead to an arms race but could not enhance security. The **Strategic Defense**

Initiative, launched by President Ronald Reagan in 1982, rejected the technological impossibility of defense against ballistic missiles and proposed a multifaceted research and development effort designed to create and eventually implement such a defensive system.

Subsistence — a standard or style of living in which only the basic material needs of a people (food, clothing, and shelter) are met on a regular basis. In modernization theory, the **subsistence stage of development** is one in which the means of production or the organization of productive activities allows a society to meet only its basic material needs.

Summative evaluation — feedback from an evaluation process that comes at the end of a project and is designed to measure whether or not the project has achieved its objectives.

Superpower — a term used after World War II to acknowledge the dominant military, economic, and political power of the United States and later the Soviet Union. The term reflected the fact that since the 1600s no state had been so overwhelmingly strong militarily and economically as the United States was after the war.

System — any collection of people, things, or parts that work together to form a unitary whole. The concept of a system originated within the engineering sciences but has been widely used within the social sciences and history to look at how individual actors (people and organizations) fit together into a whole (an economy, a society, or a polity), which in certain respects exists apart from those individual actors and extends beyond their lifetimes. The concept of a mechanical system has also yielded some insights into the properties of social systems, including interdependence and the effects of change.

Technology — the tools and techniques used by people to accomplish desired ends. While Americans normally associate the term with the latest science-based tools, such as computers, satellites, rockets, and robots, even the stone tools of Paleolithic hunters represented technology.

Technology, appropriate — tools and techniques that are well suited to the level of development and resources of a society. For example, in countries experiencing labor shortages, labor-saving machines may represent appropriate technology. However, such machines may not represent appropriate technology in countries experiencing chronic, large-scale unemployment or underemployment.

Terrorism — the use of violence by individuals, groups, and even some states, in order to promote fear in a target audience and thereby achieve political ends. In the abstract, terrorism is considered illegitimate by most international actors. However, specific cases are always controversial; one person's "terrorist" is often another person's "freedom fighter."

Tertiary industry — a type of economic activity aimed at producing services rather than goods. Examples of service industries include the commonplace (e.g., housekeeping and restaurants) and the not so commonplace (advertising, research, computer analysis). When service industries become the chief source of growth, income, and employment within an economy, that economy is said to have reached a **tertiary stage of development.**

Third World — a term used to refer collectively to the more than 140 states and colonies in Asia, Africa, Central and South America, the Middle East, and the Pacific Basin. While these states vary tremendously in their political systems, level of economic development, and cultural heritage, all exhibit some aspects of underdevelopment. Equally important, the term reflects a political unity among these states with respect to such international issues as colonialism and foreign aid.

Totalitarian — a state or society in which the political rulers control virtually every aspect of private and social life, as well as political life, such that individual liberties and decisionmaking are virtually nonexistent.

Trade, international — the exchange of goods and services across state boundaries. The contemporary international trading system is organized along capitalist lines and began to develop as the new capitalist economies of Europe started looking for direct trade routes to Asia. The post-World War II trading system was founded on the principles of free trade and comparative advantage, although restrictions to free trade in the form of quotas, tariffs, and administrative regulations still exist.

Turning point — a historical period in which fundamental changes occur in the distribution of capabilities among the world's civilizations or in the trends that dominate the course of future events. Turning points may coincide with culture crests.

Underdevelopment — a condition in which a country has not been and is not capable of fully utilizing its economic and human resources. Underdevelopment is considered a syndrome common to all Third World countries. It results from a varying set of factors, including (1) economic dependence on primary industries and the export of primary products, (2) low levels of economic productivity and domestic investment, (3) low levels of literacy, (4) high levels of unemployment and underemployment, along with high rates of population growth and low standards of living, and (5) political instability.

Underemployment — a condition in which people who seek full-time work have only part-time employment available to them. Underemployment is distinct from **Unemployment,** in which people who are looking for jobs cannot find them.

Uneven development — the pattern of economic inequality between different world regions. Some areas, characterized as the "more developed countries," tend to be highly industrialized and urbanized, have high per capita Gross National Products, are technologically sophisticated, and have slowly expanding populations. Other areas, characterized as the "less developed countries," tend to be minimally industrialized, have low per capita Gross National Products, are technologically unsophisticated, and have rapidly expanding populations.

Urbanization — the process through which the population of a society comes to be increasingly concentrated in towns and cities rather than in rural areas and comes to be engaged primarily in non-agricultural activities.

Urban revolution — a fundamental change in historical cultures, brought on by the emergence of cities. More densely populated local areas, in which people from diverse clans were often mixed together, required new forms of social organizations (e.g., government, taxes). Cities also created new opportunities for specialization and interaction that may have facilitated the development of new crafts and writing and made possible a more complex division of labor.

Violence — the overt use of physical force to achieve a particular goal or to compel another actor to do one's bidding, as in war or terrorism. Some social scientists also talk about **structural violence,** referring to social, economic, or political repression and deprivation that result from the operation of coercive economic, social, and political systems.

War — a type of large-scale organized violence that states use to advance or protect their vital national interests. War has long been regarded as a legitimate tool of international politics. Yet perennial concerns about what constitutes a "just war" also indicate that war is not regarded as legitimate under all conditions.

Western civilization — the set of values and institutions that were initially formulated in the Mediterranean world in the first millennium B.C., took root in

Europe during the first millennium A.D., and expanded into the Americas and Northern Eurasia during the last 500 years. Contemporary nations that are the heir to these traditions include those in Europe, some in Latin America (e.g., Argentina), some in the British Commonwealth (e.g., Canada and Australia), the United States, and the Soviet Union.

Westernization — the process through which cultural elements developed within Western civilization come to replace traditional cultural elements in other culture regions. Cultural changes involving the adaptation of Western cultural elements to non-Western settings may also be seen as Westernization, but that may be an ethnocentric interpretation of the normal process of cultural diffusion and change.

Index

DATE D